T0159510

Maggie's Hammer

How investigating the mysterious
death of my friend uncovered a
netherworld of illegal arms deals,
political slush funds, high-level
corruption and Britain's thirty-year
secret role as America's hired gun

Geoffrey Gilson

MAGGIE'S HAMMER: HOW INVESTIGATING THE MYSTERIOUS DEATH OF MY FRIEND UNCOVERED A NETHERWORLD OF ILLEGAL ARMS DEALS, PO-LITICAL SLUSH FUNDS, HIGH-LEVEL CORRUPTION AND BRITAIN'S THIR-TY-YEAR SECRET ROLE AS AMERICA'S HIRED GUN
Copyright © 2014/2015 Peter Geoffrey Gilson. All Rights Reserved.

Published by:
Trine Day LLC
PO Box 577
Walterville, OR 97489
1-800-556-2012
www.TrineDay.com
publisher@TrineDay.net

Library of Congress Control Number: 2015941100

Cover Design: Ed Bishop
Author picture: Kelly Bell

Gilson, Geoffrey
Maggie's Hammer–1st ed.
p. cm.
Includes index and references.
Epub (ISBN-13) 978-1-63424-010-9
Mobi (ISBN-13) 978-1-63424-011-6
Print (ISBN-13) 978-1-63424-009-3
1. Simmonds, Hugh John (1949-1989) 2. Conservatism -- Great Britain -- History -- 20th century. 3. Great Britain -- Politics and government -- 1979-1997. 4. Military-industrial complex -- Great Britain. I. Gilson, Geoffrey II. Title

First Edition
10 9 8 7 6 5 4 3 2 1

Printed in the USA

Distribution to the Trade by:
Independent Publishers Group (IPG)
814 North Franklin Street
Chicago, Illinois 60610
312.337.0747
www.ipgbook.com

This story is dedicated to my mother,
Patricia Louise Gilson
(December 7th, 1926 – October 24th, 1999)
She never stopped believing.

For now we see through a glass, darkly;
But then face to face: now I know in part;
But then shall I know even as also I am known.

Corinthians I, 13

Acknowledgments

IF I TRIED to thank everyone who has helped to bring this work to fruition, I'd miss someone. And then I'd feel awful. You all know who you are. And you all know how I feel about you. Thank you.

There are three individuals, however, whom I will single out. And of the three, the first is the most important: my twin sister, Maggi. Then, there are my almost-ghostwriter, Simon Regan (now deceased), and Hugh's father, John Simmonds (also deceased).

There were many times I doubted myself. These three were always there to see me through – primarily Maggi. If this book in any way defines me, it is because she showed me the way. I do not have the eloquence to do proper justice to the gratitude and love I truly feel. But, thank you.

Well, that was the writing part. Now I come to the publishing experience. And front and center, I thank Kris Millegan, without whom, well, you wouldn't even be reading this. It's a huge risk gambling on books some folks don't want published. Kris took that risk, before he even met me. Thank you. And thank you to David Wayne, who introduced me to Kris, and who was a great supporter on so many other levels too.

Many thanks to Ed Bishop and Bob Passaro for their detailed work, Ed on the cover and Bob on the story editing. Also huge gratitude to Peg and her wonderful staff at Booth Media for their indefatigable assistance in letting the world know about me.

Thank you all,

Geoffrey Gilson
Carrboro, 2015

Contents

Prologue

At the age of thirty-two, in November 1988, I was living in the same small English town that I'd been in all my life. I considered myself to be a reasonably ordinary guy, going about a reasonably ordinary life.

I had met my friend Hugh Simmonds as we fenced with each other on the local political scene in our mutual hometown of Beaconsfield, Buckinghamshire. We became close friends, and set about our rise through the ranks of the British Conservative Party, then led by the redoubtable Margaret Thatcher.

We shared an ambition to become Members of Parliament, mine being a step or two behind Hugh's because of our nine-year age difference. Hugh then managed to screw up a couple of opportunities in safe Conservative Parliamentary seats. So, while waiting for his third chance, he had set up his own law practice in Beaconsfield, and I became his senior employee. Like I said, an ordinary guy, leading an ordinary life.

Then one fateful November morning, I found myself staring down at Hugh's dead body, in the clearing of some local woods, and I couldn't for the life of me work out why he might have committed suicide. But the weirdness had only begun. Back at the law office, I discovered that some £5 million ($7.5 million) was missing from the firm's Clients' Account.

I was devastated by Hugh's death, confused by the apparent theft, and concerned for his children, who were left with no suicide note. Any of these would have been enough reason to hunt for the truth behind Hugh's death. But the primary reason I started poking around was much more prosaic – I needed to clear my own name.

Society needed a scapegoat – who was alive. I fit the bill. My response was to ask questions. And that's when I was launched onto my rollercoaster adventure of international mystery and intrigue, an odyssey which continues even now. As innocuous as I thought my questions to be, they provoked a powerful response in very high places – all around the globe.

I was shot at, chased through the streets, warned off by the CIA, and threatened by Israeli and British intelligence officers. Even the FBI lied to me. Blatantly. But not before I discovered that Hugh was a senior officer in and a contract assassin for MI6 (Britain's equivalent of the CIA), and that he was part of a small specially selected team close to Margaret Thatcher, seemingly tasked with arranging arms deals in support of covert foreign policy and funneling illicit arms' commissions back to her and other senior figures within the British Conservative Party.

On further investigation, it became clear that, whatever the private and personal ambitions of the British Prime Minister, there was wider purpose for the team. Namely, and with the open support of the British Government, to smooth the path for Britain's military and intelligence services and its defense industry, as they surreptitiously engaged in their clandestine role as hired gun for the US government, waging unconventional warfare around the globe in aggressive pursuit of covert US foreign policy.

But I get ahead of myself. For the moment, let's just go back to the beginning ...

CHAPTER ONE

An Ordinary Death?

"SO. THAT'S WHAT a dead body looks like." I tried to think of something more sensitive to feel. But I wasn't feeling very sensitive at all. In fact, I wasn't feeling very much of anything. My mind was numb. The only thing it could register was that I'd never seen a dead body before.

***

It had begun as another ordinary day, in my otherwise very ordinary life: November 15, 1988.

I collected the post, as I always did, at 8:15 A.M. from the Beaconsfield Post Office, and opened the law offices of Simmonds and Company at 8.30 A.M. The proprietor, Hugh Simmonds, was not in, but this had become increasingly common since he started his own Wine Bar company, City Jeroboam Ltd., in 1986.

The staff of Simmonds and Company arrived at about 9:00 A.M., followed closely by the directors of City Jeroboam. There was a Board Meeting of City Jeroboam scheduled for that morning. Martin Pratt, a close friend of Hugh's and one of the directors of City Jeroboam, came into my office shortly before 10:00 A.M. and asked if I knew where Hugh was. I replied, with a nod and a wink, that if he was this late he was probably visiting his mistress, Karen George.

Shortly after this conversation, Jill, the receptionist, rang through to say that she had a hoax caller on the telephone. She wanted me to deal with it. The caller said he was a police constable and that the police had found one of our shared company cars with a dead body in it. It appeared to be suicide. I was skeptical, but since he persisted I agreed to meet him at the local woods where he said the car had been discovered.

I arrived at the spot and was directed to the scene by another policeman. It was only as I got out of the car that I realized I'd never seen a dead body before. I had no idea what sort of grisly spectacle to expect. I mentioned this to the policemen standing nearby. They were very understanding and explained that the body would simply look like someone had fallen asleep. I wasn't going to be in for a nasty shock. In this prediction, they would prove to be only partly correct.

***

I entered the woods, and quickly came across the small company car. Perhaps too quickly. The car was sitting all on its own in a clearing. Looking back over my shoulder, I noticed that at a certain angle, the car could be seen quite clearly from the road. The thought swiftly passed through my mind that anyone wanting to commit suicide in this location would have had trouble with inquisitive passers-by.

That thought was quickly snuffed out by my first glimpse of the motionless body in the car. I couldn't see any facial features, but the clothes were the same ones Hugh had been wearing the night before.

I've always heard that shock causes everything to slow down. At that moment, the world around me seemed to float along in silent slow motion. The birds may have been singing, but I didn't notice. All I could hear was the thumping of my own heart and the swish of my feet through the long, frost-covered grass.

I spent some minutes circling the car at a distance, working up the courage to glance inside. Sunlight filtering through the gently swaying trees danced and bounced off the metal and glass. My breath formed little clouds in the crisp November air.

Finally, I strode up to the driver's side and crouched down using the door for support. The policeman had been right – Hugh looked as if he had simply fallen asleep. His head was leant back over the upright seat, his arms dangling gently between his legs. Save for the open mouth, and the half-closed lifeless eyes, he could have been having a nap.

I noticed a heavy book lying on the floor next to the accelerator pedal and a length of garden hose on the back seat.

That was when the shock hit me. I wanted to feel something. But I didn't know what, or where, or how. All I knew was that my very best friend was gone, and I couldn't for the life of me work out why.

The scene was lifeless. The air was still. His body was clay. And my mind was ice. Then, as I glanced once more at his immobile face, the whole frozen façade shattered like a dome of many-colored glass.

***

On the face of it, Hugh John Simmonds, CBE was the epitome of '80s' Thatcherite ambition: forty years of age, tall, dark and handsome; a cross between Pierce Brosnan and Dan Ackroyd on their good days. He was top heavy with charm and charisma, and he used both shamelessly to fill his bed with a seemingly endless supply of conquests.

But life was not all play for Hugh. He balanced pleasure with a serious commitment to serve in Margaret Thatcher's Cabinet, before she concluded her time as Britain's most radical, right-wing Prime Minister.

For seventeen years, his life had been a calculated agenda, artfully designed to bring him to Parliament as a Conservative M.P. in early middle age. From a prep school background, at age 27, he had become a partner with Wedlake Bell, a small and exclusive firm of London solicitors.

The following year, he served as Mayor of Beaconsfield, his and my hometown in the rural County of Buckinghamshire. He married Janet, the nearest thing to a childhood sweetheart that he could find. Small, slightly dumpy, with an elfin face and brunette hair, she was an absolute wizard at organizing an office.

Hugh religiously paid his dues on the British equivalent of the political chicken circuit, putting in seventeen-hour days as he kissed babies, charmed old ladies and arranged for various local government departments to fix sewers and potholes for the constituents of his municipal council district.

In the General Election of 1979, the election which first brought Margaret Thatcher to power, he served the obligatory role as a losing Conservative Party Parliamentary candidate in a safe Labour seat – a grim and grimy seat called West Leeds. Hugh did, however, manage the distinction of achieving the largest swing to a Conservative candidate in the entire North of England. No small success in Leeds, a decaying leftover from Britain's industrial greatness.

This put him in excellent stead to be awarded a safe seat, and indeed, he landed one of the five safest in 1983. True, he was then de-selected from South West Cambridge because his wife, Janet, opposed fox hunting – the Cambridge Hunt being one of the oldest in Great Britain.

He then doubled his misfortune by being de-selected from another safe Conservative seat, South Warrington, in 1987. On this occasion, his illegitimate son was the stumbling block. But these were the Energetic '80s. Cabinet ministers fathered children out of wedlock and became Foreign Secretary. Hugh's hiccups were no more than colorful episodes in his burgeoning biography. And a variety of different paths to political success lay just another hiccup away.

In 1988, he was still one of Thatcher's favorite speechwriters; the youngest ever recipient of the CBE (one notch below Knighthood); and a sometime and hugely respected member of the Conservative Party's National Union Executive Committee.

He had used his "sabbatical" to establish his own law practice in Beaconsfield; he was developing City Jeroboam, a company that then owned five wine bars and a pub, and had a turnover of several million pounds; and in the previous six months, he had been negotiating a loan of £25 million ($37 million), with which to buy 100 pubs from Whitbread, the UK's largest hospitality company.

Wealth and political fame lay just around the corner. So why kill himself? I had no time to consider the answer. I was fast approaching the outskirts of Beaconsfield and had no idea to whom or how to bear the ill tidings. His mother seemed a good place to start.

***

Beaconsfield was typical of the stockbroker suburbs dotting the Green Belt surrounding London. Overly large houses, in undersized plots. Lots of trees and pubs, virtually no racial mixing, and none of the urban problems prevalent just 30 miles away.

Beaconsfield had a rich history as an ancient market town on the crossroads of two of England's oldest highways. It had a 700-year-old street fair and an "Old Town" that looked as if it had come straight off the back lot of a Hollywood period movie.

"Dormitory" was the technical description used by the Census Bureau, but "sleepy" is how Beaconsfield liked to think of itself. You went to work in London, you came home, shut the door and ignored the rest of the world.

Hugh's parents, John and Gwen Simmonds, lived in a comfortable manse on one of the sleepier cul-de-sacs, just a couple of streets away from Hugh. Their only son liked to affect an upper-crust south of England heritage, but Hugh's parents' rolling burr of an accent gave the game away. Both were non-fussy genteel folk, clearly hailing from solid North-of-England stock.

John Simmonds, whose short frame and sandy hair bore little physical resemblance to Hugh, was a self-made man. He had helped to develop the early radar, which protected Britain from the hordes of German bombers in the Second World War. He had established a string of small but successful civil engineering firms, and had served as President of the National Institute of Electrical Engineers. Hugh claimed that his father had been offered, but had refused, a knighthood.

Gwen Simmonds, known to her friends as "Lyn," was a short, busy lady, with facial features that were a dead ringer for Hugh's, and later her first granddaughter, Juliet. Lyn didn't spend much time at home, which more often than not was empty, what with Hugh being the only child, and John spending so much time staying over at his Gentleman's Club in London.

But she answered the door that morning. I stood nervously in front of her, not knowing how to break the news. A couple of false starts, a quick outburst, and a half bottle of brandy later, we were in the main sitting room, comforting each other with silence.

"I don't get it," I blurted out, "why would he kill himself?" We'd already determined from his Harley Street doctor that he hadn't picked up a terminal nasty from his exotic sex life. "It can't have been about money; he had all that money he made trading Ferranti stock." "What money?" came the gentle response. "The Ferranti stock was his father's, to be left to the grandchildren, Juliet and Tanya. Hugh didn't have a penny. In fact, he had to borrow £400,000 ($600,000) from his father just a couple of years ago."

Oops.

I needed to get back to the office. Fast. Lyn agreed to do the honors with Hugh's wife, Janet, and help to collect the kids from school. I wasn't one of Janet's favorites, and she needed someone she would feel comfortable sobbing against. I headed back to the looming disaster.

Before pulling out of the driveway, I paused for a moment, and risked one more glance back at the front door. Lyn stood there, dwarfed by the huge oak frame, hugging herself tightly. The bustling matron was long gone. All I saw now was a frail old lady, forcing a smile into her face, as the light slowly died in her eyes. Her only child was dead.

***

It didn't take long to confirm the worst. Waiting for me at the office was a representative from the Law Society, the national equivalent of a State Bar Association. Chap bore a distinct resemblance to Uriah Heep, all bone, gristle and six feet tall, with a few hairs greased over a balding pate.

Clients were complaining about not being able to get their money.

"Is there a problem?" came Uriah's smarmy enquiry.

"Not unless a dead body constitutes a problem," came the equally smart-ass response. Pleasantries aside, we quickly ascertained that the law firm's Clients' Account was shy about a million pounds, and that this had gone "shy" in the past year and a half.

So, that was that. Bastard. He'd got bored with waiting for Parliament, blew a bunch of pocket change and scampered, leaving the rest of us to pick up the pieces. Not very nice, but actually, not all that surprising.

The rest of the day was a slow-motion swirl, fueled by regular visits to a bottle of vodka one of the secretaries rescued for me. Curtains were pulled, curtains were opened. People came, people left. And the City Jeroboam Board stayed closeted in the conference room all day, wringing their hands in total, useless despair.

Even more clueless was Hugh's close buddy and sometime business partner, the aforementioned Martin Pratt. Hugh had a weakness when it came to extended families. Martin was a poster boy for fat and seedy, thirty going on fifty. It was a toss-up as to which battle he'd lose first: the one with his waistline, or the one with his hairline. He quarantined himself in his small corner office, darting out from time to time, with the strangest expression on his face, before disappearing again, to get even drunker than me.

I was left to comfort Hugh's mistress, Karen, who had burst into the office wailing, crying and bemoaning the fact that Hugh would not now be fulfilling his promise to move in with her and their two-year-old son, Paul. Hugh had begun an affair with Karen, who was one of England's leading show jumpers and horse trainers, after the loss of South-West Cambridge, in 1984. She too was small, a little dumpy, with an elfin face, but blond hair.

John Simmonds visited long enough to declare that there was nothing he could do. And then we played games with the curtains again. What the hell was the deal? I just didn't want the whole of Beaconsfield peering into a dead man's office.

At last, darkness fell. Everyone left. I was on my own. My twin sister, Maggi, arrived from London. She was visiting from Australia, helping to promote a play for a guy who wrote a couple of the episodes for the TV version of "Mission Impossible."

Maggi is a little smaller than me, with a full figure, a boyish cut to her hair, John Lennon glasses, and a sweet pixie face. That's how I always think of her – as a wood nymph, one of Peter Pan's mischievous pals.

She had never liked Hugh. She was repulsed by his cocksure chauvinism and his arrogant amiability. However, she had responded immediately to my telephoned plea for support, which was itself out of character for me. All my life, I had regarded myself as far too self-sufficient to need help of any kind, let alone emotional attention. Yet here I was openly embracing it, and from Maggi of all people.

Notwithstanding the fact that we were twins, I had never considered us to be very much alike. We didn't look alike. And I could find little that we had in common, save for our birthdate. She was artistic; I was a material cynic. She was definitely Venus; I was undoubtedly Mars. She was one in harmony with all the world's dimensions; while I was restless and unsatisfied, driven to experience all the world's glittering prizes. Bless her heart, she'd had good reason, on many occasions, to think of me as little more than a self-promoting poseur. And yet, she had dropped everything to come and be with me.

She sat down opposite me and encouraged me to talk. I was pretty brusque. I didn't have the time. There was a mess to clean up. She insisted. Gently. Eventually we got to the point. I couldn't escape the vision of Hugh driving past my apartment, on his way to those lonely woods, and not stopping and asking me to pick up the pieces, one last time.

"I mean, all I can see … he's in his car, going past the office, past my apartment … all alone. He didn't stop … he didn't come in and talk to me. He could have come in … and talked to me. What was so bad that he couldn't come in and talk to me…?"

I sucked in a long breath, and stared deep into my twin sister's eyes, as much to avoid her as to see her. I continued in a monotone made lifeless by my despair.

"He drove straight past me, and there was nothing I could do. He went to his death alone. I just see him dying so terribly alone…"

"Now, I understand," she said, so very softly I almost missed it.

I looked up. "What?"

"All the way here on the train, he was nagging me." Maggi was serious in her claim to have a psychic streak. "He kept saying, over and over, tell him it's OK, tell him I'm fine, he's not to worry."

My hands went limp in hers. "But I wasn't there for him."

"Oh yes you were," was her immediate yet soft retort, "And he knows that. And whatever happens from now on, he'll be there for you. Always. For the rest of your life."

The day's self-control finally snapped. In the privacy of Hugh's personal office, in the safety of my twin sister's protective embrace, the emotional dam burst. I collapsed into her arms and cried. The confidence and the arrogance were gone. In their place, the simple and honest anguish of a shattered human soul.

***

After what seemed an eternity, we separated. She went to make some coffee. With everyone else gone from the office, I wandered about, gently gathering files and records that I hadn't shared earlier with the Law Society. I'd had no cause to worry beforehand. Hugh was rich after all, right? But now I wanted a more careful calculation of what had been going on the past year and a half.

The answer chilled me to my roots. There was some £5 million ($7.5 million) missing. There was no way Hugh had spent this over a year and a half. It would have amounted to throwing away £40,000 ($60,000) a week.

***

Hugh should have been an actor. Take away his stories of personal wealth, and what you were left with was a life that was one hell of an act. He was the "almost" man, the "not quite" guy.

He wasn't quite a gentleman. He had the tailored suits, the law firm, the fancy car, and membership in the Reform Club. But he was really from the wrong side of the tracks. His father was self-made, and maybe Hugh resented this. All of this. Both the fact that his father was a financial success, and that he was cut from the wrong cloth for Hugh's ambitions.

It was as if Hugh was always trying to prove himself, but was never quite making the grade. His favorite trick was regularly snatching victory from the jaws of defeat, and then just as regularly, tossing it straight back into the slavering jaws.

He could talk himself out of any situation, but never saw the impossibility of the mess he was creating, a mess he normally left me to clean up. He was great at employing successful tactics, but could never grasp the larger, strategic picture.

Hugh believed he could do anything. He was ruthlessly ambitious, and wholly single-minded about achieving an objective, whatever the cost. This is why I'd been attracted to him. I had no political background in my family. He was going somewhere I wanted to be. And I was having my own success in his wake, in elections and in the Party, up to and including the national level.

He never thought twice about cutting corners. And maybe this was the problem. Maybe he'd grown restless at having spent seventeen years with a political game plan that was now on hold, but which in the meantime, had sidetracked him from emulating, or exceeding, his father's monetary success?

This then was the theory that quickly took hold with friend and foe alike, and which was splattered all over England's national press. Namely that Hugh, fabulously talented but flawed young Conservative star, had emptied his firm's Clients' Account, in the *single largest defalcation in the history of the Law Society*, to finance some "get-rich-quick" scheme that then went wrong. Most everyone was agreed that he hadn't simply spent the money – but that there was some "investment."

That's where everyone else left it, but not me. They had an answer for his death: the missing money. But I didn't have an answer for the money going missing. I had no illusions about Hugh's character. No rosy-tinted spectacles for this boy. I knew better. And what I knew left two burning questions in my mind about the allegedly stolen money: why hadn't Hugh run away with it, and why had he thought he could get away with it in the first place?

**

There was no more I could achieve staying in the country of my birth. Eventually, news of the missing money would hit my small hometown. And even though I knew I had not been involved, my fellow townsfolk would not look upon me with generosity. Time to move to the second nation where I hold citizenship: the US of A.

A few days before I left for good, I had lunch with Hugh's father, John Simmonds, whom I had been helping to pick up the scattered family pieces of Hugh's life.

At the end of lunch, with no warning, he turned to me, and in a deadpan voice told me that he'd been approached by two gentlemen he preferred not to name, who had told him that Hugh had taken all of the money "to get an agent out of a foreign country."

I realized I had never included in my equations the fact that Hugh had mentioned to me from time to time that he was a senior officer with MI6, Britain's foreign intelligence service.

That's when I had a sudden vision of blinding clarity. It was the look on Martin's face. I had finally identified it. It wasn't shock, surprise or even anger. Those would have been understandable. It had been fear. Cold, naked, unreasoning fear.

Perhaps if at that point I had listened to the voice that was beginning to nag in my mind, I would have avoided what was to come. I would have continued with my ordinary life. But would I truly have wanted that?

CHAPTER TWO

British Intelligence

I T WAS A DULL and overcast Saturday, the sort for which Britain is famous, contrary to its reputation as a green and pleasant land. I had known Hugh just a few months, having met him at some worthy function or another in Beaconsfield in late 1975. He was just a Town Councilor then; I was still a lowly Youth Club leader.

We'd done lunch in one of the older hostelries in the historic part of Beaconsfield, and were now off on a meandering journey through the rural delights of western England. To be precise, the road signs stated that we were approaching the outskirts of Hereford, just a little to the east of the Welsh border.

Drizzle, another British specialty, was just beginning to spray as we pulled up to the doors of one more ancient drinking hole. "Wait here," Hugh commanded, "I'll be back in a minute." And a minute and a half later, he was back, with a small, wrapped package in his hand.

"You seem particularly uncurious," he stated, with an amused twinkle in his eye. I just shrugged, and returned my gaze to the vibrant but soaking wet landscape. I'd got used to episodes of strange goings-on when with Hugh. He had made no secret of his involvement with British Intelligence. Seemed a little weird to me. Wasn't this all supposed to be shrouded in secrecy? Why tell me? His retort was always the same. I was his insurance – just in case something happened.

Eventually we stopped at a turn-out, on top of a spectacularly bleak and abandoned hill. We had been there no more than five minutes when an Army Land Rover pulled up behind us. Hugh again told me to stay put. He got out with the package.

He advanced slowly towards the Army vehicle. Three soldiers, in full camouflage got out, two with down-turned rifles. They took up positions on either side of the turn-out, facing outward, scanning the surroundings. The third, clearly an officer of some sort, met up with Hugh. They had a few moments of conversation. Then, just as Hugh was handing over the package, two extremely large and extremely noisy fighter aircraft came out of nowhere, and passed immediately overhead.

Hugh got back into the car, and we drove home. Not a word passed between us, save for one humorous aside from Hugh, "I love it when things go off according to plan."

I later learned that Hereford is the home base for the SAS, the Special Air Service, Britain's elite Special Forces unit, the one that had so dramatically rescued the hostages from the Iranian Embassy in 1981, on primetime national television.

**

I could fill a book with similar occurrences. So could other friends of Hugh's. Why did he tell us? Oh, I'm sure that some part of it had to do with that "insurance" idea of his. But the primary reason was that he wanted to impress upon us his vision of himself as the swashbuckling renaissance hero.

Hugh was attracted to the romance of espionage. Certainly, he was loud and brash and obnoxious; and ruthless and driven and ambitious, too. And I'm sure the intelligence services offered all manner of scope for those less attractive features of Hugh's character. But more than that, Hugh was an incurable romantic and dreamer.

Alexander was his hero. Arthur his passion. He devoured Tolkein and Asimov and Arthur C. Clarke. His dreams were the stuff of quest and conquest. Loyalty and honor. Passion and pride. If there were still a Big Game out there, and room for a latter-day Lawrence of Arabia, he wanted in. I felt sure he believed that the best chance of finding it was with the clandestine services.

For certain, the Chairman of the Beaconsfield Conservative Association, when Hugh first became active in local politics in his early twenties, was one Colonel Ian Lapraik, a former Commandant of the SAS. Both of his political mentors, Sir Ronald Bell, the late Member of Parliament for Beaconsfield, and Enoch Powell, the former Conservative Cabinet Minister, had served in British Military Intelligence during the Second World War. And Hugh hung a Ceremonial Sword over his mantelpiece. Attached to it was the Scabbard Sling of the Black Watch, a secretive Army Regiment with close ties to the SAS.

In 1985, at the tender age of 37, Hugh was appointed the youngest-ever Commander of the Most Noble Order of the British Empire (CBE). Ostensibly, Hugh was awarded his CBE in gratitude for his service to the Conservative Party. Indeed, he was recommended for a Knighthood, but the then Chairman of the Conservative Party, one John Selwyn Gummer, found himself on the opposite side of the debate from Hugh about membership in the European Union, and so had downgraded the honor. Most solely political honors were specifically designated "for political service." Hugh's was described as "for political and public service."

On the evening of his Investiture, relaxing back at home with a tumbler of Scotch in hand, but still wearing his formal penguin suit, Hugh regaled his closest friends with every Seinfeldian detail of the day's events: his conversation with the Queen, the color of the drapes, the size of Buckingham Palace. Eventually, everyone but Janet and I had drifted away. Then, even Janet grew tired at the fifteenth recounting of the tale. She had, after all, been there as well.

When he was sure that Janet was in bed, he handed me the satin inlaid box holding the medal and supporting neck ribbon. I remember the pattern clearly. Grey silk ribbon, with salmon edging. Then, he lifted the satin inlay, to reveal a second ribbon. This one was the same pattern, but with a salmon stripe down the middle as well. I was later told by an expert on military decorations that this second ribbon was the ribbon for the military CBE. The first was the civilian equivalent.

Hugh told me that it was not usual for civilian officers in Intelligence to be honored. You can hardly have supposedly secret members of a government service wandering about town with a breast laden with hardware. However, in view of his civilian honor, the powers that be had decided that it would be appropriate to take the opportunity to honor him with the military appointment to CBE as well.

After his chit-chat with the Queen, and while Janet was occupied elsewhere, Hugh had been taken to a private room within Buckingham Palace, and was there secretly appointed.

***

The coroner's inquest on Hugh had been held on March 20, 1989. The verdict had been death by his own hand. It was on this occasion that the Law Society revealed for the first time the full extent of Hugh's defalcation. Interestingly enough, they didn't report it as £5 million ($7.5 million), but only as £3.8 million ($5.2 million). Why was someone not claiming their money?

Most of the articles were stodgy and boring. But one had headlines describing me as fleeing the country. The body of the article referred to the fact that I was refusing to return to the UK to answer questions. I telephoned the journalist, one Chris Hutchins (then of London's *Today* tabloid; currently a well-known royal biographer). I was all piss and vinegar. Acidly, I asked him who his sources were. He told me that they were the police and the Law Society.

I rang their representatives, and proceeded to have tart "conversations," which crammed as much Shakespearean vulgarity as it was humanly possible to remember into the short time allowed to me before they hung up. Feeling much better, I then returned to Chris Hutchins to set the record straight.

I explained that their judiciously placed red herring had all been a consequence of the fact that they'd been unable to turn up anything substantial. "So, do you have some theories of your *own*?" was the immediate comeback. Tabloid journalists may be the scum of the earth, but they can spot a story a mile off, with blinkers on, and their heads shoved in a lead-encased toilet bowl.

Chris knew he had gold dust when the pregnant silence dragged on for more than two seconds. I was nervous sharing what might appear to be outlandish fantasy about MI6 and agents in foreign countries. But Chris proved to be psychic. And quite gentle. Well, like a kick in the head from a rodeo bull is gentle. "Does it have anything to do with the D-Notice that was slapped against Hugh's story?"

What?

Britain doesn't have a First Amendment. The media can print anything it likes, provided the Government likes it. Every media outlet has a civil servant from the Ministry of Defense on site. All articles have to be vetted by him. If he believes an article contains something that might endanger national security, he can yank it, or slap a D-Notice, a Defense Notice, on it.

Chris told me that a friend of his, a TV producer with the BBC, had told him that they had done a half hour segment on Hugh for *Newsnight*, the BBC's nightly, one-hour newsmagazine show. The segment had been D-Noticed. I told Chris to check with his source.

If the source confirmed the D-Notice, and could give details, I'd think about talking to him.

About an hour later, Chris called me, in a very agitated state. A tabloid journalist gets ruffled about as often as an angel descends and goes on a shoplifting spree. Chris told me that the TV producer was not only now denying there had been a D-Notice, he was even denying he'd ever spoken to Chris about one.

Some years later, I was told that the most serious level of D-Notice is called a Category A, D-Notice. This is the one they use when there's a war on, or a spy defects, or the Queen is photographed in bed with the President of the United States. A "Category A" D-Notices the offending article, and then it D-Notices the D-Notice. Then it D-Notices the D-Noticer and then, just for good measure, it wipes all the fingerprints off the ashtrays. My source told me that the Hugh D-Notice had to have been Category A.

So. We were now definitely out of the realm of wine-induced speculation. Kansas had been left a long way behind. Something was afoot. Something was being hidden. And it was up to me to find out what it was, because somebody had me firmly in their sights, possibly as the next fall guy. I needed to get information, any way that I could.

***

It was then that I remembered Hugh had sometimes mentioned his pal-in-arms, a bloke who went by the unlikely name of Reginald von Zugbach de Sugg. I'd met him once, at one of Hugh's summer garden parties. Last I'd heard, he was in Glasgow. Time to return to Great Britain – if by a circuitous route, for safety. Why the concern? Well, it was at about this time that I started experiencing weird echoes and clicks on the telephone.

Chapter Three

Reginald von Zugbach de Sugg

I HAD NO IDEA WHAT TO EXPECT in Great Britain. Better safe than sorry. So, I brought with me my six-foot brother-in-law, Gregg. Our plane touched down in Belgium in the late afternoon. As we made our way up an escalator, after our dealings at the immigration desk, I looked back, and noticed a nondescript man emerge from a door behind the desk, walk over and collect our papers, before disappearing back through the door.

We walked to the nearby railway station, to catch the subway to the ferry, which was to take us across the English Channel. The station was a typical Old European mock-Renaissance monstrosity, all chandeliers and huge staircases, with enormous balustrades. At the top of the staircase leading to the subway was a man, standing around, doing nothing, with a newspaper tucked under his arm.

Nothing wrong with that. Except that when we got down to the subway and turned around, there he was, about twenty paces behind. Gregg and I looked at each other, went back upstairs, passing "Newspaper Guy" on the way, and waited up top. Sure enough, Newspaper Guy followed us, and renewed his perch at the head of the staircase. We shrugged, and went downstairs again. Whereupon, the routine was repeated. Without shame.

From that moment on, and indeed for the next couple of months, there was clear evidence of being followed almost all the time, either on foot or by car. Undeterred, we made our way to the beckoning mysteries of Glasgow.

***

Gregg and I arrived in Glasgow, Scotland, on a Friday. A more depressing city you cannot imagine. All goth and grime. It was as I imagined some of the worst Soviet cities must have looked. We made a beeline for the Public Library, to try to find a home address for Hugh's intelligence buddy.

After some difficulty, we succeeded. We'd been looking under 'Sugg,' and there he was under 'Zugbach' all the time. The first thing I noticed was that he lived in the town of Dumfries, which was barely a stone's throw from Lockerbie.

Further research indicated that Dr. Reginald von Zugbach de Sugg had once been a British Army Major, but at the time was a Professor in Management Studies at the University of Glasgow. Reggie (which was how I remembered Hugh always referring to him) had published a book, called *Power and Prestige in the British Army*. The book was critical of management structures within the services, and it had aroused the interest of senior officers in the French Army.

Reggie's home address was deserted. A neighbor told us that Reggie and his wife were getting divorced and that they had both moved out in December. Rats. We'd have to wait until Monday, and try to catch him at the university.

We had time to kill, and almost got killed by a roving band of drunk Glaswegians. We were saved by my brother-in-law's timely impersonation of Crocodile Dundee. Although in this case, the 12-inch knife he produced like magic was hidden in his cowboy boot. I have yet to work out how he got it through airport security.

***

Bright and early Monday, I telephoned Reggie at the University. He had no idea who I was, but agreed to have lunch with me at the Glasgow Royal Automobile Club. He met me midday at my hotel, and we walked the few streets to the Club.

Notwithstanding the Teutonic name, Reggie bore all the hallmarks of a classic British military officer. Just watch any period movie about the British Empire in India, and you have Reggie in your mind's eye. Six feet tall, cropped hair, ramrod back, the arrogant stain of Empire still evident on his hard, upturned face.

We set off at a clip for the RAC. Reggie didn't look at me, just fired questions. Who was I? Why was I here? Why did I want to see him? Had Hugh been murdered? This last one stopped me. Reggie carried on a few more paces, before noticing that I was no longer in step with him.

"Why the last question?" I asked, matching Reggie's hardness with my own.

Reggie came back, and leaned down into my face. "I don't yet know who you are, but I knew Hugh. And he was not the type to take his own life." He hesitated for a second. "But if he did, he was under some mighty duress."

We circled each other for a few moments. "I'm here because I'm trying to make sense of his death," I offered as a challenge.

"But how can I help?" he responded warily.

"By confirming he was in British Intelligence," was my quick retort.

"How could I do that?" Reggie now had a half smile on his face. "By confirming that you are," a smile advancing over my face as well.

With this, Reggie thrust his hands into his pockets, and wandered over to me, slowly. He whispered gently into my ear, "Problem is, laddie, if I am, the Official Secrets Act requires that I deny it. And if I'm not, then I have to deny it anyway. Try something else."

And so the games began.

***

I merrily responded to Reggie's invitation by regaling him, throughout lunch, with all of the anecdotes Hugh had told me of their derring-do, while the two of them were in Czechoslovakia together. That had been in 1968, the year the Soviets had invaded that poor, repressed country, in order to re-impose Stalinist-style Communism.

The one I liked the best was the one where Reggie and Hugh had been captured in a barn. Reggie had been shot in the back. And later, while the Soviet guards were doing something particularly nasty and painful to Reggie's fingernails, the only pleasure he had given them was when he finally screamed, "Shit, that hurts!"

Reggie had feigned indifference for going on an hour by this point. But with this last story, he put down his fork, studiously wiped his mouth with his linen handkerchief, and, mustering a thousand years of combined Teutonic and British pride, archly pronounced that, being a gentleman, he never screamed. Thank you. "And the word I used was 'ouch,'" he concluded, with an aristocratic sniff.

He then got up from the table, and motioned me to follow. We entered the men's toilet. Reggie locked the door, checked the window, and ran a couple of the faucets, I assumed to deter any listening devices. How exciting. Just like the movies. Yawn.

Reggie looked thoroughly amused. "It seems Hugh was a little indiscreet."

"Not really," I rejoined, "It served its purpose. No-one else believes me; but I know enough to be here engaging you."

"Hmm. Maybe." He looked at the floor for a few minutes, obviously deep in thought. It's a good thing that all the other RAC members were constipated. Finally, he looked up. "OK. I can tell you this much, but no more: I was in a military branch of British Intelligence, and Hugh was in a civilian equivalent."

At last a nugget. A tiny crack. I was ecstatic. So much so that I found myself babbling about all sorts of nonsense. Ending with the declaration that this probably explained why I had been followed all the way to Glasgow by what was clearly a very professional outfit.

Suddenly I was aware that, except for the echo of my own voice, there was no other sound in the bathroom. I glanced over at Reggie. His face had turned white, and he was muttering to himself. The aristocratic sneer had disappeared. "...damn, I thought I'd got rid of them, but you've brought them back..." This last comment was directed at me, and the hard stare was back in his eyes.

He grabbed my arm, unlocked the door, and shuffled me towards the Club entrance. "Look," he barked, "if you value your life, you will do exactly as I say." And with that, we were into the sunlight, and onto a chase scene that was more bizarre and twisted than anything any scriptwriter ever could have devised.

***

As we crossed the road in military two-step, he whispered harshly in my ear, "Stay to my side, don't look up, they may not recognize you." We maintained the brisk pace all the way to the car in the parking lot, with Reggie giving me a running commentary: "You were right. They're out in force. One on the corner over there. One on the other side of the road. No, don't look," he hissed. "I wonder if they're after you or me? Oh very clever ... one behind us dressed as a police-woman..."

Once in his car, he told me to lock my door, and then locked his own. We made our way slowly across the parking lot, Reggie glancing in every direction. He stopped briefly at the exit. "Roll down your window," he commanded, "And just stare obviously at that man standing on the corner, over there on the left."

Hey, what did I know? I did as Reggie suggested. The man, apparently on cue, turned away. At which point, Reggie swung the car violently to the right, tires squealing. We would have sped off down the road, if we hadn't been stopped by the traffic lights. Not the way it happens in the cinema, at all. A car tucked in behind us. "Damn," came Reggie's muttered oath.

The lights changed. And we entered a realm of fantasy driving, not to be found on the daytime menu of your average downtown driving school. My heart was pretty much firmly lodged in my mouth. Indeed, this time a whole series of scenes did flash before my eyes. But they weren't about me. They were about Hugh.

***

It was the British General Election of 1979. Hugh was the Conservative Parliamentary Candidate in that safe Labour seat of West Leeds. One of Margaret Thatcher's closest lieutenants, Airey Neave, was assassinated by an IRA bomb, which had been positioned underneath his car. It was generally known that Neave had been in British Military Intelligence during the Second World War. In fact, he was something of a hero, having been imprisoned in Colditz, Germany's top-security prison castle.

The day after Neave's assassination, a nondescript little man appeared at our campaign headquarters. He spoke to Hugh in urgent whispers, and then disappeared for an hour or two with my brother Jon, who was helping out by being Hugh's campaign driver.

Later that night, Jon, unable to contain himself any more, revealed to me that he had spent the afternoon with this guy, who did not offer his name, learning all sorts of driving tricks with Hugh's Rover sedan.

How to perform a 180-degree emergency-brake turn. How to judge and navigate sharp corners, without braking. And best of all, how to know which parts of the car were least vulnerable to being hit.

"Why?" I asked Jon, already guessing at the answer.

"So that I know which parts of the car I can use to ram other cars, if we're in a trap," he exclaimed, the look of a happy five-year-old plastered on his beaming face.

That same year Lord Mountbatten, the Queen's cousin and a Field Marshal in the British Army, was among those killed in a rash of IRA assassination.

I remember standing by Hugh as he gazed sadly at the television set, recording the funeral of Lord Mountbatten. Softly, as if I was not there, he murmured that the IRA had good sources because they were killing off all the former British Intelligence desk officers for Northern Ireland.

That was some years before the Good Friday Peace Accord, brokered by a combination of Northern Irish Catholic and Protestant politicians, and midwifed by Bill Clinton, John Major and Tony Blair. Before the Accord, the '70s and '80s had been a time of regular IRA bombing campaigns on the UK mainland.

The first IRA bomb, aimed at civilians in Great Britain, had been planted in the '70s, at the Old Bailey, in London. The Old Bailey is England's premier criminal court. A bomb scare was telephoned into the central desk. All the courts were immediately emptied onto the street fronting the building. Some moments later, the massive bomb exploded. But outside, not inside the building, catching innocent bystanders, who thought they had reached safety. Hugh had been at the Old Bailey that day, and was standing outside when the bomb exploded. He was unscratched, save for some temporary hearing loss.

As the years passed, the British public became much more safety-conscious, decades before the American public had to go through the same routine in response to 9/11 and the threat from radical Muslim militias. Police were alerted to suspicious packages left on trains; over-parked cars were blown up with controlled explosions.

This was why I had suspected, instantly, that the subway bombs, in London, in 2005, had to have been the work of suicide bombers. The British public had become far too aware of terrorist threats to allow five separate bombs to sit around unquestioned. Those bombs had to have been introduced in a fashion that would have gone unnoticed, and then been detonated by people in close proximity.

Some years after the first IRA bombing campaign in London, Hugh found himself dining one evening with a friend, at an exclusive restaurant in London, called Wilton's. Suddenly, there was a crash of glass, and a heavy object came tumbling in through the shattered window. Hugh was quick to react. He upended the heavy table at which he and the friend were sitting, seized his friend, and took cover behind the table.

His friend had been a little faster. As Hugh was reaching for him, he grabbed the open and expensive bottle of claret they had been drinking, and hit the floor, cushioning the precious bottle with his body. The IRA bomb exploded a second later.

Again, both Hugh and his friend were unhurt, but as Hugh recounted cryptically some years later, there weren't too many "civilians" who found themselves in the midst of two IRA bombings. I still wonder whether Hugh's initials are carved somewhere on that Northern Ireland desk. I wasn't doing much wondering at the time, though. I was more focused on Reggie's exotic driving skills.

**

Reggie had us circling blocks. Dodging through parking lots. In and out of driveways. Stopping. Starting. Doubling back. Down one street. Up another. Until we found ourselves trapped in a dead end.

I glanced at Reggie. He smiled wanly. "It really doesn't happen like this in the movies," was his weak explanation.

He reversed hurriedly, the engine screaming, the gears grinding. At the last moment, Reggie swung the car around in a perfect 180-degree emergency brake turn, just missing the car that had been on our tail. "Yup," I thought to myself, "that's how Jon did it." A couple of Middle-Eastern looking swarthies leaned out the windows, cursing and spitting, and waving handguns at us.

Reggie was into his groove now. We went the wrong way down one-way streets. Turned right, while signaling left. Slowed down; speeded up. In and out; roundabout.

Halfway through the pursuit, a third car joined in. Although for the life of me I couldn't work out if they were chasing us, or the car behind us. No matter. We all continued with the stomach-churning nonsense for a further twenty minutes until Reggie lost all of the pursuers.

Reggie then pulled into the parking lot of a rather seedy apartment complex. As we entered his apartment, he rummaged around behind a small cupboard by the front door, extracted a six-shooter, and tucked it into his coat pocket. As he was doing this, I couldn't help but notice the gold signet ring on his left pinky finger. Engraved as it was with the crest of a double-headed eagle.

***

I know I should have been terrified, but I wasn't. I found myself unusually calm, with everything happening around me in a kind of warm slow motion. I sat in a chair in the corner of his living room, and just watched Reggie with detached bemusement.

He was making a telephone call. Didn't say very much. Just a couple of words. Then hung up. Finally, he turned to me. The confident air was gone. However I might have been feeling, Reggie was clearly now a very agitated man.

He sat down on the edge of a sofa, nervous and twitchy, and the words came tumbling out of his mouth. Hugh and he had not met accidentally. The implication was that he had had something to do with Hugh's original recruitment. Reggie confirmed that he had been with Hugh in Czechoslovakia in 1968. He even confirmed the "ouch" story, though he embellished it somewhat.

I got the feeling Reggie was trying to convince me of something, but I couldn't work out what or why. Frankly, he'd had me at "ouch." Nevertheless, Reggie continued unchecked. He stated that Hugh had been involved in some "interesting bits and pieces" before his death. Reggie did not believe that Hugh was a crook. And he repeated that he did not hold with the line that Hugh had committed suicide. "Not with all we've been through," was his heartfelt explanation.

Reggie mentioned that he'd been threatened in a local telephone call, made to his then home, in Dumfries, in October 1988. The message had been picked up by his answering machine. The chilling message had stated, matter-of-factly: "We are going to get you, Doctor." He handed the tape over to the Police. I could check. Both Reggie and his wife had received continuing telephone calls, always threatening. His house had been broken into, on a number of occasions. So had his car. Papers had been taken. His mail had been interfered with.

Although Reggie did not discuss his wife, he did say that, since the end of 1988, he'd had to move from apartment to apartment, in order to keep his night-time location a secret. Every evening, he'd go through the same rigmarole I'd just experienced in his car, just to get home safely. No one would bother him during the day, in the open. That would invite unwanted attention. No. The cloak and dagger routine was reserved for the dark hours, away from public gaze.

"But they're in the open today," I countered.

He looked at me darkly. "Yes," he spat, "and you brought them with you. I thought they'd lost interest in me last April. Now, I can't work out whether they want me, or you."

Reggie held my gaze for a second longer, and then dropped his head in his hands. He explained that he'd been in fear of his life since before Hugh had died. That's why he'd been hiding out. "God," he cried out, flinging his arm around the tiny room, "you think I choose to live like this?"

I asked him why he thought he was in danger. His stumbling response wasn't very convincing. There were things he was not prepared to tell me. He began chopping and changing his routine, one minute alluding to the things in which Hugh had become involved, the next, affecting ignorance of anything and everything.

I asked him who he thought was causing all the trouble – MI6 (Britain's foreign intelligence service) or MI5? For the first time, he laughed out loud. "Neither," he exclaimed, with genuine amusement, "whoever they are, they're far too sophisticated for British Intelligence."

He paused for a second. Then continued. "Look. I'd like you to see me and my new girlfriend, later this afternoon. Say about 5:30 P.M?"

I wondered why.

"I want you to repeat everything to her," he reasoned, "about Hugh, about the missing money, about your suspicions. I want her to hear it from someone else. I want some insurance. OK?"

I shrugged my shoulders. Why not? How much further could I descend into Wonderland?

After this, Reggie went silent. Then, he made another abbreviated telephone call. This time, he did more listening than talking. By the time he hung up, his facial expression had hardened. "Right," he said coldly, "time to go."

He reached into a desk drawer, and pulled out a passport. Tucked it into another pocket of his coat. I asked him where he was going: "Away for a while." What about the meeting with your girlfriend? "Canceled," came his taut reply.

We went back to the car. There was a man standing by the entrance to the parking lot, watching us. We got into the car, locked the doors, and drove past the man, without looking at him. As we pulled into the street, a new car slipped in behind us. And so the circus act began again.

There was no further conversation between Reggie and me. He concentrated on his alarming driving regime. Finally, we approached a multi-story car park. As we sped into the basement, he shouted more instructions at me. "When I say 'jump,'" he ordered, "you get out fast."

We swerved around a couple of pillars, and then as we came up to a dark corner, he yelled at me to jump. I flung open the door, and launched myself out. The car was still moving, and I staggered for a few steps. But I quickly steadied myself, and then looked back at Reggie's car.

He had brought the car to a halt, and was leaning across the passenger seat. Aiming his gun at me. Without thinking, I threw myself towards a half-open door, nestled in the dark corner, about five feet away. The last thing I heard, as I disappeared through the welcoming doorway, was the sound of two ear-splitting explosions behind me.

CHAPTER FOUR

Law Society

GREGG WAS VERY UNDERSTANDING, but forceful. He had not signed up for guns. I gave him the airfare home, and wished him well. I tried Reggie at the University a couple more times, but no one had seen him.

I left messages and returned to London, there to stay with Rissa, a delightful friend of my younger sister, Susannah, the sister who was married to Gregg.

I whiled away the time getting acquainted with those who seemed hell bent on implicating me in Hugh's defalcation. Quite aside from anything else, I wanted to know if they were exploring the MI6 angle. First stop, the Law Society.

***

The Law Society, headquartered in Chancery Lane, finds itself surrounded by the gothic spires and turrets of London's ancient High Court. Perhaps inspired by surroundings that date back to the Middle Ages, my meeting with the Law Society turned out to be something akin to the Spanish Inquisition.

There were six of them, including Geoff Hughes, the lead investigator of Carratu International, the firm of fraud investigators appointed by the Law Society to track down the money missing from Hugh's Clients' Account.

Geoff had a tape recorder on the table in front of him. I had one hidden in my jacket pocket. It proved to be a singularly frustrating get together, the reason for which was established with the first exchange: "Why are you here?" asked the Law Society's head honcho, who did not introduce himself.

"Well," I replied, "I've always liked England in the summer; the cool climate, the languid afternoons, the sound of leather against willow at a village cricket game…"

"No, Mr. Gilson," the no-name interrupted curtly, "why did you want to see us?"

"Oh," I feigned surprise, "to clear my name. But more to the point, to find out why you were the ones who decided to start dragging it through the mud? You told me I was in the clear."

"Yes. Well. We've determined in the last few months that Simmonds must have had help," was the short reply, "and it was decided that you were the most obvious candidate."

After that, they pretty much clammed up. They quite openly took the view that the only reason I was there was to throw them off my trail. "But here I am, do your worst," I countered. To no avail. They were convinced I was trying to pull something clever. If they only knew.

I hammered away for an hour. I was riding a confident streak after my episode with Reggie. I had nothing to lose.

They did admit that they hadn't recovered any of the missing money. In fact, after some gentle baiting, they grudgingly confessed that they hadn't even traced any of the missing money. What's more, they had no clue as to why only £3.8 million ($5.6 million) of the £5 million ($7.5 million) stolen had been claimed.

I was beginning to see why they were turning the spotlight on me. They had run out of alternatives. In some exasperation, I finally wondered aloud why on earth they were even bothering to spend time with me that morning.

In equal frustration, a little weasel of a desk clerk, John, suddenly piped up from the back: "Because we think you know where the £10 million ($15 million) came from."

Except for the quite audible sound of leather shoe impacting on the clerk's exposed ankle, you could have heard a pin drop in that room.

"Come again," I said. "I thought we'd just established that you hadn't traced any money?

Silence.

"And now we're talking about some £10 million extra?" Another pregnant pause, broken by the no-name head honcho.

He cleared his throat noisily: "We appear to have found some £10 million that does not belong to any of Simmonds' clients. We wondered if you had any ideas…?"

I'd had enough for one morning. I gave them Reggie's telephone number, and suggested, my voice icy with sarcasm, that they give him a call. As I was leaving, I noticed out of the corner of my eye Geoff Hughes, looking quite amused. He signaled me to have a word with him. I had mentioned in the meeting about my being followed. Geoff told me he wanted to take up a hidden vantage point in the parking lot before I made a move for my car. I obliged, waited a few, and then drove off, quite obviously being followed by a fake taxi.

A couple of days later, I telephoned Geoff and asked him if he had seen the taxi. "Oh yes, the taxi," he answered softly, "and the other two cars as well."

In Geoff's opinion, I was being tailed by what he described as a classic three-car tandem formation. I asked him to define what he meant by "classic." He hung up. Geoff was no pen-pushing desk jockey. His first career had been as a Senior Inspector with Her Majesty's Customs and Excise.

***

On which note, my next port of call was a Senior Inspector with Her Majesty's Police Constabulary. I was in no mood to be trifled with. If I was to be so openly held in suspicion, I might as well tackle the accusers head on. Specifically, I met with a Detective Inspector Lambert and a Detective Sergeant Brown. Another inconclusive conversation followed.

The police had already cottoned to the fact that Hugh appeared to have been messing around with more than just his clients' money. Lambert said that they too were now openly looking for an accomplice. However, he didn't seem to be making any real effort to find one. Except for continually asking me if I was yet ready to tell him where the missing money was. He almost visibly yawned when I suggested that he might find the answers with British intelligence agencies.

Lambert did, however, confirm that I was being followed. Not by them, he hastened to add, with a heartless chuckle. But by a car that followed me into the police parking lot. An officer had been dispatched to talk to the driver, but he'd driven away before they could catch him. The police in England aren't much into Cops-style TV chases.

I gave Lambert a list of license plate numbers for the cars that had been following Gregg and me. A few weeks later, Lambert informed me that two of the plates were "odd." One belonged to a firm of private investigators in Surrey; the other to a company that "doesn't exist." When asked to explain what that meant, he wouldn't say any more. He sounded somewhat embarrassed.

Not half as embarrassed as when he had to admit that the tape recording of our initial interview didn't exist because his recording machine hadn't functioned.

This might have had something to do with the phantom "Detective Sergeant Brown." Nick Brown, as he'd been introduced to me, had contributed nothing during my interview with Lambert. When I called the police station the first time to speak with Lambert about the tape recording, I was told Lambert was not in the station. When I asked for his assistant, Sergeant Brown, I was told that they'd never had a Sergeant Brown in the station.

MI5 is the domestic counterpart to Britain's foreign intelligence service, MI6. However, it should not be confused with America's FBI, which is a national law enforcement agency, as well as a spy-catching operation. MI5 can only go after foreign spies. It has no "every-day" law enforcement capacity. It cannot arrest or even question criminal suspects. For this to be done, it has to get its officers to "pretend" to be police officers, so that they can sit in and listen while real police officers question suspects. As has been proven time and again by investigative journalists, the tell-tale sign of such MI5 "sit-ins" is their subsequent "disappearance" when inquiries became a little too intrusive.

Curious. If I was so far off base with my enquiries, why was MI5 interested in me? As a lark, I contacted Geoff Hughes, and asked if I could have a copy of the tape recording Carratu International had made of our meeting at the Law Society: "Um, funny thing, Geoff," Hughes told me, "but that tape recording's been lost…"

***

Rissa had been the perfect hostess, even attempting to take an interest in what I was doing. I don't think, however, she believed a word of it. So it was with enormous surprise that she flung open the door that evening to tell me breathlessly that Reggie had called and would be calling later: "Oh my goodness, Geoff, he exists; he really exists!"

***

"It's a good thing you're a fast runner, and I'm a lover of mankind." I'll say this for Reggie, he certainly knew how to start a conversation in style.

"So, what was the parking lot all about," I asked, my calm voice belying my frantic heart, which was tapping a merry tattoo on my ribs.

"I had my orders," Reggie replied. Those orders were to kill me. Not because someone knew what I was doing, but because no one knew what I was doing. Better safe than sorry. But Reggie had doubts. He wanted now to play a double game. Pretend to be getting information from me, while actually trying to find out what was going on.

"I'll be in touch," was his last comment before hanging up. I'd had no time to get a home telephone number, or come to think of it, quiz him as to how he'd found out Rissa's telephone number.

***

Well, that was a somewhat shorter conversation than I had hoped for. Time for a quick review: no money; no bodyguard; Reggie on "walkabout." My name still mud. And the Law Society and the police not prepared to look at MI6, and taking the view I have no right to be poking my nose into any of this. What was a chap to do?

I came up with the bright idea that maybe I should be poking my nose with a little more depth and breadth. So, while waiting on Reggie, I decided to spend my time and my money making the rounds of as many of Hugh's friends and acquaintances as I could, to see what they might know.

***

Neil Relph, Hugh's former accountant, was the classic success story of Margaret Thatcher's attempts in the '80s to turn Great Britain into an enterprise economy like America's: a country which had its own dream, to which every ordinary Joe could aspire through hard work and dedication. Neil hadn't been to the best schools, but he'd earned his college degree, studied to be an accountant, found a working balance between charm and sweat, and was now next in line to be Senior Partner of Rouse and Company, Beaconsfield's largest firm of chartered accountants.

Neil raised the first suggestion that I'd heard of about potential political involvement or protection at a high level. He stated that on the same day that the Law Society had informed Hugh they wanted to meet with him (the day before he died), Hugh's primary bank, National Westminster, had given him notice that all of his bank accounts were to be foreclosed upon – the kiss of death to any practicing solicitor.

But intriguingly, Neil impressed upon me, it had not been the local manager's idea to foreclose on Hugh's bank accounts, and not on that particular day. The instruction had come directly from the Office of the Chairman of National Westminster, Lord Thomas Boardman, who had served as a Treasury Minister in a former Conservative Government, and had been Joint Treasurer of the Conservative Party in the early '80s. Coincidence, or a coordinated dropping of the blade?

Boardman, later, had to resign as Chairman of NatWest in 1989 because of a scandal involving a large British company, what was then called Blue Arrow plc. NatWest's stockbroking subdivision had been involved in illegal activity with regards to a huge share issue for Blue Arrow in 1987. Martha Stewart and Enron did not invent stock and accounting fraud in the second stock boom in the '90s. They'd learned their skills from all those who cut their teeth doing the same things in the first stock boom in the '80s.

***

The Law Society had covered all of its bases. They had appointed their own solicitors as administrators of Hugh's estate. A firm by the name of Charles Russell, out of Hale Court, in Lincoln's Inn, London. Between them and Carratu International, the Law Society had monopolized all the information on Hugh's financial affairs.

I checked with the Probate Division of the High Court in London, where Hugh's will was registered. A signed copy of Hugh's redrafted will had never been found. So, the original one had precedence. The two named executors in that latter Will, Peter Smith and Philip de Nahlik, had revoked their positions as executors within days of Hugh's death. This left the estate adrift, and Janet pretty much adrift too. Peter and Philip had been Hugh's closest friends. To my knowledge, Janet never heard from them again.

The Probate Division records indicated that Hugh had left bona fide assets of some £1.6 million ($2.4 million). Not bad for a forty-year-old, who had dedicated the major part of his adult life to the "non-profit" pursuit of politics. It was also something of a dose of cold water for those who kept referring to Hugh as "failed."

Problem was that the Law Society, as was their right, had made a claim against the estate for the £2.7 million ($4 million) they had already had to pay out to Hugh's former clients in compensation. This had bankrupted the estate, leaving Hugh's family penniless. It was only John Simmonds' unfailing generosity and loyalty that saved Janet and Karen, their houses, and their children's childhoods.

As soon as the Law Society made their claim against the rudderless estate, they were entitled to appoint their own administrators of the estate, and this they had done. Technically, it is not the Law Society or their investigators (in this case, Carratu International) which recovers money. Technically, the estate's new administrators "decide" to hire the Law Society's investigators, who hand over all the information they have gathered about the whereabouts of any money and assets, bona fide or otherwise. It is then the estate's administrators, on behalf of the estate's creditors, who take the action necessary to recover any money, and dispose of the assets.

Taking up Geoff's suggestion, I went to have a rather useless meeting with Patrick Russell, one of the appointed administrators, and a partner of Charles Russell. We had an initial spat about his responsibilities. He took the view he was beholden only to the Law Society. I reminded him that, regardless of who had appointed him, he was now responsible to all of the estate's creditors, and that included me.

Once we had cleaned the testosterone off the walls, Patrick became a little more forthcoming. But only a little. The estate had only been able to liquidate or recover some £100,000 ($150,000) of genuine assets or missing money. But, I exclaimed, the estate's administrators had themselves reported to the Probate Division that

Hugh had left £1.6 million ($2.4 million) of legitimate assets. Patrick's only response was to stutter that Carratu International was on the trail of property on the other side of the Atlantic, and the estate remained hopeful. I'd heard more likely promises from presidential prospects in the Iowa caucuses.

But I thought I'd push Patrick a little harder on the property angle. I think he felt a tad embarrassed, because he revealed more than he probably ought to have done. A condominium had been located in Florida. There was some sort of shopping center "investment" out West, maybe California or Colorado. And a hint of something exotic in the Caribbean.

I was reminded of a trip that Martin Pratt and Hugh had taken to America in 1985. The primary purpose had been to accompany Martin, who is an accomplished chemical engineer, to a NASA conference in California. All military brass and champagne. Martin was presenting a paper on bio-systems in the space shuttle. However, the trip was rounded off with a visit to Florida, and a quickie cruise through the Caribbean.

One consequence of the estate's continuing failure to recover money or assets, with which to repay the Law Society the £2.7 million ($4 million) it had paid out to Hugh's clients, was that, for the first time in its history, the Law Society had to institute a special, once-off "Simmonds Levy" of some £1,000 on each and every solicitor in England and Wales.

**

As I drove away, I got to thinking about Wedlake Bell, the boutique law firm in central London, of which Hugh had been a partner, before setting up in business on his own in Beaconsfield in 1982.

Did they also have some sort of protection, as I believed Hugh may have had for his "operation?" Was the source the same, and were the reasons the same? Had Wedlake Bell been a "cover" for Hugh during his years with them? There were one or two interesting connections that suggested the possibility.

The senior partner of the firm, when Hugh had joined, was a crusty old patrician, by the name of Harry Ellis. Harry didn't take a lot of bull. He took to Hugh instantly. So much so that he asked Hugh to be one of the named executors in his will. Apparently, there were special responsibilities that went with the job. Harry was a named executor for the solicitor who, in turn, had been the named executor for the solicitor who had acted for the Duke of Windsor (formerly King Edward VIII).

In 1936, the then newly crowned King Edward VIII had abdicated the throne, in order to marry his American love, Wallis Simpson. The King's constitutional advisers had told him that under no circumstances could he marry Wallis as King because she was a divorcee. As head of the Protestant Church of England, the King could not yet condone divorce. We were many years away from Charles and Diana. The King was told he would have to make a choice.

The decision to abdicate threw the Royal Family and the upper reaches of the British body politic into a panic. The problem is that every new King or Queen not only inherits the title, they also inherit a huge fortune in land and holdings, and centuries of secret knowledge, which could cause untold damage if it was to find its way into the wrong hands. Edward VIII had already inherited all of this. No one could force him to un-inherit it. All the family could do was to negotiate with him.

It was a delicate balancing act. On the one hand, you could ask nicely, he could say "no," and you were no further forward. On the other, you could be "mean," force a deal out of him, leaving him bitter and near penniless, when he might go and spill all the beans. As it was, the newly designated King, Edward's brother and about to be George VI, and his advisers took the "mean" route. Edward was effectively exiled, with just enough money to live in reasonable comfort, with a new title, the Duke of Windsor, and a new job, as Governor of Bermuda.

According to Harry Ellis, the treatment of Edward VIII had been brutal. Never underestimate the Royal Family when it comes to protecting its own. An aspect that would be revisited when it came to Diana, Princess of Wales, many years later. Before he had been allowed to become a named Executor, Harry Ellis had been sworn to keep secret all the information that was divulged in the estate he would be administering, including all the details of the deal done under the abdication, and a not insignificant amount of the "secret knowledge." Apparently, Hugh had had to engage in a similar sworn declaration. It made me wonder if Hugh had been chosen because of his "second career," and if Wedlake Bell made a habit of harboring "sensitive" individuals.

***

In between all this fascinating background check, Reggie kept in touch. But with overly melodramatic and rather useless, staccato snippets. Here one minute. Gone the next. I was never certain if this act was to impress me, or if he was genuinely as scared as he made out.

He indicated that he was not prepared to say too much on an open telephone line. And at first, he didn't want to confirm too much of anything in any event. On these occasions, I took the lead in asking questions, since so little had been achieved in our previous telephone conversations.

Reggie claimed not to have any idea who was following me. Or him. He did not believe it was anyone "official." He believed that Hugh had become involved in something "non-kosher" in the lead-up to his death. Reggie was pretty certain he knew the broad outlines, but he was not being upfront in sharing it with me.

I pushed Reggie to tell me who had recruited Hugh. He went all enigmatic on me. Whether this was because it was him, or he did not want to name names on the telephone, I couldn't tell. Certainly, there was ample opportunity for recruitment to have been by way of the British Army.

On the outskirts of Beaconsfield is a large British Army base, called "Wilton Park." It is one of the worst kept secrets in Beaconsfield that the seemingly innocuous base is, in fact, the home of the Army's Languages School, which trains the Army's spies. Wilton Park also houses a huge underground bunker, which would have been used by the government if nuclear bombs had begun to fall.

Reggie finally admitted that he had indeed "invited Hugh to the party," and that the year 1968 was important. All I could think of was that this was the year in which the troubles in Northern Ireland had begun heating up again, and was also the year in which the Soviets had invaded Czechoslovakia.

Reggie said that he wanted to help me, but that it depended on the risk. He felt that the matter might never be resolved, and he did not want to attract too much attention to himself in a useless cause.

He became very agitated when I wondered if he and Hugh had fallen out, "Why, who's suggesting that we did?"

I was becoming a tad frustrated by this game of allusion and illusion. I got to the point. Open telephone or not, I set out the scenario that John Simmonds had presented to me, oh so long before. Bluntly asked Reggie if Hugh had been involved in an operation trying to get an agent out of a foreign country.

Again, the reaction was instantaneous. "How do you know this?" Reggie hissed. "Who are you? You're so very close." A pause. "You have no idea how close. Look, you're in no danger at the moment. But if you keep on messing around, you're going to start pissing off someone. My advice to you is to go home." Then without warning, Reggie hung up. Scared, or pissed off?

***

Well, on a scale of 1 to 10, I called that a near-certain 9 that this all might well have had something to do with getting an agent out of a foreign country. Time to get out the reading glasses and bone up on any and all matters current then in the world to do with agents, hostages and foreign intelligence services.

Of course, I didn't have far to look.

CHAPTER FIVE

Hostage To Fortune?

A LITTLE RESEARCH QUICKLY LED ME to the most famous hostage crises of the late '80s, those involving Americans and Europeans held by radical Shiite Muslims in Lebanon. The practice of taking hostages in the Middle East had begun with the Crusades, and has proved to be a source of trouble for the West ever since.

Back in 1982, Israel, under its then-Defense Minister, Ariel Sharon, invaded Lebanon to clear out the Palestine Liberation Organization.

Sharon had let his Lebanese Christian militia pals loose into the Muslim Palestinian refugee camps, where they had indiscriminately massacred men, women and children.

The West sent peacekeepers to stop the fighting. The problem was that nothing was black and white. There weren't just good guys and bad guys. There were lots of different guys and loads of different factions within the Christian, Muslim and Palestinian camps.

Often, different factions of the same religious or ethnic type hated each other more than they hated other religious or ethnic types.

The intelligence efforts of the incoming peacekeepers could not keep pace with the complexity of the situation. As a consequence, peacekeepers found themselves being blown up or taken hostage by all sorts of different groupings of all sorts of different religious and ethnic factions.

Remember now, at the time, Britain's radical right-wing Prime Minister, Margaret Thatcher, and America's equally radical right-wing president, Ronald Reagan, were both giving the same tele-prompted "get tough" message to the world's media: "We do not negotiate with terrorists."

The reality is that they were both negotiating like crazy – and willing to pay any price to avoid the embarrassment Jimmy Carter suffered with the fifty-seven US hostages held in the American Embassy in the capital of Iran from 1979 to 1981.

Indeed, such negotiations had given rise to the scandal known as "Iran-Contra": The US agreed to sell arms and military equipment to Iran, which desperately needed them to fight off Iraq, which had invaded Iran in 1980.

The problem was that such sales were in breach of a UN embargo, which had been instituted to prevent the supply to both Iran and Iraq of any equipment and technology that could be used by either country in an offensive military capacity.

Being oil rich, the radical Muslim mullahs of Iran were prepared to circumvent the UN embargo by paying well over market price for military goodies. The US then used the profits to supply the Contras fighting the Communist Sandinistas in Nicaragua (something which the US Congress had already banned the US government from doing with US taxpayer dollars) – and of course, to fatten secret bank accounts in Switzerland and the Cayman Islands.

Finally, the US used the goodwill generated with Iran to encourage them to persuade their allies in Hezbollah, a newly formed military and political organization in Lebanon that was behind many hostage-takings, to free their captives.

In 1984, Thatcher and Reagan were particularly eager to gain freedom for one William Buckley, the recently arrived CIA Head of Station in Lebanon. Early on in the peacekeeping effort, in 1983, the US Marine barracks had been blown up by one or other of the Lebanese Muslim militias, causing the death of 168 of America's finest. The same militia had also exploded a bomb outside the US Embassy in Beirut, killing among others at least eight serving officers of the CIA. Buckley had been stirring up trouble for a couple of years in Angola, a country in the midst of a civil war, where the CIA was supporting a nasty piece of work named Jonas Savimbi, against the left-leaning National Liberation Front of Angola.

Buckley was called back to Langley and given special responsibility to go to Lebanon and seek revenge for the deaths of the Marines and the CIA officers. Unfortunately, the Lebanese Muslim militias had better intelligence than the West had bargained for, and Buckley was taken captive soon after arriving.

This case drew my attention for a number of reasons. First, it fit the bill of "getting an agent out of a foreign country," the scenario Hugh's father, John, had told me about, and that Reggie had suggested was "so very close." And it made me wonder if one or more of the

British hostages might not also be a British "foreign agent." The more I looked into it, the more it appeared Buckley was in cahoots with a renegade British spy-cum-mercenary named Leslie Aspin.

I started digging around to learn a bit more about Aspin.

Les Aspin, sometimes acting with his wilder brother, Michael, and sometimes not, was first a contract agent for British Intelligence. Later on he defected to the United States, and acted under the direct authority of William Casey, Reagan's director of the CIA. Les had been up to all sorts of naughty no-no's in Angola with Buckley, and had gone on to work as an "adviser" for one of the Lebanese Christian factions. And he had a night job smuggling arms to Iran.

When Buckley was taken hostage, Aspin became the lead contract agent in efforts to find Buckley and negotiate for his release or break him free.

The most interesting aspect of the Aspins was their role as "contract agents." Every intelligence agency has regular employees. When serving abroad, some are attached to their embassies, but are generally given titles that bear no resemblance to their real work. Others operate free of the embassy, but are still bona fide employees of their intelligence agency.

Then there are contract agents. As the name suggests, they are offered jobs on a "contract" basis. They are not full-time employees. This allows the agency in question to disavow any knowledge of the agent. Oops, no, we don't employ "X."

After all, when one is essentially asking someone to lie, steal, cheat, or kill it's convenient to temporarily sign on a person with a shady background. They won't shy away from the job, and it's easy to destroy their credibility later if there's a need to clean the "dirty laundry."

So while the world believed that the British Government's efforts to free British hostages was being undertaken by Terry Waite, the Archbishop of Canterbury's special envoy to Lebanon, the government's real work was being done by Aspin, the "hard man" heading up the "unofficial," behind-the-scenes, far less-principled effort to free hostages. Governments place far more faith in the barrel of a gun than they do in prayer, holiness and a quick rendition of "Kumbaya." The British Government was simply using Terry Waite as a stooge.

By the time I'd unearthed this information, Les was dead. Otherwise I'd have tried to make contact with him. His brother, Michael, served time in jail for fraud, although throughout his trial, he claimed that the money he had stolen had been taken to finance a deal to release hostages in Lebanon, an operation that had the full sanction of MI6 and the British Government.

The coincidence between Michael Aspin's story and the rationale advanced to John Simmonds for Hugh's defalcation was intriguing. Indeed, there were a number of other matters that gave me cause to ponder the possible connections between the Aspin boys and Hugh.

I remember watching the television with Hugh when the Special Air Service freed the hostages from the Iranian Embassy in London in 1981. As the black-clad and hooded SAS soldiers were leading the freed hostages to safety, a rogue cameraman followed an ill-kempt bloke, up to all sorts of strange behavior. He was wearing jeans, had long hair, and was darting from car to car looking underneath. "Oh dear," exclaimed Hugh, "we really shouldn't be seeing that."

Hugh explained later that the gentleman in question was with a "civilian unit" of the SAS. And that would be...? Hrrmph, came the unexpected response from the normally talkative Hugh. He did tell me that, during the Second World War, British Military Intelligence had begun a practice of forming ad hoc civilian units, which went out and hired whoever was appropriate for a particular job. Thus, if we wanted to steal some important designs from a factory in Occupied France, we went down to the East End of London and hired a couple of safecrackers for the night. He left the rest to my imagination – an imagination that was now beginning to wonder if Hugh had been a senior member of a similar unit. I learned that Les was formerly with the Special Air Service. He also owned a large house in Buckinghamshire, not far from Beaconsfield. One of his banks was the Barclays Bank branch in Stanhope House, Park Lane, London. Hugh did all of his City Jeroboam financing with the same bank, same branch.

The Aspins were heavily involved in gun-running around the Mediterranean. The favorite triangle was: guns from Yugoslavia, Bulgaria or Czechoslovakia; deals done in Marbella, the jet-set location on the south coast of Spain; and then, guns to Palestinian or Muslim militias in the Near or Middle East, by way of Marseilles, or some other port along the south coast of France.

The Mediterranean coast was a place Hugh spent a good deal of time.

Hugh had told me that he spent some time early in his intelligence career serving undercover in Marseilles.

Between 1986 and 1988, he had a major client in Marbella: a timeshare operation called Paradise, whose two partners were Paul and Victor. Paul came from a lot of textile money in the North of England, and had his own offices at 16 Pall Mall, London. Victor was an expatriate Italian. No one knew much about where he'd come from, or where he eventually went.

Hugh and I visited the south of Spain from time to time. Usually to do business, but we also spent a lot of time just wandering around the port area of Marbella, looking at boats. On one occasion, Hugh had remarked that one of the fancier motor yachts belonged to Robert Maxwell, the billionaire British publisher who owned London's *Daily Mirror* and the *New York Post*, and ended up taking a fatal dive off the very same boat. I never stopped wondering how Hugh recognized the yacht. In the dark. From the other side of the harbor.

In about 1987, Hugh and Martin Pratt spent a deal of time in Provence, just to the north of Marseilles, scouting possible small vineyards to buy. Finally, in the summer of 1988, a couple of months before his death, Hugh, his family, and I had gone for a two-week holiday in Cannes, just down the coast from Marseilles.

It was obvious Hugh knew the area well, and had an especial fondness for the locality and its people.

***

What of Hugh and his specific operation? After a deal of soul-searching, and what I would describe as rigorous intellectual analysis (others might call it a couple of bottles of ice-cold Frascati wine), I came up with the following ideas. Their primary attraction is that they do a better job of starting to square the anomalies of Hugh's theft and death than the rather half-hearted versions previously offered.

Hugh was somehow involved in an operation to free a hostage in Lebanon, part of his duties included making funds available, which he apparently stole from his Clients' Account. The operation had the nod from the powers that be, which was why he felt he was protected. The funds would be replaced after the operation, either from profits from the operation or by the same powers.

Something went wrong. Since the money was not replaced, one has to conclude that the "something" interfered with the funds in some way. Either the very fact of it going wrong, or perhaps the fact that the funds were interfered with, which prevented the operation from happening, caused the powers to remove the protection, and left Hugh to his own devices.

This hypothesis worked. But only to a certain extent. A major question it posed was why did Hugh remain silent when it all went wrong? Why not leave some clue, at least as to where the money might be found? The silence left his family burdened with the most extreme stigma and financial cost.

I could say he was doing his "duty," but it just didn't feel right, in all the circumstances and with everything I knew of Hugh's complicated character. I can think only that some sort of threat must have been made against one or other members of his family.

Hugh had made the art of his own survival a living extension of his own irrepressible arrogance. There was no situation he could not deal with. Every problem was merely a challenge. One swing of the sword, and any knot, however complicated, could be severed. However, this dictum applied only to his own survival, not that of his loved ones. Their care and concern came ahead of all else. Hugh was not all hardhead. He had a heart. He just kept it well hidden. Frankly, he was a psychological nightmare. A kaleidoscope of contradictions.

Loving and affectionate to friends, yet diabolically cruel to rivals. Desperate for love, yet the only true loner I'd ever met. Loud, brash and boorish in public, yet civilized and attentive in private. Always needing to be the center of attention when in the company of an audience, yet solicitous and loyal when dealing with an individual's personal problems. Utterly convinced of his own invincibility, yet almost childish in his incomprehension of why things went wrong, as regularly they did. Charismatic and flamboyant, extravagant and petulant; yet kind and generous to a fault.

Hugh was also the most responsible father I had ever witnessed. If there was one matter more than any other that did not ring true, it was that he had left no suicide note. In particular, nothing for

Juliet. At 11 years of age, she was the son he had always wanted. Serious, smart, his features, but with blond hair. Tanya, at age 8, had her grandfather's sandy hair and freckles, and her mother's infectious laugh. She was going to break a lot of hearts. Paul, age 5, was all Karen in looks, and all Hugh in his attitude.

Hugh loved his children dearly. And he cared for them. And the two are not the same thing. Everything I understood about Hugh screamed at me that he would have found some way to tell his children what was going on. Mind you, there are days when I think I am the suicide note.

No one just "liked" Hugh. He did not inspire casual emotion. You either loved him or hated him, as my sister Maggi had found out. And he returned the compliment four-fold. So, I had no difficulty believing that, faced with the possibility that his continued existence on this mortal coil would, of itself, have placed one single member of his extended family in harm's way – even for a single second – he would have chosen silent self-execution as the noble alternative.

Indeed, looking more closely at his health history at this time, his illness during the summer of 1988 broke down into some interesting phases. He fell suddenly ill in May. Maybe this was when the major financial disaster occurred? He was bed-ridden for a month. Then, he picked up, and from July through September, he was almost frenzied with activity. Looking back, maybe he thought he had found a way to escape the trap? Martin Pratt told me that, during this time, Hugh was constantly discussing business schemes with him, to try to make money quickly. Then, in about October, Hugh seemed completely to give up. Was this when possible threats began?

At one stage, Hugh had left Janet to live with his mistress, Karen. But he then returned to Janet, for the sake of his daughters. After this, he kept Karen somewhat at arms length. Yet, in the few months before his death, the steamy relationship with his steamy mistress was once more rekindled.

Janet lived in a large house, in the middle of a busy neighborhood, heavily covered with burglar alarms and motion-operated lights. Indeed, the neighbors had complained more than once about the "Hollywood Effect" every time Hugh and his family returned home. Karen, by contrast, lived in a much smaller house out in the middle of the country, her only protection a couple of teenage female horse-grooms.

After Hugh's death, Karen's mother, not Karen, told me that Hugh had told her in the week before his death that he was planning to move back in with Karen. Like Hugh's parents, neither Karen's mother nor father are given to flights of fancy. Indeed, her father was a professor at a local university and was held in some esteem by John Simmonds. Karen's parents expressed as much surprise as I that Hugh had told them this.

***

Jimmy Carter's presidency was crippled in its waning years by its perceived impotence in the face of the capture by Khomeini's Iranian Revolutionary Guards of fifty-seven American hostages in the US Embassy in 1979. Carter had tried everything to secure the release of his countrymen, including an ill-fated rescue attempt in the middle of an election year, 1980.

The Republicans were convinced that Carter would pull an "October Surprise," securing the hostages' release just in time for the goodwill to sweep Carter to a second term. There were too many in the military and, in particular, in the CIA – which had been devastated by Carter's wholesale assault on their Operations Directorate – who wanted to do all they could to prevent Carter's re-election. JFK déjà vu, all over again.

A plot was hatched. The initial core consisted of ex-CIA officer Miles Copeland Jr. (whose primary public claim to fame was that he was the father of Stewart Copeland, drummer for the British rock band The Police); William Casey, ex-CIA and close friend of the new Republican presidential candidate, Ronald Reagan; and Robert McFarlane, a former Marine Colonel, senior aide to Texas Republican Senator John Tower, and later, one of the chosen fall guys for the Iran-Contra debacle.

Part of the deal struck between Reagan and George H.W. Bush, which allowed the latter so graciously to accept the vice presidential nomination, was Reagan's agreement that, as vice president, Bush would have de facto control over all sensitive foreign relations matters. For which read "covert operations." Bush wasn't waiting for Election Day. There was work to be done immediately, and he very quickly linked up with Casey's mob.

There was even assistance from inside Carter's administration. Donald Gregg was a member of Carter's National Security Council. He was later accused of leaking the Democrat's debate briefing book to the Reagan team, allowing Reagan to best Carter in the first, and ultimately deciding, presidential debate. He also regularly briefed Bush and Casey on Carter's moves in regards to Khomeini and the hostages, in the months leading up to the presidential election.

All of these machinations culminated in a hugely secret meeting in Paris, on October 12, 1980, just under a month before the US presidential election. In attendance were Bush, Casey (soon to be the next director of the CIA), McFarlane, Gregg, Robert Gates (who became CIA director under President Bush Sr., and Defense Secretary under Presidents Dubya and Obama) and one George Cave. Cave had been officially purged from the CIA in 1977, as part of Carter's cleansing of the agency. However, he remained "unofficially" active until 1989.

The Americans were in Paris to meet with a delegation of Iranians, led by a man called Mehdi Karrubi, who was there as the personal envoy of the then Iranian President, Hojjat al-Islam Ali Akbar Hashemi Rafsanjani. A Devil's Deal was struck that day: In exchange for $52 million in cash; the unfreezing of Iranian assets in America; and guarantees of arms sales to Iran (desperately needed to stave off Iraq, which had invaded Iran earlier that year), the Iranians personally guaranteed to Bush and his team that they would delay the release of the American hostages until after the presidential election. Thus, it was that Bush supplanted any possible Carter "October Surprise" with a surprise of his own.

Bush and his team were flown to Paris in a BAC-11 owned by King Khaled of Saudi Arabia, and piloted by one Heinrich Rupp, a former employee of the Saudi national airline. Arrangements were made through Four Seasons Travel, an alleged front company for the CIA.

No records of the airplane, or its flight plan, were ever logged on the Federal Aviation Administration computer database. However, there was one overlooked piece of paper evidence: a manual card index containing details of the airplane and its flight plan. This card index was filed away with other FAA archives in the Alfred P. Murrah Federal Building in Oklahoma City, which was destroyed by a truck bomb in 1995.

Meanwhile, Reagan and Bush were elected in 1980. Reagan kept his word and put Bush in charge of covert operations. Bush kept his word, and began the flow of arms to the Iranians. McFarlane became Reagan's National Security Adviser. Casey became the Director of the CIA. Gregg became Bush's National Security Adviser, while Bush was vice president. Carter returned to Plains, Georgia. And Miles Copeland continued listening to his son's pop records.

Quite aside from the secret sale of arms to Iran, which was banned by international law, there were all sorts of other covert actions that Vice President Bush wanted to instigate – and that he simply did not want to have Congress knowing about. Because of all of the misdeeds of the CIA up to and including the Vietnam War, Congress had created various oversight committees.

So, Bush had to find ways to get things done outside of the CIA and "normal channels."

The first thing Bush had Reagan do was set up, under top-secret National Security Decision Directive (NSDD) #3, a new intelligence organization, under Bush's control, with the specific purpose of waging covert wars. This organization was known as the Special Situation Group/Standing Crisis Pre-Planning Group (SSG/CPPG). Congress had no control over this group.

Despite the new organization, Bush Sr. still thought it wise to use surrogates to do the illegal arming of the militant Muslims in Iran. The Israelis, led by the right-wing Likud Party and its die-hard Prime Minister Menachem Begin, were happy to oblige. Begin had never forgiven Carter for embarrassing him with his Camp David Peace Accords with Egypt.

So the Israelis supplied Iran with American military hardware they had previously bought. The Americans then re-supplied the Israelis from NATO stockpiles in Europe. Everything was fine until a Palestinian terrorist group assassinated the Israeli Ambassador to the UK, Shlomo Argov, on the streets of London. Israel invaded Lebanon in 1982, to clean out the Palestinians from that country. The "cleansing" took a nasty turn in the Palestinian refugee camps in Beirut. Western peacekeepers arrived. Muslim militias blew up the US Embassy, the Marines' barracks, and a couple of other embassies. The US retaliated with William Buckley. And the Muslim militias started taking hostages.

Then somebody noticed that the same Muslim militias were being openly backed by Iran, and got the bright idea of using the arms sales as a bargaining chip to release the hostages in Lebanon.

Meanwhile, Congress had stopped the CIA funding of the Contras' attempts to overthrow the leftist Sandinista Government in Nicaragua. So Bush had had to find some other way of financing the Contras. He did this through SSG/CPPG, using the enormous profits from the arms sales to Iran, among some other rather creative sources of money. And so the ugly triangle of Iran-Contra was established.

As the '80s progressed, this triangle expanded to include other covert operations around the world, all of which needed to be conducted out of sight of the Congressional Oversight Committees. Ships were needed for transporting weapons; tame banks were set up to launder money; every conceivable aspect of logistics was considered and provided for. Bush's SSG/CPPG became a huge global business, and was known variously as either "The Enterprise" or "Octopus."

***

Armed with all of this new information, I now felt fully equipped to have a productive conversation with Reggie, if only he would overcome his sulk and contact me. And if only I could keep him on the telephone long enough. We began a cat and mouse game that lasted through August 1989.

I telephoned every day, both at his home and at the University. I left messages on his answering machine and with his assistants. I heard nothing, or his staff would say that he was "popping in from time to time." It was most frustrating. As the month progressed, it also became quite worrying. I wondered if he might be in serious trouble. Finally, Reggie called late one evening. He said he was in Germany, "helping to test a new weapon." Sometimes, I felt that Reggie, like Hugh, was trying desperately to impress me with all this cloak and dagger. The problem was, it made as much impression on me as it had with Hugh – namely, nada. I had a single item on my agenda: finding the truth.

On this occasion, Reggie was very abrupt. He seemed a little distracted. "I've got problems," he explained, "Friends are causing me problems," he added cryptically. "I left the country two days ago … hang on … I'll call you back." He hung up.

I wondered if he was just messing me about. A few minutes later, he called again. He had just begun to talk again when there was an electronic sound on the line. "What was that?" he asked sharply. "This is your cellular, right? Blast. I'll call you back on the regular line. They've picked us up on your cellular. Too easy." The phone went dead again. James Bond never had it this difficult.

A few minutes later, Reggie was back. "Right. We've got one and a half minutes. That's how long it takes to trace. Then, we'll switch back to your cellular. And so on." Blimey, it was like a high school science project. Reggie claimed he had tried to send me something, but the chemistry hadn't worked. His life was worth nothing now. Mine even less. He would try to meet with me in London.

I asked him baldly what his intentions were with regards to me. He hesitated for a second: "To give you information, without breaking the law. I will send you something. But because of events, there are certain people who do not want some 'snot-nose' snooping around." I flushed with embarrassment at the compliment. "So steer clear of dark alleys," he concluded, ominously, "particularly around Leicester Square." He might just as well have given me detailed directions. Talk about your red rag to the bull.

***

Leicester Square is one of those wonderful melting pots you seem only to find in the heart of truly vibrant cities. It is the spot where all of London's movie premieres are staged. Yet, in 1989 certainly, it was also the gathering place for a sizable section of London's homeless people.

I arrived early the following morning, cheap throwaway camera in hand, eager to see what I could find. It didn't take me long. There, on the northern side was The Swiss Centre, home to all manner of Swiss chocolate and fancy lederhosen, in the ground floor tourist shop, and to the Swiss Bank Corporation, in its upper levels. Coincidence was becoming a daily part of my routine.

As I made my way through the dark alleys around the exterior of the building, I noticed that the office area was singularly impenetrable, even for a bank. As I was aimlessly wandering along, peering up at the top of the building, I bumped into a man walking fast in the opposite direction.

I recognized him, but could not remember a name. He clearly recognized me also, but said nothing. Just brushed past me and disappeared into The Swiss Centre. After a few minutes standing still, scratching my head, I recalled that I'd seen the man with Hugh at Wedlake Bell years before, but I still could not grasp a name.

By the time I'd completed my circumnavigation, I found another man waiting for me. With the ever-ready, but unread newspaper. I was bored. I decided to have some fun. Strolled around the Square, just to make sure that he was following me, and that he was staying close. Then, when we hit an open patch, I turned abruptly, and began to snap away with the camera.

This was clearly something they'd not covered in spy school. The poor chap went all Peter Sellers on me. First one way. Then the other. Doffed his hat. Went bright red, and stalked off in the direction of The Swiss Center. At which point, I noticed that I'd picked up two more gentlemen with ever-present, yet unread newspapers.

***

The following morning, while in the depths of a searing hangover, I had a brainstorm. Maybe if Reggie had a "document" of mine, to which he could refer obliquely on the telephone, he would find it easier to talk to me.

I spent the day crafting a letter for Reggie. I set out everything I thought I knew, and then everything I knew I thought. And then for good measure, I put in a list of questions about the things I thought I thought. Reward was swift. At the end of September 1989, Reggie finally opened up.

CHAPTER SIX

Reggie Unplugged

IN ANTICIPATION OF REGGIE being more forthcoming, I had invested in a small microphone and a tape-recorder. The mic wasn't sophisticated enough to attach to a telephone earpiece. So, I had to engage in an acrobatic exercise, balancing the microphone between the earpiece and my ear.

During the ensuing conversations with Reggie, this would occasionally prevent my being able to hear Reggie, so I had to plead deafness, and ask him to repeat himself.

I was no longer staying with my sister's friend, Rissa, and had somewhat ironically returned to my unsold apartment in Beaconsfield. I had no telephone in the apartment, and so used the public telephone at the local railway station. When a train came into the station, I'd lose Reggie altogether, or the microphone would swing loose.

Not for the first time in this adventure, I had cause to wonder if real-life spies had half this much trouble. However, the upshot was that I had a full transcript of the evening's conversation, and all the other evenings of enlightenment that followed:

> *Geoffrey*: "Did you get my letter?"
>
> *Reggie*: "Yes. What can I say? I think you're on very dangerous ground."
>
> *Geoffrey*: "Because I'm close to the truth?"
>
> *Reggie*: "Yes. And because you're still in England. Can I direct your reading?"
>
> *Geoffrey*: "Yes."
>
> *Reggie*: "Go to the last chapter of *The Messianic Legacy*."
>
> *Geoffrey*: "All I can find is the Knights of Malta."

Reggie: "Got it in one."

Geoffrey: "So, it's not British Intelligence; it's the Knights of Malta?"

Reggie: "I'm not saying that. I'm saying no-one is acting alone."

Geoffrey: "So, it's British Intelligence-ish?"

Reggie: "Ish."

Geoffrey: "Knights of Malta-ish?'

Reggie: "Ish. But not alone."

Geoffrey: "Ish?"

Reggie: "Ish."

Geoffrey: "CIA-ish?"

Reggie: There was a pregnant pause. "Beautifully said on my telephone. Well done."

Geoffrey: I persevered. "Ish?"

Reggie: "Ish."

Geoffrey: "Ish." It felt like we were in a mosque. I almost began to chant. "Ok. So, Hugh takes the money, which, from various sources, I gather to be about £5 million [$7.5 million]..."

Reggie: "...£15 million [$22.5 million]..." Well, he fell neatly into that trap.

Geoffrey: "£15 million. Ok. In 1987 and 1988. Probably more 1988."

Reggie: "From May 1987." He was giving away a lot, wasn't he?

Geoffrey: "Doesn't spend it. Stashes it. Hides it. We know he's hidden it, because the combined forces of the Law Society and the police can't find it."

Reggie: "No. The combined forces of the Law Society, and one or two other unnamed institutions, can't find it."

Geoffrey: "So. We're in November 1988. Something's gone wrong. Why doesn't he put the money back, or run away? Why does he kill himself?"

Reggie: "I don't believe that Hugh killed himself. I believe that Hugh went out to that location, wherever it was, to meet somebody, and I believe they killed him."

Geoffrey: "Why can't we just stop messing about? Why can't you just tell me?"

Reggie: "It's not as simple as that. I'm a soldier. I signed things. And they may be taping this."

Geoffrey: "Tell me something."

Reggie: Long pause, broken only by the occasional sigh. "Look. I believe that what he was doing ran counter to what some other people were doing. And I believe that he was taken out accordingly. Or that some other people wanted it done."

Geoffrey: "There were two things going on?"

Reggie: "There were lots of things going on. The problem is that you're seeing it through a very simplistic lens. How does it go? Try seeing it through 'a glass darkly.' You're assuming that all of the parties are working together to the same end. Not the case. Today some parties may be working together; tomorrow against each other; the day after they're friends again. If you want to name names, for the time we're talking about, I would see two groupings. I would see America, in the form of the CIA. I would see Mossad and they working together. And I would see the Knights of Malta with them. On the other side of the fence, there is another grouping. There are two Protestant versions of that organization. I'd investigate the Knights of St. John and the Knights of Lazarus. Then, other institutions of a British and German origin ... I believe they are in opposing camps."

Geoffrey: "What can I do?"

Reggie: "I believe Hugh was ... when you came to see me in Glasgow, I didn't know. But now ... my contact with Hugh had been quiet for a long time. I believe that he was involved in something quasi-official. That money was being used for that purpose. It was not stashed away for personal gain. There was some 'higher purpose.'"

Geoffrey: "What was going to happen at the end of the day? Was he going to be paid back?"

Reggie: "I don't know ... I can only ... look ... I've got to be cautious..." He sounded genuinely nervous. "...I mean my advice is to ... Counsel's Opinion is to fuck you off ... I wouldn't walk down any dark alleys if I were you..."

Geoffrey: "...you mean like around The Swiss Centre, in Leicester Square?"

Reggie: "...you know what 'wet operations' are? Well, that's where one of the London centers is..."

Geoffrey: "Can you tell me anything else?"

Reggie: "Well, I hadn't quite finished actually. There are two sides to this, and I believe Hugh got caught up in the middle. I think in a general sense your scenario was probably right. But my contact with that part of the world stopped in February. When I had a warning not to go on a trip I was planning to take. A friend of mine, called David Heald, who is well known about the world of economics, gave a lecture in Pakistan fairly recently. He is well known in the Islamic world. His advice to me was not to go to Beirut. Got similar messages when I started poking around on your behalf. Was told to steer clear of Buckley, and stay the hell away from Waite. The view on him is that he can rot in hell. I believe that Hugh was involved in some plan, much along lines we've discussed. He was the lynchpin of the whole thing. As you've suggested. And he was taken out because of it. By people who didn't want it to happen. Now that's a slightly different picture to the one you're painting.

Geoffrey: "Ok. That makes a lot more sense."

Reggie: "Have you read any of those books yet?" [*Holy Blood, Holy Grail* and *The Messianic Legacy*]

Geoffrey: "Some." Um. The Introduction.

Reggie: "I'm going to draw your attention to a particular passage. In the hardback version [of *Holy Blood, Holy Grail*], it's on page 190. Hugh was not a Freemason. Therefore, he missed a lot of things. Chapter 8. Twenty pages in. The paragraph begins: 'Initial inquiries were undertaken by an Englishwoman...' Then, there's a sentence that starts: 'One journalist...' Read that, and take note. I don't think you can prove anything. I'd be hard put to know where to start."

Geoffrey: "Do British Intelligence know about it?"

Reggie: "Yes."

Geoffrey: "But they can't find the money."

Reggie: "At this stage, I think the money's irrelevant. It's merely a means to an end. Without the money, there's no action. Without Hugh, there's no action. One or the other."

Geoffrey: "Ok, you have lost me."

Reggie: "Look. Hugh was involved in something. Other people didn't want it to happen. It doesn't happen if either Hugh disappears or the money disappears. Someone with Hugh was a crook, or worse. And made one or the other happen."

Geoffrey: "Do you know who?"

Reggie: "I'm not sure it's not you." Said in a dead quiet voice.

Geoffrey: "Oh. And I'm looking for the money?"

Reggie: "No. You know where it is." The chitchat was definitely over. A much harder voice had taken its place.

Geoffrey: "But … if I know where it is, why would I be wandering all over England?"

Reggie: "Because you didn't know where I was. And I might know something."

Geoffrey: "Fair enough."

Reggie: "You remember that afternoon in Glasgow? I was taught to be cautious. I made a telephone call. I was given instructions. My military record shows an interesting background. I was a marksman with a pistol, until 1969. Then, I was made a 'bare pass.' To … er … hide me. It became useful. We weren't sure you weren't there to eradicate me."

Geoffrey: "So British Intelligence knows about me?

Reggie: "Oh, you figure pretty high on one or two lists. Europe's not a very safe place for you at the moment."

Geoffrey: "But why? Why would anyone consider me a threat?"

Reggie: "It's not so much who you are. *As what you're doing.* You fly in from nowhere. No one knows who you are.

And you're poking around places no one wants anyone poking around. And then, you come looking for me. Anyway. I've got to go. Watch yourself, mate."

For the first time in this whole saga, I was truly scared. I didn't leave the well-lit telephone kiosk for at least fifteen minutes. I then quick marched all the way back to my apartment. It was only a few minutes walk, but it was the longest "few minutes" of my life. I kept glancing over my shoulder. And nearly freaked when I dropped my key at the front door.

I locked the door, piled a month's worth of trash against it, and wedged a broomstick under the door handle. I grabbed a bottle of wine, and disappeared into a closet. In the comforting darkness, I got well and truly drunk and cried myself to sleep. All I cared about, at that point, was getting someone to help me help three small kids. As for all the cloak and dagger stuff, on that particular evening, I was convinced I was not cut out for any of it.

**

When I had originally left for America at the beginning of 1989, I'd put my apartment on the market, and had switched off the electricity. Without money, I was unable to reverse the process. So along with everything else, I had no light, no heat, and no hot water. Ever resourceful, I spent the next few days hiding out in my lair, working on a routine to cope with my poverty. I felt like Rowan Atkinson in *Mr. Bean.*

Fall was underway. I still had a mattress and a down-filled comforter, which I'd left in the apartment when I'd moved to America. But no bed, sheets or pillows. I'd wake up, making little spiral freeze clouds with my breath. Every morning was a struggle to convince myself that I really did want to leave the warmth of the goose down. The shortest time on record for this exercise was fifteen minutes.

I'd dash to the bathroom, to perform my morning ablutions, singing at the top of my voice. There was no radio, and the singing took my mind off the cold. It also took the neighbor's minds off whatever they were doing, usually evidenced by loud thumping on the walls.

The previous night's clothesline would be removed from over the bathtub, which I'd fill with freezing cold water. It's a strange phenomenon. However cold the ambient temperature, it tends not to be as cold as water from a pipe. So, although entering the bathtub would be accompanied by much screaming and cussing, along with more in tempo thumping from the neighbors, getting out was a gas. The apartment would always seem quite warm by comparison.

No matter how many times I did it, the sensation always struck me anew. For the few minutes that the warm sensation lasted, I felt quite exhilarated. And usually got dressed to more loud singing. And even louder thumping.

With nothing else to do but wait for Reggie's continued "revelations," I used what little money I had left to buy reading material, which kept me occupied for most of the day. I'd eat out of cans, and drink water. As night drew in, and the light faded, I'd pull the apartment's one chair closer and closer to the window, and the street-light outside. In the evenings, I'd stay warm by adding more layers of clothes, and downing a bottle of "El Cheapo" from the nearby liquor store.

Since the first letter to Reggie had made him so loquacious, I took the view that a second could do no harm. I set out all the different ways Reggie might be able to help me, and made a list of all the potential candidates for the individual who had double-crossed Hugh.

**

I was minding my own business one dark and chilly evening. As usual, I had taken up a post by the window nearest to the street-light, and was quietly imbibing a warming glass of red wine. As the wine took effect, the thoughts swirling around my head gently coalesced into a picture of Reggie, dressed as a warlock, muttering incantations on a lonely hillside in Scotland.

My reverie was broken by the sound of furious thumping on my front door. For the first time, I experienced what it meant when they say "your heart is in your mouth." Either that, or I'd just swallowed the cork. I peered carefully out of the window. It was nothing more harmful than Hugh's friend Martin Pratt. Who had suddenly become very talkative.

We went to a nearby pub, where Martin poured forth. It turned out that he had been sacked earlier that day by City Jeroboam, and he wanted someone's shoulder to cry on. That, at least, was the reason he gave. But I think he had other matters he wanted to get off his chest, since he talked about nothing but Hugh.

Martin now confided that he had known all along that Hugh was in MI6. And that he, Martin, had on occasion done one or two things for British Intelligence. However, he still clung to his claim that he knew nothing of what Hugh had been involved in before his death.

Martin did, however, have much to say about Philip de Nahlik, the friend of his and Hugh's who was known to us to be a Polish Papal Count, and who had been married in the Temple Church in Lincoln's Inn, London, a former chapel of the Knights Templar.

Philip was apparently always talking to Hugh about the Knights of Malta and Freemasonry: "Philip wanted Hugh to join all sorts of secret societies." Martin's last comment, as he staggered to his car, was that I should stay away from Philip, "he's more dangerous than he seems."

***

A series of abbreviated, late-night conversations with Reggie followed. The second letter had indeed proved to be most useful.

First, Reggie told me that two of Hugh's close friends were connected to British Intelligence, and that one of them was also a Knight of Malta. Hello. Got there first.

Then, somewhat cryptically, Reggie sent me greetings from a colleague who knew me, but did not wish to be revealed at that time. I really was making some people quite jumpy. The colleague wished only to be identified as "Charlotte."

Apparently, this was a Square in Glasgow, which at that time was regularly frequented by the local yuppies and preppies, or as they are known in Great Britain, the "Sloanes" and the "Hooray Henry's." In her time, Princess Diana had been the Queen of the Sloanes in London.

Reggie's information was that Hugh had at least £3 million on him at the time of his death. And more stashed away elsewhere. British Intelligence had not the slightest interest in knowing the details of Hugh's operation, nor what had gone wrong. Their interest was singular: contrary to what Reggie had told me in our last conversation, British Intelligence were now keen to know where the money was. Join the queue. But why on earth would British Intelligence be so interested in what I understood, at best, to be no more than £15 million? Were they that hard up? Reggie would not or could not enlighten me.

Reggie did however startle me with his assertion that he had been told that Hugh had been killed by the Mafia, working on instructions from the CIA. The reason for Reggie's continuing fear was that he believed that the CIA were now after him. And possibly me. His immediate preoccupation was with further investigation. And with getting rid of the mortal threat. Communication with me would continue to be spotty, at best. But he promised that he would try.

***

In the meantime, the noble quest was about to take a dramatic turn. It was the fall of 1989. Momentous events were shaking the very foundations of the global political structure that had existed since the end of the Second World War. And Reggie was involved at the sharp end – in East Germany.

CHAPTER SEVEN

Smuggling Over Berlin Wall?

RONALD REAGAN rode to power in 1980, vowing to bring down the "Evil Empire" that was the communist Soviet Union. He instigated a massive arms build-up, daring the Soviet Union and its satellites in Eastern Europe to bankrupt themselves trying to keep pace. He exacerbated the economic squeeze by ending the policy of easy credit to those wishing to do business with Russia.

He supported covert military actions specifically designed to wear down the communist Soviet military machine on as many different fronts as possible. The gloves were off: Nicaragua, Angola and Afghanistan, where the US poured a billion dollars a year into the mujahideen in the successful effort to drive the Russian 40th Army out of that occupied country.

Eventually, in the fall of 1989, the Polish Government announced that it would be holding partially free Parliamentary elections the next year. It was a foregone conclusion that Solidarity, under the direction of its charismatic leader Lech Walesa, would win those elections and end the dominant role of communism in Poland. Everyone around the world held their breath, waiting on Moscow, which did nothing. And with that, the floodgates opened. Hungary declared that it too would be holding elections. Czechoslovakia opened its borders to thousands of East Germans who finally sensed freedom. And East Germany, under enormous pressure, tore down the Berlin Wall. All in the space of a few months.

No one, not even Reggie and his pals, had foreseen the collapse of communism in East Europe happening that fast. The Velvet Revolution staggered the world with its speed, and, for the most part, its lack of bloodshed. "We thought maybe 1991, 1992," exclaimed an overjoyed Reggie, "but not this soon."

***

Reggie had gone "missing" for a couple of weeks again, but then, in November, it was all I could do to keep him off the telephone. He had been operating day and night out of a base "a few minutes away from Templehof," an airport near West Berlin, deep in the heart of what was then still communist East Germany. (Quite separately, I discovered that, in Berlin, MI6 regularly used as a base of operations the otherwise empty Olympic Stadium, which Hitler had built for the 1936 Berlin Olympics.)

Reggie had been taking large amounts of money clandestinely into East Germany for the CIA. "All is forgotten and forgiven with respect to Lebanon," Reggie explained. Whatever trouble Reggie had been in was now gone. His enemies had become his friends. He had a talent: He could speak German in whatever dialect his new friends fancied.

Reggie had also been given new and completely different information in respect of Hugh's activities. The Lebanon scenario had been a smokescreen, used to deflect Reggie before he became one of the "chosen few." In fact, Hugh had been laundering large amounts of money into Bulgaria and Yugoslavia. For whom, Reggie would not or could not say. However, according to Reggie, Hugh had made at least two visits to Bulgaria and Yugoslavia in the ten months before his death.

This money was to be used either to bump someone off, or to buy them out. Whatever or whoever it was, "others" had not been in favor of the operation. Steps were taken either to deny Hugh access to the money, threaten him, or kill him. What remained the same was that the villains were unchanged. They were still the Mafia, acting on behalf of the CIA.

This complete change of direction was more than I could handle after only one bottle of wine. I threw something of a wobbly at Reggie over the telephone. He was impervious. He kept jabbering away about seeing friends of his from Lazarus and British Intelligence on the TV news, parading around the streets of the former East Berlin, rejoicing at the fall of the Wall.

"I keep telling you, dear boy," he laughed, "you've got to read those two books. It's the only way you'll understand what's happening. We're about to win a war we've been waging for a thousand years." I knew I wasn't all that good at history, but it was my impression that Eastern Europe had been under the communist yoke for only fifty years.

***

"There are all sorts of interesting people, with all sorts of interesting agendas, running around Eastern Europe, trying to recreate it in their own image," declared Reggie. "It's not just what you're reading in the newspapers."

Reggie was adamant that my concerns and interests were now lost. Hugh was history. As was I. At one point, I was proving useful "to one or two organizations of a Christian bent." My investigations, while irksome to some, were seen as a boon to others, precisely because they were an irritation to their enemies. But the dramatic change of events in Eastern Europe had rendered me insignificant. I tried my hardest to figure out who might once have been "friends," and who "enemies." Plus, what they might be now. But it was all to no avail. When he wasn't talking to me in parables, Reggie might just as well have been speaking in tongues. A typically cryptic comment was his declaration that "all the forces of Christendom had been allied against 'The Bear' [Russia]. And it wasn't even against 'The Bear.' Because they were on our side, too."

I couldn't even pretend to understand. But I attempted valiantly to swing the conversation back to me, and to Hugh. Reggie was more animated than he had ever been. And was equally dismissive. No one cared. All the focus was now on Eastern Europe. And the Priory of Sion, along with their attendant Fraternal Orders, including the Knights of Lazarus, were right in the thick of it. Slugging it out with the "secular" intelligence agencies of the West and East, and with each other.

"We've been preparing for this battle for a thousand years," Reggie exclaimed, "and this time, we're going to be victorious." The Knights of Malta were organizing in Hungary. Reggie had not only been carrying money into the East for the CIA. He had been in Dresden, East Germany, the week before using US dollars to free half a dozen Knights of Lazarus from jail.

I could make no further impression on Reggie. Like a man transformed, he stated that he had undergone a "spiritual rebirth" in the previous week, and that there was now no turning back for him. I concluded I was wasting my time.

"Remember, I gave you a warning about the double-headed eagle?" Reggie asked. "Well, the eagle on my ring is from a different branch, but the same 'family' as Otto von Hapsburg [the reputed heir at that time to the bloodline of Jesus]. That's what it's all about at the moment. This is no longer about Hugh, or me, or you. It's about major changes in the world political balance. On levels you can only begin to imagine. Read those books. Hugh missed a lot because he was not a Freemason. And you're missing the bigger picture, as well."

Reggie had one more personal warning for me before he hung up for the last time: stay away from Philip de Nahlik. This was the close friend of Hugh's, whom Reggie had identified as being both British Intelligence and a Knight of Malta, "although his primary allegiance is to the latter, and the two loyalties have now probably come into conflict."

**

I was lost in thought as I climbed the stone stairs to the darkened balcony fronting my apartment, and I did not immediately see the two figures huddled by my front door. They were dressed in police garb and, as I drew near, I noticed that they were in fact looking at what had previously been the window to Hugh's office. The office and my apartment had been, quite conveniently for me at the time, side by side. The window in question was wide open.

I paid the two apparent policemen no heed, until one stopped me as I was about to enter my apartment. "You used to work here, didn't you – Mr. Gilson?" I had not given him my name. I had served on the Beaconsfield Town Council for four years. Beaconsfield is a small town. But I did not recognize him, or his mate. Plus, I hadn't told any policeman that I had returned to Beaconsfield. I tried to hurry on past.

The policeman made to stop me again. "Can you tell us why this window is open? We couldn't help but notice it from the street." The balustrade to the balcony was too high for the window to be seen from the street. And it was too dark to see anything anyway. I had no idea what these two were up to, or what they intended to do next. But I knew that I intended to find myself in the safety of my apartment just as quickly as possible. Which I did. I spent most of the night shaking. As soon as it was light, I checked the window to Hugh's office. Whoever my two visitors had been, they had not seen fit to close the window. I never saw nor heard from them again. Nor from any other policeman following up on mysteriously open windows.

**

I was done. I was tired. I was cold. And Reggie was not going to give me anything more. It was time to return to America. I began my round of farewells. Hugh's former accountant Neil Relph was first on the list. He had another interesting nugget from Carratu International: a nameless client reported that Hugh had shown him a briefcase one day, stuffed with cash. Hugh was apparently taking the cash to Geneva, "to consummate a deal."

***

I also had a last visit with Geoff Hughes. He was courteous as always. He reported that, although the Carratu investigation would be continuing (someone had to keep trying to find the missing money), the police had finished with their enquiries. They were no longer looking for an accomplice. They had simply concluded the accomplice was me. However, since the police didn't have any proof, they couldn't do anything about it. But they would be delighted just as soon as I felt fit to let them know where the money was. As would Geoff, the Law Society and the estate.

The tally for recovered money and assets to date remained a paltry £100,000 ($150,000). I gave Geoff a long letter re-iterating my belief that the best hope for recovery still lay with either twisting the arms of Hugh's closest friends or prodding British intelligence. I continued to get the impression that he believed he might actually be doing both simply by talking with me. Sigh. Definitely the weirdest "investigation" I'd ever encountered.

Geoff did break down a little and confirmed Neil's story about the cash in the briefcase. Geoff had not, however, been able to establish whether or not Hugh had actually traveled to Switzerland. Mind you, there was evidence he had made trips to Europe in the year before his death. Yugoslavia or Bulgaria, I wondered aloud? Geoff went shifty on me. No one had been able to find Hugh's passport.

As I was leaving, Geoff came over to shake my hand. He held on a little longer than normal. "I shouldn't say this, but you're a decent guy," he said, ever so softly. "I'd probably be getting further without interference from the Law Society. You're not so wrong. It will all come out. Just not in the timeframe you might wish." He would say no more. But he wished me well. And that was that.

***

It was the depth of winter in Rhode Island, and conditions seemed to be little different from those inside my apartment in Beaconsfield. Well, save for the three feet of snow on the ground. But at least I had the luxury of enjoying hot showers morning, noon and night.

I took the opportunity to contact every media outlet I could track down in Great Britain, in a vain attempt to rustle up interest in my discoveries about Hugh. I kept it simple. The press release I used focused on Reggie's second scenario [Eastern Europe], with a little embellishment of my own.

I told the media that Hugh had been working for persons unknown, but with the knowledge of British intelligence, to launder money into Yugoslavia and Bulgaria, to help foment the Velvet Revolution in those countries. The CIA had become unhappy, either with Hugh or his "masters," and had had him bumped off, via the good offices of their Mafia buddies.

I sparked interest from only two quarters. The first came by way of a telephone call from a Paul Halloran, claiming to work as a journalist for *Private Eye*, a well-known satirical and investigative journal in Great Britain. The conversation was as strange as it was short. Halloran evinced no interest in Hugh, British Intelligence, or the CIA. He was concerned solely with determining if I knew where the money was, and if he could be my exclusive media contact when I found it. When I asked him why, he hung up.

The other interested party was the CIA, which introduced itself to me almost as soon as I returned to England. This I did when my money finally ran out in America. Because England, at that time, remained the only country in the world where I knew how to survive when broke.

Chapter Eight

I Meet The CIA

WHENEVER I AM POOR, I feed myself by selling advertising space. So it was, on my return to the fair shores of England in the summer of 1990, that I found myself doing just this for a bunch of cowboys in the West End of London. We all worked in a circle, in an open office environment. Our basic tools were a desk, a telephone and a stack of directories. We telephoned companies worldwide, aiming to speak with presidents or CEOs. We sold pages in a non-existent trade annual, at $5,000 a pop. When we had enough sold, an editorial team downstairs would concoct the trade annual, we'd shove the artwork in, send it to the advertisers and move onto the next group of industry suckers.

I made it past the first week of fire-walking only because I got drunk one morning, and managed to persuade the South African Chamber of Commerce that President G.H.W. Bush and Margaret Thatcher were about to lift economic sanctions on South Africa, and my trade journal would be the first opportunity their member industries would have had to advertise to the international community in over a decade. I hit the motherlode. We couldn't beat them off with an M-1 tank. In general, however, success for rookies was as scarce as a six-pack at an AA meeting. As a consequence, we tended to have about a 100 percent turnover of staff every 10 days or so.

At the beginning of my second week, our group was joined by an African-American guy, who called himself Roy Thomas. He was in his late twenties. At lunchtime, we'd all go out to a local hostelry, and mess about while wolfing down food as quickly as possible. Bit by bit, Roy let his story slip: first, he'd been in the US Navy; then he'd been in the SEALs (the US Navy's elite special forces unit); finally, he'd been on loan to the CIA, while still in the US Navy. This last one caused my ears to perk up. I got him alone walking back to the Tube one evening, and told him I wouldn't mind having a chat with him sometime. Alone. Socially. He suggested his house that coming Sunday afternoon.

Roy had rented an old Victorian townhouse in Fulham, London. He lived there with his wife and two-year old daughter. He had just left the Navy, and was taking a year or two to see something of Europe. We spent about an hour that Sunday afternoon chatting and drinking a couple of glasses of wine. He showed me pictures of his family, and we played with his daughter for a while. Then, his wife discreetly left us alone.

I got straight to the point. I wondered what he could tell me about his service with the CIA. Roy was very professional. He said that he could not tell me much. He said that his primary attachment had been with the Navy and the SEALs, but that he had performed some work for the CIA as a "Watcher." The occupation is exactly what it suggests. The CIA contracts thousands of individuals, on a part-time basis, as and when they are needed, to watch people and places, and report back. Roy was not allowed to tell me, or anyone else, who or what he had been watching.

I ran the "I've got a friend" line, and then, without mentioning names, proceeded to tell him all about Hugh and Reggie. My theme was that this friend had information that might embarrass the CIA, and that he was interested in meeting with someone from the CIA to discuss the information. How did one go about meeting the CIA, without getting shot? I asked Roy.

Again, Roy was very professional, and did what in cricketing terms is known as "keeping a straight bat." He would not give anything away. We danced around. I could give him the information. No, my friend would rather do it direct. Well, the CIA doesn't just "have meetings." They probably knew the information already. Highly unlikely. Well, don't worry about it, the CIA has thousands of Watchers; my friend was probably already being watched; if the CIA really did feel that they were about to be embarrassed, they would find a way to get a message to my friend, to warn him off. At which point, the best thing my friend could do … would be to listen to the warning.

It became quite clear that either Roy did not believe me, or that he was too wise in bureaucratic ways to be of any use to me. We looked at some more photographs, chatted about my relatives in America, and after a suitably courteous interval, I made to leave.

Roy silently accompanied me to the front door. As I stood on the doorstep, he gently pulled the door closed behind him, and tapped my shoulder. I turned.

"Ah, Geoff," he began softly, "you know I said I was a Watcher? Past tense?"

"Yes," I answered, completely unsuspecting.

"Well, I'm still very active," Roy continued, "and the message for you is this: if you know what's good for you, stop with your investigations … bye now." And with that, he shut the front door.

I never saw Roy again. As far as I know he never came back to work. I was only at the advertising sales firm for a couple more days. Personal safety was one concern. The other was that I can only lie for a living for about a month before my conscience gets in the way.

***

Geoff Hughes wanted to meet. As it turned out, he didn't have all that much to tell me, but what he did was fairly explosive. The Law Society had brought the Carratu International investigation to a halt. The total monies recovered by the estate had topped off at £166,000 ($250,000). Yet evidence had been uncovered suggesting that Hugh had been laundering money for at least a hundred "entities."

This did not surprise me. When Hugh had been with Wedlake Bell, money laundering had been Hugh's specialty. But back in the days of socialistic Britain, when top tax rates ran at 80 percent and rising, this sort of laundering was still legal, and it went by the more sanitized description of "Money Management and Tax Assistance." I remember a huge chart on Hugh's office wall, showing all the interconnecting lines between Jersey, the Isle of Man, Switzerland, Liechtenstein, Luxembourg, Hong Kong, Liberia and the Cayman Islands, to mention but a few.

Geoff became more coy when I asked for details of names and quantities of money. He was prepared to confirm that no one had had less than £30,000 ($45,000) laundered. I responded by stating that no one was going to follow me for over a month in England for £30,000. Geoff slipped, and replied that they might for a few million. I did some quick mental math, and declared that we could be talking about a total of anything from £30 million ($45 million) to

£100 million ($150 million). Geoff did not reply. The meeting was over. He wished me well. And left.

Geoff did mention that the Law Society was in receipt of Carratu's final reports, but that they were unlikely to be released. I devised a ploy. I sought a legal opinion, and drafted a lawsuit against Hugh's estate (i.e., the Law Society) for damages. My novel argument was that a special trust existed between a Solicitor and his senior staff. That trust was recognized by clients and other employers alike. Hugh had broken that trust by stealing clients' money. I had been rendered unemployable by that breach.

One of the monopolies that Maggie Thatcher never broke up was that of the legal profession. Not surprising since she was a lawyer herself. The Law Society has omnipotent powers over the practice of law by Solicitors. It trains them; gives them their practicing certificates; oversees their finances; acts as their trade union; and when they've been naughty, performs all the functions of a kangaroo court, acting as judge, jury and executioner. This is not where it ends, however. The Law Society is also the organization that administers Legal Aid.

In my impecunious state, I found myself in the unusual position of applying to the Law Society for Legal Aid with which to sue the Law Society. They responded with the evenhandedness that I would have expected. They refused me. They knew very well that the first item of discovery in any trial would be the entirety of the folder from Carratu. Yet, their double-dealing did not go unnoticed. I appealed. And won. I had spent a week with my sister Maggi practicing my hour-long speech to the Independent Appeal Tribunal. They didn't give me a chance even to get out my notes. Almost as soon as I walked in the door and sat down, the Chairman declared that he'd never read such a load of ... nonsense as the reasons given by the Law Society for refusing me legal aid. Appeal allowed.

Unfortunately, that was as close as I ever got to seeing the Carratu reports. I dropped the suit. I had become involved with a consortium applying for one of the new UK Commercial FM radio station licenses then being offered in public auction pursuant to the Tories' deregulation of the BBC Radio state broadcasting monopoly. I expected to be the focus of some local public attention, and did not want to mess up our chances. It was a difficult choice. Rendered more poignant by the fact that the first business of the investors

I attracted to our bid was to ditch me for their own candidate as Managing Director.

***

I kept trying Reggie. But he'd gone cold on me. I was all set to engage in some more background reading, in the hope that I might find some mention of anything that rang a bell with what I knew so far. But as luck would have it, related scandals started popping up all over the daily newspapers.

***

In October 1990, one of Britain's brightest corporate stars, a company called Polly Peck, surprisingly went into the British equivalent of US Chapter 11 bankruptcy. No one had seen it coming. Soon enough it became clear that millions of pounds were missing. The former head of the firm, Asil Nadir, fled to Northern Cyprus, where he'd been born, shortly after it was announced that he faced 66 charges of theft amounting to £34 million ($47 million).

Nadir was safe in northern Cyprus, because Great Britain had no extradition treaty with the unrecognized northern half of the divided country. Not so lucky was the Conservative Party. A veritable soap opera played out in Britain's tabloids over the ensuing weeks as it became clear how close Nadir was to the Leadership of the Party. Hundreds of thousands of pounds in contributions from Nadir and Polly Peck were revealed. The scandal was so far reaching that the then Conservative Minister of State for Northern Ireland, Michael Mates, a close lieutenant of Michael Heseltine, resigned over his links to Nadir.

These developments marked the beginning of the years of Tory "sleaze," behavior that would be central to the public's eventual loss of faith in the Conservative Government. Yet, even though these episodes proved to be visceral and fascinating, in terms of the amounts of money involved they proved to be mere appetizers for what was to come later in 1991. Great Britain was about to become center stage to a couple of scandals that between them would represent financial "holes" totaling in the billions. And Hugh had connections to both scandals.

***

The actual genesis of the Bank of Credit and Commerce International is a little uncertain. It depends on who is telling the story – and on the affiliations and agendas of the person telling the story. There is no such thing as an objective writer. Some say it was the personal brainchild of a Pakistani banker called Agha Hasan Abedi, who ultimately sought the patronage and financial support of Sheikh Zayed bin Sultan Al Nahyan of the United Arab Emirates in order to establish the world's first global Muslim bank. Others say that British intelligence used their puppet Zayed as a front to set up a conduit for transferring money undetected around the world. The rest was mere cover.

Whatever the case, after its founding in Pakistan in 1972, BCCI grew quickly, and operated on two quite separate levels. On one level, it was what it claimed to be: a bank where Muslims in all participating countries could safely deposit their money with an institution whose traditions were the same as theirs. In particular, Muslim expatriates found it useful when wiring money to their families back home. In this regard, BCCI established a firm footing in England, and ultimately registered itself in Great Britain, where it fell under the supervision of the then Government-controlled Bank of England.

Such friendly supervision, whether a consequence of chance or design, proved most convenient with regards to the second and more clandestine function of BCCI, that of money-launderer for MI6. BCCI's usefulness developed quickly, and it soon became the center of a network, used not only by MI6, but also by the CIA and by Bush's SSG/CPPG. Since these bodies were themselves doing business with all manner of criminals, drug-traffickers and crooked money-launderers, the network became, in short order, a vast international underground trading exchange.

Intelligence agencies, organized crime, and terrorist groups could feed into the network, or feed off it. All you needed was something to trade with and some thing to trade for – hostages for arms; money for guns; drugs for political influence – and the network and its friendly bank, BCCI, would set up the trade, provide you with the financing, and even a ship to transport it. BCCI was nicknamed the Bank of Crooks and Cocaine International. I have come across no name for the wider network, and so have christened it – the "International Terror Network." When, at the end of the '80s, so much evidence of other nefarious activities was "cleaned away," the International Terror Network remained. It still served a purpose. And besides, its activities had become self-generating.

BCCI was not so fortunate. The charade began to fall apart in 1988, after two men linked to the bank were indicted in Miami for drug-running and money-laundering. BCCI's auditors, Price Waterhouse, engaged in a massive exercise in deception, trying to fool banking authorities in both the US and the UK that everything was fine, but eventually, even the Bank of England had to open its eyes, and finally shut down BCCI in 1991. Thousands of small Muslim depositors, in Britain and around the world, lost their money. When eventually the cobwebs of duplicity were brushed aside, it was discovered that there was a huge hole at the center of BCCI's finances, amounting to several billions of dollars.

The dramatic collapse of BCCI was all over the front pages of the British press in 1991. Most of the attention at that time was focused on the terrible hardship imposed on the thousands of Muslims who had lost their money. But details were emerging about the illegal activities of the bank, not least the evidence that the bank had been used by companies in the US and the UK to finance illicit sales of military technology to Saddam Hussein and Iraq in the '80s.

Notwithstanding the charges that the Democratic candidate for the US Presidency in 2004 did nothing while serving in the Senate for twenty years, Sen. John Kerry was in fact at the forefront of efforts to investigate the activities of BCCI. It was the scrutiny of his Senate Foreign Relations Subcommittee on Terrorism, Narcotics and International Operations that helped to uncover links between BCCI, Manuel Noriega, and the laundering of drug profits by the one for the other through Panama. This information led, in part, to the indictments in Miami in 1988.

Purely on a hunch, I telephoned Geoff Hughes, and asked him if Hugh had had a bank account with BCCI. After a deal of huffing and puffing, Geoff confirmed that Carratu had uncovered evidence of an account with BCCI, at their Park Lane branch.

***

A story that circulates about immigrants to Great Britain is that, having arrived at London's Heathrow Airport, they then travel west, along the arterial M4 motorway, as far as their money will allow. Leaving the truly poor to make it only as far as a bedsit in a dingy, light industrial town called Slough, just at the end of Heathrow's flight path. Slough will be known to US television viewers as the location of the UK version of the show, *The Office*, starring Ricky Gervais. Yes folks. That Slough. And yes, it is as depressing as it is portrayed.

Slough was my destination when finally in 1990 I landed back in England with no money. And having no money, I couldn't afford even a telephone for my bedsit. Mind you, even if I'd had the money, living in a slum, it was best not to draw attention to the fact that one might have more than food stamps in one's back pocket. I made all of my telephone calls courtesy of the High Street wine bar where I hung out, and which number I never gave out. So, it was with some surprise that I arrived there for lunch one day to be told that someone had called for me.

The caller was one Sushma Puri, who, when I returned the call, claimed to be an Associate Producer with *This Week*, a well-known documentary program on Thames Television, London's leading commercial television station. She had heard of my investigation and told me that her producer was interested in doing a slot in an upcoming show. I didn't want to ask how she knew, and she didn't bother to explain. We agreed to meet in London.

I recognized the front entrance to the Thames Television building from the credits they ran at the beginning of their evening news programs. Sushma was a slip of an Asian girl, with pretty features and long dark hair. She seemed to be much the same age as me, in her thirties. I was a shade bemused when we didn't go to a conference room or a private office. Here she was, supposedly the Associate Producer of the station's flagship news magazine, and we ended up perched on a desk, in a tiny cubicle, lost in a vast ocean of open-floor office space. I couldn't even find a plaque with her name, and I wasn't convinced that this was where she normally worked.

Without any chitchat, she asked to listen to the tapes of my conversations with Reggie. I had prepared some clippings of the more exciting stretches, while leaving out the details. If there was to be a documentary, I wanted to have some control over eventual content. Small I may be; stupid I'm not. She quickly lost interest in the edited version. I indicated that there wouldn't be time to listen to all six hours of the total tapes. She wondered if she could have a copy for her Producer. Which led me to wonder where he was, since we were supposed to be meeting him.

Sushma then completely changed tack, and began grilling me about my knowledge of Hugh and the "missing" money. What had been his schedule; foreign visits; bank accounts; spending patterns, etc. I desperately wanted a major media outlet to take an interest in my investigation. But Sushma was making me feel uncomfortable. Once again, I felt that I was talking to someone who had an unhealthy interest only in the "missing" money. I think Sushma sensed my jitters. She brought the "interview" to an end, mumbled something about needing to talk to her Producer, and directed me back to the front entrance. I never heard from Sushma again. Indeed, I telephoned Thames Television a couple of times, and they seemed completely unable to locate her. According to information, available on the Internet in the winter of 2014, she was a researcher at *This Week* for five stories during 1990-92.

In the entire BCCI affair, no entity has been more mysterious and yet more central to the bank's eventual collapse and criminality than Capcom, a London and Chicago-based commodities futures firm, which operated between 1984 and 1988. Capcom is vital to understanding BCCI because BCCI's top management and most important Saudi shareholders were involved with Capcom. Moreover, Capcom moved huge amounts of money, billions of dollars, which passed through the futures markets in a largely anonymous fashion. Capcom was the piggy bank inside the piggy bank.

Capcom was created by a young Pakistani named Syed Ziauddin Ali Akbar, the former head of BCCI's Treasury Department and a protégé of BCCI's founder. The company was staffed primarily by former BCCI bankers, and the major investors were almost exclusively Saudi and were largely controlled by Sheikh A.R. Khalil, the then chief of Saudi Intelligence. Capcom numbered among its financial advisers and auditors Price Waterhouse, National Westminster Bank, and American Express.

Along with the original Treasury Department of BCCI, Capcom was one of the single largest sources of the eventual financial "hole" associated with BCCI. Capcom proved to be a convenient financial conduit both for siphoning off assets from BCCI, and for laundering billions of dollars from the Middle East to the US, and to safe havens around the world. It was while I was studying Cap-com, some months after my ostensible episode with Thames Television, that I came across the information that Akbar had had a close female associate called Sushma Puri.

**

In October 1991, the famed American investigative author Seymour Hersh published a book, *The Samson Option*, exposing Israel's program to build a nuclear bomb. From a British perspective, the most sensational aspects of the book were the allegations by a former Israeli spy that Robert Maxwell, billionaire owner of London's *Daily Mirror* and Labour Party stalwart, had been for many years a critical agent in the service of Mossad.

The Israeli spy was one Ari Ben-Menashe, who was to become a figure of some controversy in matters relating to the '80s and '90s. He had been arrested in the US in 1989 for conspiring to sell military aircraft to Iran. At first, Israel disavowed all knowledge of him. However, he was later acquitted of all charges when the Israeli Ministry of Defense had to fess up that Ari's allegations that he was a spy acting on instruction from the Israeli Government were, in fact, quite true.

In many ways, the story of Robert Maxwell was more the stuff of the American Dream than something one associates with the stuffy upper crust of Great Britain's class-ridden society. This might account for the perverse pleasure he so often gained shocking that society with his vainglorious behavior. Maxwell was born a Jew in Czechoslovakia and fled that country after the Nazi invasion in 1939. Most of his family had been killed in the Holocaust. Like so many other Central European refugees, he was attracted to Great Britain, where he enlisted in the fight against Hitler. He rose to the rank of Captain in the British Army, where he served with some distinction in Military Intelligence.

After the Second World War, Maxwell stayed on in his adopted country, changed his name, and set about making his fortune. With trademark energy and ebullience, he soon owned a controlling share in Pergamon Press, which he built into a successful publishing house, specializing in trade journals and technical and scientific books. Based partly on that success, Maxwell won a seat in

Parliament, serving as a Labour MP from 1964 to 1970. Even after his electoral defeat, he continued to be one of the Labour Party's leading benefactors. Through the '70s, and into the '80s, he focused on massively expanding his publishing empire on both sides of the Atlantic, increasingly using the financial tool that came to define the later corporate scandals of the '80s, the leveraged buyout. In this way, Maxwell gained control of the left-leaning *Daily Mirror*, Macmillan (a large US publisher) and the *New York Daily News*.

Hersh's book told how Israel became a secret nuclear power, recounting Israel's clandestine mission, from the building of the Dimona reactor site in the remote Negev desert during the late '50s, to the establishment by the late '70s of a nuclear capability that targeted and threatened the Soviet Union.

Ben-Menashe's contribution was to state that Maxwell had been a spy for Mossad, as well as the British, almost from the time he had landed on English soil. Through Maxwell's extensive global contacts, and particularly relying upon the friendships he had forged with the Communist dictators of Eastern Europe, the Israelis had used Maxwell for a number of important secret missions.

In reference to the subject matter of his book, Hersh alleged that Maxwell had conspired with Mossad to kidnap Mordechai Vanunu, the Israeli technician who broke the story of the Dimona reactor to London's *Sunday Times* in 1986. Vanunu was lured to Rome, where, apparently under the supervision of Ben-Menashe, he was abducted and taken back to Israel, where he was put on trial and imprisoned for espionage. Vanunu was released in 2003, after 16 years in prison, but is free only on the basis of the strictest parole conditions, which include not talking with any media.

Ben-Menashe also revealed that Maxwell, together with the Foreign Editor of the *Daily Mirror*, Nicholas Davies, arranged to buy arms for Iran as part of the Iran-Contra-Lebanon triangle. Allegedly the arms-buying had been effected through a company called Ora Limited, a company registered in London, and of which Ben-Menashe and Davies were both Directors.

Maxwell's *Daily Mirror*, along with the *Sunday Times*, lost no time in savaging the credibility of Ben-Menashe in their respective newspapers. However, just a few weeks after the original revelations in Hersh's book, Robert Maxwell's huge naked body was found floating face up in the chilly Atlantic waters off the Canary

Islands, near the south coast of Spain. Twenty-four hours earlier, the crew of Maxwell's yacht, which had set sail from Gibraltar a few days beforehand, reported the flamboyant publisher missing. The autopsy ruled out death by drowning, due to the absence of water in Maxwell's lungs, and settled on heart failure.

Maxwell's body was flown to Jerusalem for burial in November 1991, on the historic Mount of Olives, the resting place for Israel's most revered heroes. The burial service had all the trappings of a state occasion, attended by the country's government and opposition leaders. No fewer than six serving and former heads of the Israeli intelligence community listened as the serving Prime Minister, Yitzhak Shamir, eulogized: "He has done more for Israel than can today be said."

***

In 1992, my younger brother, Jon, called from Atlanta to invite me to come and help market his computer software company. It didn't take me long to accept. I had, once again, come to the end of my finances. Notwithstanding its blandness, Slough had proven to be a good home, and I was sad to leave it. However, as was happening with increasing frequency, I was about to find myself traveling to exactly the right place, at exactly the right time. Revelations aplenty awaited me on the other side of the Atlantic.

CHAPTER NINE

Arms To Iraq?

B Y THE TIME I GOT to Atlanta in 1992, a scandal was hitting the press there. It involved the indictment of a banker named Christopher Drogoul, who in the late '80s had run the Atlanta branch of the Italian Government-owned bank, Banca Nazionale del Lavoro (BNL).

BNL had been wrapped up in the illegal arming of Iraq in the '80s by the US and the UK. It wasn't fully clear at the time, but this storyline would eventually lead back to Hugh. First, there was some more history to take in.

Saddam Hussein came to power in Iraq in the early '70s. One of his first priorities was to use the profits from Iraq's oil wells to build up his armed services. Saddam needed a strong military to maintain control over the fractious factions within his own country, to intimidate the neighboring Arab nations, and to keep Israel at bay.

At first, Saddam was content merely to buy a ready-made arsenal from the Soviet Union, which had been supplying all of the Arab nations, in order to maintain a balance of terror with the American-armed Israelis. However, after the Yom Kippur War of 1974, fought between the Israelis and the Arabs, when Israel came close to launching its nuclear bombers, Saddam decided he needed to diversify his sources and extend the focus of his purchasing.

The Soviet Union had taken to using its position as sole source of supply as a lever to "encourage" client countries like Iraq to follow its line on foreign policy. Saddam was less concerned about having an independent view on world affairs than he was determined to have a military machine that was under no-one's control but his own. First, he sought merely to buy weapons from France as well as the Soviet Union. However, in 1981, the Israelis bombed his Osirisk nuclear reactor, which was just beginning to produce plutonium for Iraq's nascent attempts to build an Arab nuclear bomb. At this point, Saddam set out in earnest to create an indigenous military industry for Iraq, not only producing basic weaponry, such as artillery and shells, but also making available a nuclear, biological, and chemical warfare capability.

Saddam put in motion a global effort to purchase the component parts for his wide-ranging military effort. The concept was not merely to buy the tools necessary to build weapons, but also to become the owner of foreign companies engaged in this industry, so that the blueprints for their machine-tooling could be exported back to Iraq. Saddam was determined to have an Iraq-based military industry that would ultimately be immune to interference from other countries, whether by military action or economic sanction.

The man put in charge of Iraq's covert and worldwide military-purchasing effort was Hussein Kamel, Saddam's son-in-law and the head of the intelligence service, Amn al Khas (Special Security Organization). It was primarily from Kamel that the West and the United Nations learned of the full capability of Saddam's weapons of mass destruction, when Kamel defected to the West in the '90s. Back in the '80s, Kamel's first order of business was to purchase front companies, and find tame banks, behind which Iraq could hide its true intentions.

There were few countries that did not hop on the illegal Iraqi bandwagon, particularly those from Western Europe. However, much of Kamel's trawling was done in the United States, and it was here that, alongside BCCI, he found a great banking asset. The young and brash Christopher Drogoul, who had become manager of BNL's new Atlanta branch in 1984. Between then and 1989, when it was finally seized by the FBI, he illegally lent Iraq some $5 billion, all of which was used to buy illicit military technology. Almost all of the loans were underwritten by US Government export credit guarantees. Thus eventually, the entire tab was picked up by the American taxpayer.

Government export credit guarantees are the same the world over. They work like this: A company wishes to sell a product to a foreign country with a less than stellar financial history. First, the country places an order for the product. The company then issues an invoice. Before the product is shipped, however, the company has to obtain an export license and an end-user certificate from its own government, confirming that the product is either military or not, and that, if a military product, it is not going to end up with a foreign country that is a no-no. This process is pretty easy to circumvent.

During the '80s, billions of dollars of illegal military business was regularly being done with Iran and Iraq, while the countries were at war with each other, and both of which had had an arms embargo slapped against them by the UN. The favorite scam was for a US company to buy a UK company, and produce a legal export license and end-user certificate, quoting the UK company as the end destination for the product of the US company. The product in question would then miraculously disappear en route, and later turn up in either Iran or Iraq. When it was UK companies doing the selling, the process was reversed, with export licenses and end-user certificates being produced to export to US partners.

The next step in the process was to get a commercial bank to underwrite the transaction. Banks will generally only do this in the case of foreign countries with a bad credit history if the exporting country's government agrees to bail out the loan if anything goes wrong. This is called a government export credit guarantee. The product is shipped to the foreign country, the commercial bank pays the totality of the purchase price to the company, and the bank turns its attention to bringing in the monthly installments on the loan from the foreign country.

More often than not, and this was particularly true with Iran and Iraq, the foreign country defaults on the loan, and the commercial bank looks to the government to bail out the loan, landing the taxpayer with the bill. This is how the US Government finally caught up with Christopher Drogoul and BNL.

The news in 1992, as I arrived in Atlanta, had to do with the US Government trying to achieve a plea bargain deal with Drogoul, in order to keep the "real" BNL story out of the media – namely, that the US Government had been actively supporting the Iraqi attempt to build its own military machine and had been fully aware of the activities of the Atlanta branch of BNL. The US District Court Judge in Atlanta, Marvin Shoob, tried his hardest to blow the lid on the deal, but he was no match for the full weight of the US Government, even with newly elected Democrat, Bill Clinton, at its helm.

BNL turned out to be another international bank with interesting political connections. Once again, Kissinger Associates was there. BNL was a client of Kissinger Associates, which throughout the '80s used its close connections with the Reagan and Bush administrations to help BNL in Atlanta obtain export licenses for the military technology it was helping Iraq illegally purchase. During the same period, Henry Kissinger served on the BNL International Advisory Board.

***

It was not enough for Hussein Kamel to provide his father-in-law with nuclear, biological and chemical weapons. To be of any use, Saddam needed the capacity to deliver these weapons to the enemy. From the other side of the Atlantic came the news that Kamel had been searching the UK for such delivery systems.

In 1991, the UK Customs Service discovered that Walter Somers, a British engineering firm, was trying to export pieces of a huge artillery gun to Iraq. The gun, which was nicknamed the "Supergun," was being constructed under the auspices of Iraq's secret Project Babylon, led by a brilliant Canadian scientist called Gerald Bull. For many years, Bull had been at the forefront of artillery design, but had fallen on hard times when he was caught performing illicit work for the apartheid regime of South Africa, which was at that time the subject of international economic and military sanctions.

Iraq desperately needed artillery superiority over Iran, which was throwing millions of its fanatical soldiers at Iraq's eastern border in the war between the two countries, a war which had been started by Iraq in 1980, but which it was losing. Bull agreed to upgrade the Iraqis' artillery and extend the range of their SCUD-B missiles, in return for funds to develop his Supergun. Bull kept his word, and the new artillery that the Iraqis brought to bear at the end of the '80s proved so successful that the Iranians finally agreed to a ceasefire in June 1988. The UK Customs Service discovery brought the Supergun project to an end, and led to several convictions for illegal arms-trading for Bull's partners in Great Britain. Bull escaped prison time because he and his company were based in Belgium. Later in March 1990, he was shot to death with five bullets in the back of his neck, after answering the door to his apartment in Brussels.

More fortunate were the directors of another British company called Matrix Churchill. This company was a machine tool manufacturer that had been purchased in 1987 by an Iraqi-controlled company, TMG Engineering. This company, in turn, was owned by a larger Iraqi company, Technology and Development Group Ltd., which was one of Kamel's primary fronts for buying into companies with technology required for Iraq's military industry.

In the late '80s, two significant contracts were placed with Matrix Churchill. The first contract came from Industrias Cardoen of Chile, and was to supply Iraq with the machine tools to manufacture fuses for shells. The second contract was placed directly by Iraq's NASSR Establishment for Mechanical Industries, and was for a project code-named "ABA." Under the terms of this second contract, Matrix Churchill was to provide NASSR with machine tools to construct multi-launcher rocket systems. The British government granted export licenses for both of these contracts on the basis that the materials were for civil use, since that is what the export license applications had fraudulently specified.

In the spring of 1990, West German intelligence informed the British government that Matrix Churchill machine tools were being illicitly diverted to Iraqi military programs. Soon after learning of these reported breaches of British export control regulations, Britain's Department of Trade and Industry and the UK Customs service began their investigations of Matrix Churchill.

Those inquiries confirmed that the two contracts, both of which had been financed by BNL in Atlanta, had indeed circumvented British export guidelines. As a consequence, the directors of Matrix Churchill were charged and stood trial. However, the whole pack of cards came tumbling down when the nature of the relationship between Matrix Churchill and the British government was revealed.

Paul Henderson, the Managing Director of Matrix Churchill, was a contract agent for MI6, with a specific brief to report on illicit exports to Iraq. As a consequence, the British Government had known all along about the activities of Matrix Churchill. The judge dismissed the charges with the famous comment that he was damned if he was going to send to prison individuals who were acting on orders from their government.

To the surprise of most informed observers, Prime Minister John Major reacted with speed and almost unseemly propriety. He immediately ordered a Judicial Commission, headed by Lord Justice Richard Scott, to examine the whole issue of the sale of potentially dual-use technology to Iraq, to determine whether it had been used for military purposes, and whether or not the government had been aware of this fact.

The British media were not used to a politician prepared to search for the truth. Particularly when it seemed obvious that the truth would prove to be so unpalatable to the politician seeking it. As soon as the commission was announced, journalists and authors fell all over themselves in their eagerness to present the wealth of evidence apparently confirming not only the British government's awareness of illegal arms sales to Iraq, but its open encouragement of those sales.

After Iraq invaded Iran in 1980, the international community had imposed military sanctions against both countries, forbidding anyone from selling any hardware that would significantly alter the offensive balance between the two nations. The world took the view that this definition offered such wide latitude for interpretation that illicit sales to both countries began almost immediately.

Head of the queue were American companies and those from Western Europe, while their respective politicians did what they could to make the job easier. To their credit, the politicians at least paid lip service to the idea of balance. At first, the Iraqis held the upper hand. For this, and a host of other reasons, including the hostages in Lebanon and the "October Surprise," governments initially favored export licenses for Iran.

Around about 1984, luck had begun to favor the Iranians in the war. Saddam had not achieved success with his intended quick punch. The Iranians had rallied, and were now pouring their foot soldiers of Islam into the battlefields by the thousands. The Iraqis simply did not have enough weapons to kill them all. Plus, the Iranians were not proving as co-operative in Lebanon as the West had hoped. Accordingly, the political "tilt" was altered to lean in favor of Iraq.

Notwithstanding her calls to stand firm against terrorists and their allies, Britain's then Prime Minister, Margaret Thatcher, and her government were not going to be left out of the pig's trough developing in the Persian Gulf. The Ministry of Defence actively encouraged British defense contractors to enter the fray, while ministers from the Department of Trade and Industry held unofficial seminars, where they told arms dealers how to complete applications for export licenses in a manner that would circumvent the very regulations the ministers were supposed to be enforcing.

After 1987, the United States and Great Britain increased the tilt towards Iraq. Iran had proven useless in Lebanon; the need to honor the October Surprise had run its course; and both countries were, at that time, importing more of their oil from Iraq than ever before. Besides, Saddam was proving to be a reasonably "tame" dictator, and both Governments took the view that a firm hand was required in the Persian Gulf to keep the Iranians and others under control. This new policy continued after the ceasefire in the Iran-Iraq War, declared in the summer of 1988. Indeed, it was still in place when Saddam invaded Kuwait in August of 1990. British soldiers returned from the First Gulf War bearing photographs of artillery shells captured from the Iraqi Republican Guards, and marked with the imprint of British government-owned weapons factories.

London's *Sunday Times* went a step further, actually suggesting, in a series of explosive articles, that high-ranking members of the British Conservative Party and government made money off the illicit arms sales. The thrust of the allegations was that, during the Thatcher years, a group of defense contractors, businessmen, city bankers, senior civil servants, intelligence officers and high-ranking Conservative politicians had conspired to organize huge arms deals, both legal and illegal, with the covert connivance of Thatcher's government, and in pursuit of Thatcher's private foreign policy agenda. The group, which was nicknamed the "Savoy Mafia," in honor of its regular meetings at London's Savoy Hotel, included a host of well-known names, perhaps the best-known of these being Thatcher's husband and son, Denis and Mark Thatcher.

In return for expediting the arms deals and promoting Margaret Thatcher's hidden foreign policy agenda, the members of the Savoy Mafia pocketed very generous commission payments. Specifically, members were alleged by the *Sunday Times* to have earned a secret $360 million in commissions, for brokering a $35 billion agreement (known as "Al Yamamah I"), in 1985, to supply British jet fighters, naval mine hunters and ammunition to Saudi Arabia, over the ensuing 10 years.

Almost of more interest to the media than the suggestion of government corruption were the details of Mark Thatcher's involvement. For years, the British press and public had wondered how on earth this acknowledged dimwit had managed to turn himself into a millionaire. After a series of embarrassing episodes in and around Europe, Mark had been bundled off to Dallas, Texas, there to sell Lotus sports cars for a company called British Auctions, whose chairman was a member of the Savoy Mafia, and was also a personal friend of Mark's dad, Denis. Miraculously, in the mid-'80s, Mark became filthy rich, and married one of Dallas's socialite princesses.

Sources close to the Al Yamamah I deal were saying that Mark Thatcher's cut of the commissions was $18 million. The *Sunday Times* stated that this was the money he had used to set up home and business in Texas. In addition, the respected newspaper suggested that the Scott Commission inquiry into arm sales to Iraq threatened to implicate Mark as an alleged middleman who could secure arms deals at a drop of his family name.

A follow-up investigation by the *Sunday Times* then alleged that Mark was being investigated by US Customs as part of an inquiry into the illegal export of military equipment to Iraq and Libya. Agents were supposed to examine two Texas companies in which he had a holding. Aida Perez, an intelligence agent in the US Customs enforcement department in Florida, said officers were looking at allegations linking Mark to arms deals. The inquiry centered on Grantham, Mark's holding company in Houston, and Ameristar, a jet refueling company in Dallas, in which he had an interest. However, one of the primary problems experienced by all those wishing to nail Mark Thatcher, as the media at the time were the first to acknowledge, was that no-one could find a money trail.

***

The modern state of Israel is a tiny sliver of land that has existed since the Second World War mainly due to the efficiency of its armed forces. In war after war, the country has prevailed over neighbors, who seemed to want nothing more than to drive the Jewish people as far into the Mediterranean as they would go. In no small part, the military has owed its success to the excellent performance of the nation's intelligence services. And they, in turn, have lived and died by a code of silence that made the Mafia's omertà look like a friendship ritual between first-graders.

So it was with no small sense of outrage that Israelis awoke in October 1991 to read that a renegade member of Mossad, one Victor Ostrovsky, was spilling the beans on some of its more exotic training practices and escapades in his book, *By Way of Deception*. While there was considerable public and press interest in the book, at least outside of Israel, it was nothing compared to the reaction that met his second book a few years later.

The essence of his second book, *The Other Side of Deception*, was that the first book, and indeed the very suggestion that Ostrovsky was renegade, was merely a device to undermine dangerous rightwing elements in Israeli intelligence by exposing their activities. Apparently, there was a continuing struggle within the various factions of Israeli intelligence. Broadly speaking, the left-wing, openly in support of Israel's Labour Party, and with whom Ostrovsky claimed allegiance, took the view that clandestine work, on behalf of the state, should know some codes of behavior, and should pretty much be restricted to Israel and the lands of its immediate enemies.

The right-wing faction, which allied itself with the then-governing Likud Party of Prime Minister Menachem Begin, and later, his successors Yitzhak Shamir and Ariel Sharon, took the rather more aggressive stance that, in the fight for Israel's survival, all bets were off, and that Israeli intelligence could and should do whatever necessary, wherever necessary. If this meant assassinations and faked attacks by militant Palestinians, then so be it. If Israelis needed to interfere covertly with the political balance in other, supposedly "friendly," countries, in order to engender the right level of support for Israeli ambitions, then this should be done with gusto. The left-wing faction felt that the right-wing group could no longer be controlled from within Mossad alone, and this had led to the subterfuge with Ostrovsky.

All of this was so much gentle appetizer for a book published in 1992 by Ari Ben-Menashe, called *Profits of War*. Notwithstanding his protestations to the contrary, page after page seemed to be an unapologetic chronicle of some of the more outrageous schemes of the right-wing faction of Israeli Intelligence.

Both Ben-Menashe and Ostrovsky claimed they were now telling their stories because, both, in their fashion, had been dumped by their former faction leaders. Ben-Menashe was upset that his former bosses had taken so long to come to his aid, while he rotted in an American jail, sharing space with a bull redneck, who insisted on calling him "girlfriend." Meanwhile, Ostrovsky was upset because the leader of his left-wing faction, who went by the codename "Ephraim," had, apparently, found a new boyfriend, and no longer returned Ostrovsky's telephone calls. Problem was, who to believe? Ostrovsky had already run one successful disinformation campaign with his first book. Could it be that Ostrovsky and Ben-Menashe were now partners in another, more elaborate intelligence scam? As Reggie was fond of saying: "Once a boy scout, always a boy scout."

Certainly, Ben-Menashe had many detractors when it came to his personal credibility and the allegations in his book. He was labeled a professional liar, a man who always found himself at the center of every major intelligence triumph. *Newsweek's* national security correspondent, John Barry, said on CNN: "Ben-Menashe is a fabricator.... If you were talking about the American Civil War, he would tell you he was the guy who planned Lee's campaign."

It never ceases to amaze me that otherwise intelligent people seem to assume that intelligence services hire angels. They don't. Spying is about being a crook. And intelligence agencies hire crooks. Besides, when one looks a little closer, one finds that so many of those in the media who attack Ben-Menashe are the ones who may have missed out on the true events of the '80s. The fact is, whatever may be the truth about Ben-Menashe, he is still sought out by governments and intelligence services the world over. And Rafi Eitan, a respected, former Deputy Director of Operations for Mossad, has gone on record as confirming the bulk of the content of Ben-Menashe's book.

The central controversy of Ben-Menashe's book is its total rewrite of the script for the Iran-Contra and, at the time, still-developing Iraqgate scandals. Whatever may have been his true value to the Contra operation, Oliver North is described by Ben-Menashe as being mere sideshow to the real event in respect of Iran. Worse than being simply irrelevant, it is Ben-Menashe's contention that North was set up as a stooge, to attract attention away from the serious arms deliveries to Iran, which were occurring elsewhere.

The initial trade-off of the October Surprise (a limited quantity of arms to Iran, in return for delaying the release of the American hostages; executed by the new administration of Ronald Reagan replacing arms supplied from Israel's arsenal) set the scene for a much larger and more extended illegal supply of weaponry to Iran.

Whatever the mullahs of Iran may privately and publicly have thought of "The Great Satan," they desperately required The Great Satan's military technology to push back the Iraqi invasion. At the same time, the US found it in their political interests to maintain some sort of military balance between Iraq and Iran by supplying the latter with weaponry. Moreover, there were huge profits to be made from overcharging the oil-rich mullahs.

And it is hard to find a Republican who will ever refuse a profit.

Needing to keep this deeply dark and illegal arms supply effort away from the irritating oversight of Congress, the process was handled at the US end by Bush Sr. and his brand-new, private intelligence operation, SSG/CPPG. And, since the right-wing Likud Party, under Menachem Begin, was at that time in control of Israel's coalition government, the exercise was undertaken in the main, at the Israeli end, by the right-wing faction in Israeli intelligence. From 1980 to 1984, the left-wing group in Israeli intelligence was pretty much frozen out of sharing the spoils. And riches there were aplenty.

Worried about triggering Congressional oversight, the original sell-and-swap arrangement with Israel evolved into a more hands-off partnership, where Israel undertook all of the selling to Iran directly, with the US as cheerleaders in the background. Ben-Menashe was one of six individuals on Israel's top secret Joint Committee on Israel-Iran Relations, who spent their time traveling the world, buying up weapons wherever they could find them, shunting them through front companies, like Ora Limited with Nick Davies, and selling them to the Iranians at grossly inflated prices.

However, it was not long before greed overcame common sense, and, beginning in about 1984, Bush and his mob began arranging for their own parallel supply line to Iran. The combined effort was called the "Blue Pipeline," after the Danish shipping company that was used. All in all, Ben-Menashe reckons that, by the end of the Iran-Iraq War in 1988, the illegal sales to Iran had been worth some $82 billion in total.

That level of sales created huge profits, which needed to be laundered cleanly, and then hidden somewhere safe from prying eyes. Enter Robert Maxwell. Ben-Menashe and company used Maxwell's publishing firms and his contacts with the leadership in Eastern Europe to launder the profits into secret bank accounts on the other side of the Iron Curtain. At their peak, separate funds for the Israelis and the Americans each contained revolving totals of some $600 million.

During my intensive research, undertaken mostly between 1990 and 1993, I had read literally hundreds of books. This was exactly the sort of operation I had been looking for. Money-laundering is a skilled business, and I had seen nothing in either Maxwell or Ben-Menashe's CV's to suggest they knew the first thing about laundering money. Unlike Hugh.

By 1985, and under the terms of Israel's coalition partnership, the leader of the left-wing Labour Party, Shimon Peres, became Prime Minister of Israel. Almost the first item on his agenda was a demand for a piece of the Iranian arms' pie. A close associate of his, Amiram Nir, made contact with Robert McFarlane, Reagan's first National Security Adviser, and Oliver North. Ben-Menashe and his team made as if to cooperate, while keeping the "newbies" as far away from the real action as possible. In the end, North and his entourage shipped no more than 1,000 TOW missiles to Iran, for the kingly sum of $1 billion. Even this deal was rendered useless to the Iranians when it was discovered that the missiles were still imprinted with the Israeli Defense Force logo.

North went all sour grapes, and played stool pigeon on some of Ben-Menashe's colleagues, then passing through New York. The latter were jailed. Ben-Menashe responded in 1987 by spilling the beans on North and his outfit to a newspaper in Lebanon. Partly this was malice. Partly it was a "smokescreen" ploy. Congress was getting itchy. Inquiries were being made. Ben-Menashe and his colleagues took the view that, by offering up a juicy tidbit on North, Congress would become so preoccupied that it would look no further. Ben-Menashe proved to be right.

No one really knows why Congress didn't push harder. Perhaps both Democrats and Republicans privately supported the ambitions of Bush's secret agenda? Perhaps Democrats were cowed by Reagan's popularity? Perhaps no one wanted to see another President impeached so soon after Nixon? Or perhaps Ben-Menashe and his cohorts simply outsmarted them? Whatever the case, North and his comrades took the fall, yet were later either pardoned or had their convictions overturned on appeal. And the media did nothing, except call Ben-Menashe a liar, for revealing what they had either missed or refused to report while it was happening.

Ben-Menashe had been sacked for his disloyalty to the competing "left-wing" Israeli-American arms pipeline to Iran. However, even the limited disclosures in Congress about North's Iranian adventures pretty much brought all pipeline business to Iran to an end in 1987. Just in time for the Iraqis to get the upper hand with Gerald Bull's improved artillery, and bring about the ceasefire in the Iran-Iraq War in the summer of 1988. Ben-Menashe was immediately recalled for higher duties, as the Counter-Terrorism Adviser to Yitzhak Shamir, the new right-wing Likud Prime Minister.

Top of Shamir's agenda was the need to plug the separate, but equally covert, arms pipeline to Iraq, which had picked up pace in 1987, as the US and the UK became more reliant on Iraq's oil. Ben-Menashe's new role as Shamir's "bully boy" saw him traveling to the US, the UK, and Europe. Ben-Menashe's book even describes a scene where he is in the office of weapons scientist and engineer Carlos Cardoen in Chile, warning him to "back off," at which point Cardoen dramatically introduces Ben-Menashe to his new chum and partner, Mark Thatcher. Ben-Menashe takes the view that the introduction was staged to convince him that Cardoen believed he had enough friends in high places to be unafraid of Ben-Menashe.

Ben-Menashe claims also to have met with Gerald Bull, shortly before he was murdered. Bull also feigned indifference, but he turned up a few days later with five bullets in the back of his head. Ben-Menashe does little to dispel the notion that he was somehow responsible.

Maxwell took advantage of the slush funds in Eastern Europe to expand his business empire. He took out bank loans, which were underwritten by loan guarantees, permitted by Yitzhak Shamir, and with the blessing of Bush Sr., on the basis that any default in the loans would be covered by the money in the slush funds.

In 1989, an operation was compromised when it was leaked that Israel was negotiating with the PLO for the release of soldiers in Lebanon. Ben-Menashe was again blamed for the leak. Sensing another round of doom and gloom, Ben-Menashe, who was one of only a few signatories to the Israeli slush fund, began to move the money around, while making a fair proportion of it disappear altogether. This had the effect of undermining Maxwell's loan guarantees, and Shamir was furious with Ben-Menashe.

Soon after, Ben-Menashe lost his "protection." He found himself in jail, set up by the CIA, disowned by his employer and abandoned by his wife. However, he may have had the last laugh. When it came time to hand over the slush fund money, Maxwell returned most of the Likud money, but he cut the Americans out of their share, being some $780 million. Shortly afterwards, Maxwell took his last swim off the Canary Islands. Ben-Menashe is quick to put the blame for Maxwell's death on the CIA. Yet Ben-Menashe's "rival" Ostrovsky, and others with interests closer to the left-wing in Israel, paint a different picture.

They say that, in September of 1991, the vultures were circling Maxwell and his shambolic financial affairs. The UK Parliament was threatening to investigate, and the media was only being held at bay by Britain's draconian libel laws and a bevy of high-priced lawyers. Maxwell begged for more monetary assistance from the Israelis. When they balked, he threatened to expose the secret meeting he had hosted earlier in the year on his yacht between the head of Mossad and Vladimir Kryuchkov, the head of the KGB.

At the meeting, Kryuchkov had discussed his plans to stage a coup against the sitting Soviet President, Mikhail Gorbachev. Mossad had promised to use its influence with the United States and key European countries to recognize the new regime in Moscow. In return, Kryuchkov would arrange for all Soviet Jews to be released and sent to Israel. The discussion came to nothing. But the coup was staged. And failed. Revelation of the secret meeting would seriously harm Israel's credibility with the existing Russian regime, and with the United States.

Maxwell received a call from the Israeli Embassy in Madrid. He was asked to come to Spain the following day, where according to Ostrovsky, "his caller promised that things would be worked out so there was no need [for Maxwell] to panic." Maxwell was told to fly to Gibraltar, just down the road from Marbella, and to board his luxury yacht, the *Lady Ghislaine*. He was to order the crew to set sail for the Canary Islands, "and wait there for a message." The message was delivered by a Mossad hit team of two assassins, one of whom injected a bubble of air into Maxwell's neck via his jugular vein. It took just a few moments for Maxwell to die, whereupon his still warm body was stripped and then dumped overboard.

Notwithstanding their occasional disagreement over Mossad's responsibility for particularly controversial deaths, Ostrovsky and Ben-Menashe were agreed on one thing in their respective books: in the '80s, the right-wing in Israeli intelligence, egged on by its political masters, had ploughed a scorched earth path around the world, laying waste to Israel's perceived enemies with assassinations and dirty deeds. One of the truly disturbing features of Ben-Menashe's revelations, not in his own book, but as a source in another bestseller – *Abu Nidal: A Gun for Hire* by Patrick Seale – was the implication that the "dirty deeds" might have included faking terrorist incidents in order to whip up a frenzy of support for punitive action.

Abu Nidal, born Sabri al-Banna, was always regarded as one of the more vicious of the Palestinian terrorists. His organization was responsible for a series of violent acts in Rome, Vienna, Istanbul and London. Nidal's name was linked to the Lockerbie bombing, and he allegedly gave the order for the assassination in London of Israel's Ambassador, Shlomo Argov. The assassination failed, but the attempt was used as the pretext for Ariel Sharon's invasion of Lebanon in 1982.

Not all of Nidal's killings were ideological. He was for many years a hired gun for a variety of clients, including Iraq and Libya. Nidal had a close relationship with Saddam Hussein for many years, killing many of Iraq's enemies around the world. The relationship lasted until 1983, when Nidal took the view that Saddam had become too cozy with the West in his desire for financial and military help in his war against Iran.

This then was the public face of Abu Nidal, the most extreme of Arab Palestine's militant champions. Yet, Ben-Menashe and others suggest that the truth was more complex. That Nidal was, at the very least, a quadruple agent, bought and paid for variously by Mossad, MI6 and the KGB, all the while continuing to parade as the purist of Palestinian idealists. The implication was that Nidal was everyone's favorite play toy; a dangerous weapon, used as a last resort for work that had to remain beyond the undeniable.

Primarily, Mossad used Nidal to blunt the military efforts of the Palestinians. The thinking was that by staging particularly controversial terrorist incidents in Europe, the public would turn against the Palestinian cause, and formerly wavering European governments would line up behind Israel's aggressive stance. The British and the Russians had their own agendas.

The British tricked Nidal into providing them with voluminous information on the activities of all the Palestinian groupings. In this task, the British required the help of another notorious Middle Eastern criminal, Monzer al-Kassar, whose name regularly appeared as a bit player in most of the unseemly dramas in the Middle East in the '80s. Like Nidal, al-Kassar had many masters, including the British. But his primary allegiance had always been to Syria, the land of his birth.

By the '80s, al-Kassar and his brothers operated as the East Mediterranean "franchise" of the International Terror Network: they were the central exchange for the region's terrorist, arms and drug networks. They had close ties to BCCI, along with their own banking network, which they offered as a service to any that would do business with them. And everyone did. If you needed help in the Middle East freeing hostages, buying guns, placing a bomb, or simply obtaining drugs and laundering the profits to another part of the world, Monzer al-Kassar was your man. Clients included the CIA and their British contract agent, Les Aspin.

MI6 approached al-Kassar at the end of the '70s in his capacity as the "Banker for the PLO." He was enrolled in a plan to convince all of the Palestinian terrorist groups to place their funds with the Park Lane branch of BCCI, in London. He began with Nidal, who soon was in on the deal. The two then joined forces, and had tremendous success with the other PLO factions. Eventually, the British were able to monitor the greater part of the Palestinians' financial activity, giving them a heads-up on future terrorist incidents.

However, on the face of it, this advantage provided little by way of warning for the Lockerbie bombing, a proportion of the finance for which apparently came from Nidal's BCCI account in Park Lane.

Certain authors have suggested that, in order to hide the existence of the British monitoring process, it was necessary both to allow certain terrorist attacks, and to keep the exercise a secret from the Israelis.

The history of intelligence activity around the world is replete with instances of such double-dealing treachery. Mossad recruiters have been past masters at pretending to be something they were not, in order to enlist support from those who would otherwise run screaming from the suggestion that they help the Israelis.

The Brits hired themselves out to do the CIA's dirty work in Lebanon in the '80s, when the latter were seeking retribution for the bombing by Muslim militants of the American Embassy and the US Marine barracks. The CIA, forbidden by Presidential decree from engaging in assassination, used the British to take out some of the nastier of the militant Muslim leaders.

One paragraph in particular caught my attention in Ben-Menashe's book. In it he described how a Mossad hit team had traveled to Europe in November of 1988, where they had worked their way through a list of assassination targets. The list had earlier been compiled by a secret meeting of Mossad, and consisted of those involved in arranging arms deals for Iraq, or others who handled the financing and the subsequent laundering of profits.

In a moment of what seemed to me at the time to be inspiration, I wrote to Ben-Menashe, wondering if Hugh had been on the list. It wasn't so much the timing that had given me cause to ponder; it was Ben-Menashe's statement that the hit squads had been made up of Palestinians, hired by a Mafia Don, who was in the pay of Mossad. I couldn't help but think of Reggie, and his allegations about who might have killed Hugh.

***

Hypothesis seemed dramatically to have found expression in reality when I returned to my apartment in Atlanta one sultry summer evening in 1993. There on my answering machine was a man's voice, high-pitched but gentle with a sing-song cadence. It was Ari Ben-Menashe, and he wanted to speak with me immediately. He knew the name "Hugh Simmonds."

CHAPTER TEN

Ari Ben-Menashe

Ben-Menashe was in the New York offices of his publisher, and I rang him back, as near immediately as I could. I could hear my heart beating in my ears I was so nervous. Ben-Menashe wasted little time with small talk. And I wasted little time turning on my tape-recorder:

Ben-Menashe: "After I saw your letter this weekend, I got very interested. I was with my publishers in upstate New York. We were sifting through all the letters. We called you from there. That was my first call. About your friend. I already spoke to Kevin Robinson. He was the Matrix Churchill lawyer. He represents me in the UK I spoke to some friends there. What we already came up with is that he [Hugh] was somehow connected to GEC (UK) [General Electric Company (UK)]: Great Britain's largest privately owned engineering company; manufacturers of everything from warships to nuclear power stations; not to be confused with the American company of the same name]. GEC is nothing new. I testified to the [Parliamentary] Select Committee on Defence in London. The whole thing with GEC and [Gerald] Bull and the motors for the SCUD[-B] missiles came out. And your friend seems to be on some list of people who died as a result of their connection to those guys."

Geoffrey: "Are you saying that from your own knowledge, or from your belief?"

B-M: "We came up with these facts after I saw your letter."

G: "Who is we?"

B-M: "Me and the lawyer who represents me in the UK with respect to the Scott Inquiry. Kevin Robinson. He's the same lawyer that represented Matrix Churchill.

When I put through your letter, he found the name on a list.

G: "On what list?"

B-M: "People connected with GEC that died. I don't want to go into details on the telephone."

G: "Are you prepared to help me?"

B-M: "Yes. I was very interested in the letter. Of course, before I commit myself totally, I'd like to look into it some more. There is a possibility that I will be in London either this weekend or the beginning of next week. As you said at the beginning of your letter, you are not a madman. Your friend's name was on this list. I wanted first to hear you out. If you don't mind, I do have some friends in the Labour Party. One person I'm going to talk to about this, because he has been investigating it, is a fellow called George Foulkes. He's a Spokesman for Defence. I have my reasons why this is a very interesting case. Let's see what I can come up with. I will probably call you next week."

I got spectacularly drunk that night. In fact, I stayed over at my brother's house, just to make sure I didn't do something stupid, like trying to get into a car. After a welter of near misses, I seemed to have something resembling a near hit on my hands.

***

Ben-Menashe got back to me somewhat sooner – just two days later. He left a message asking me to call him and saying that he would like to meet me. I returned his call almost immediately. And again, the conversation was recorded:

B-M: "Is there a chance of getting together in Montreal next week?"

G: "Yes."

B-M: "I will be away for the first part of the week. Then, I'll be back for the weekend. I'll call you from wherever I am on Tuesday to finalize the details. Let me just tell you a little bit about what happened. I know a number of lawyers in

Britain. Your friend is known. Most of them are convinced ... let me give you a scenario: guy has a Clients' Account with £5 million [$7.5 million]. He has a lot of expenses. He has a girlfriend. He runs off with the money. He's caught. Instead of facing the music, he commits suicide. Possible scenario?"

G: "Yes. Lots of problems..."

B-M: "But that's what first comes to mind?"

G: "Yes."

B-M: "The guy is not an unknown person. In certain circles, they knew who he was. And he did live the high life. He liked traveling. But, it still doesn't add up. He was involved with a group of people who were exporting GEC motors from the UK to Iraq. That we have established already. I have spoken to somebody who knew about this involvement. Just wanted to make sure. The dates fit. Everything fits."

G: "Is this information you're going to make available to the Scott Inquiry?"

B-M: "About the Scott Inquiry. You understand that they don't have subpoena powers?"

G: "Yes."

B-M: "They have powers to invite people. And they are now on a break. I have been invited officially. This goes back to the Matrix Churchill case. That's Matrix Churchill in Ohio [USA]. The people there knew me from the past. Their lawyers asked me for a copy of the pre-publication draft of my book. They then used it in their defense [of the criminal charges in the UK against Matrix Churchill]. They didn't name it, but they used the book as the framework for the defense. They got a few people in. And then they won the case. Lord Justice Scott knows all about this. The same lawyers that defended [Paul] Henderson are representing me. Including Geoffrey Robertson, Q.C. So, he [Scott]knows all about this. He wasn't too happy to open up the subject of Mark Thatcher. But his hand was forced. Then Mrs. [sic] Thatcher was invited to testify too. But, they might limit the scope because we have given written things about GEC and other stuff. The lawyer did a lot of work. What happened was your friend's name popped up, as soon as I mentioned it, on the GEC list. That's why I got interested. Various people will know about that bit. But again, it's going to be very hard because there was a police inquiry that said that the guy was bad and committed suicide. Now, usually bad guys don't commit suicide. I'm sure he was a bad guy – so was I."

G: "That's been my point exactly. If he was so 'bad,' why didn't he do a runner?"

B-M: "I have a favor to ask. Is there any way of getting in touch with the girlfriend – and not the wife?"

G: "Yes."

B-M: "Do you know where she is?"

G: "Yes."

B-M: "Is there a way of speaking to her?"

G: "If she will speak. She's a very frightened girl."

B-M: "Does the wife have money? Does she work?"

G: "She works. The girlfriend trains show-jumping horses."

B-M: "Is she on the dole [Unemployment Benefit]? What?"

G: "No. Neither of them do that. In so far as they are short of money, they are looked after by Hugh's father."

B-M: "Why am I asking these questions? Is there any trace of the £5 million [47.5 million] anywhere?"

G: "The answer to that is 'yes; and the Law Society have it'. The Law Society is sitting on it, and not telling anyone what they've found."

B-M: "How much?"

G: "I don't know. But what I do know is that, in the course of their investigations, they discovered that Hugh had been laundering money for other people..."

B-M: "Yeah. Ok."

G: "...from 1984 on. Anything between £3 million [$4.5 million] and £100 million [$150 million]."

B-M: "Does the name Guy Lucas ring a bell? He's a lawyer in England. He's indicted right now. He was working with a couple of Indian businessmen that were working on arms sales to Iran. Indian brothers in business together in London. Now there's a civil lawsuit against them because they were involved with BCCI. The lawyer is indicted for laundering money. His name jumps up with your friend's name."

G: "I've heard of the name, but I'm not aware that Hugh knew him. You obviously know more about these matters than I do. Do you have a definitive answer as to what was Hugh's fate, or do you just have some interesting circumstances?"

B-M: "I don't have any definitive answers yet, but we probably could get to it. But I need more information. I will know what his fate was. I will know that. If I end up thinking he just committed suicide, I'll tell you that. But it seems strange. The guy was involved with a person that was selling motors to Iraq for the SCUD missiles. They replaced the motors ... the SCUD motors ... the Russian ones ... with GEC motors to make their range longer. The project was being co-ordinated by Gerald Bull. He's now dead. But some of his assistants are still alive. One of them is extremely angry at the British government because he was arrested for a while. A fellow called Dr. Cowley. He knows a bit about this stuff. Then there was a lawyer who was dealing with the money transactions that knows your friend. An English lawyer that I spoke to."

G: "I don't know what his [Hugh's] involvement was, but I would think that he would have had some involvement with money transactions. That was his specialty when he was a tax lawyer in the '70s. When we had a Labour Government, he designed complicated tax avoidance schemes. Now, of course, they're pretty irrelevant because the tax structure is much more lenient. As I pointed out to the Law Society's investigators, nowadays you only launder money if the money itself is illicit. They agreed. Which means that all the money Hugh was laundering was illicit."

B-M: "Quite. You aren't hiding money from the tax authorities. You're hiding it because its source is funny. Anyway, the GEC connection is very strong. There's one more comment: you don't gas yourself in a car; it's very nasty. Would you gas yourself in a car?"

G: "No. Only people who have no imagination do it that way. I couldn't sit there knowing what was happening to me. I'd get a bottle of Scotch, a few bottles of sleeping pills, a couple of my favorite videos, and do it that way."

Ben-Menashe and I then made arrangements for a meeting in Montreal. Frankly, I was too numb from input overload to know how I felt.

***

Montreal is a cold city. Even in balmy September. But it's not the city that lacks warmth. It's the people. The French as a species are renowned for their rudeness. And their cousins in Montreal live up to the reputation. They seem to delight in torturing visitors by firing French at them. Only giving up when the poor victims turn red in the face from frustration.

The city itself is pleasant enough. Particularly the historic district, down by the river. All French bunting, cobblestones and horse-drawn buggies, full of gaping tourists. Ben-Menashe owned a smart townhouse a block away from the historic district, and I took a taxi there straight from the airport.

Both Ben-Menashe and his wife Haya were out when I arrived late afternoon, but Ben-Menashe's mother was visiting from Israel. She was small, with prominent Semitic facial features. And she was the first friendly person I'd met since crossing the border into French Canada.

Ben-Menashe and Haya returned in the early evening, and immediately swept me away to a nearby Indian restaurant. I got the impression there were things Ari did not want to talk about in front of his mother. We sat in a quiet, candle-lit corner of the restaurant. And like all good spies, Ben-Menashe chose a seat facing the rest of the room, and with easy access to a nearby exit. Except most spies do not have a pretty wife hanging on their arm.

Ben-Menashe was small and round, and for all the world, looked like Jason Alexander, the tubby guy from the TV comedy series, *Seinfeld* – but with a head full of wavy black hair. His voice never seemed louder than a murmured whisper, and rose and fell like a snatch of New Age music. He seemed utterly harmless. But then I remembered Hugh telling me that the best agents are those whose seeming blandness allows them to lull their opponents into a false sense of security.

Haya was petite and pretty, and in many ways reminded me of Julia Louis-Dreyfus, also from *Seinfeld*. I had Jerry's whiny voice and mop of curly hair. If the waiter had looked like Kramer, we'd have had the whole cast gathered around that table, in a small Indian restaurant in Montreal.

I should have been nervous. In fact, at first I was expecting to be clobbered over the head, and dragged off to some warehouse on the river, there to be interrogated until the last breath left my body. But it was a little difficult to be scared sitting opposite George and Elaine. Particularly since Ben-Menashe's "George" had such a delightfully impish sense of humor.

The scene was made that much more surreal when the conversation turned to serious matters. There we were chatting about life, death and international arms sales as casually as the *Seinfeld* ensemble would talk about a clogged toilet, while having breakfast in the neighborhood diner.

At first, Ben-Menashe stuck to peripheral issues. I think he was feeling me out. However, one or two interesting things did crop up:

He mentioned that he had been in England, and that he had asked around about Hugh, to find out how well known he was. Ted Heath [former Conservative British Prime Minister] had indicated that he knew him, but had only bad things to say. Something along the lines of: "I knew that shit would always end like that." Heath and Hugh had crossed swords a few times, for instance over Hugh's strident stance against a "Federal Europe." I was intrigued that Ben-Menashe had managed to discover this nuance of Hugh's standing within the upper reaches of the Conservative Party.

Ben-Menashe mused at length, and with no apparent purpose, about the activities of the Conservative government in general. How under Thatcher, and now Major, it seemed continually to be following a pro-Arab, anti-Israel line. Ben-Menashe "and others" were worried about where this might all lead. In particular, they were concerned about who might succeed Major as figures of power in the Conservative Party and government.

The subject of David Mellor arose. The latter had been a senior Cabinet Minister and one of Major's chief political allies, before resigning in some disgrace in September 1992 after lurid publicity about an extra-marital affair with one Antonia de Sancha. One of the more outrageous tidbits had been that Dave liked to have sex wearing Chelsea Football Club stripe.

There had been some speculation that the tryst with Mellor was a deliberate set-up. That de Sancha knew that her apartment was being staked out by the press. That there were other elements behind the set-up. And that the introduction of Mellor to de Sancha by Paul Halloran had itself had undertones of some sort of revenge.

After a bout or two of conversational aerobics, Ben-Menashe admitted that Mellor had been set up in an Israeli-sponsored sting. Mellor was considered to be much too close to the Palestinians, and the Israelis were terrified that he might become the next Conservative Prime Minister. Besides, Ari added with a wink, Paul Halloran was way upset that Mellor had cut him out of a lucrative arms deal.

These last utterances tempered my earlier favorable impression of the political savvy of Ben-Menashe and his friends. Anyone who knew anything about British politics at that time knew that Mellor was a clown, a lightweight. He'd struck lucky by backing Major early in his ambition to be Leader of the Conservative Party. But Mellor had about as much chance of being Prime Minister as the Devil had of taking up permanent residence in a shady suburb of Heaven.

Ari and his friends apparently saw Hugh in much the same light as Mellor: a fast-riser in the Party, and someone who was not unduly friendly towards the Israelis. Ben-Menashe also stated that it was well-known that Hugh was close to Thatcher. *In many different ways*, Ben-Menashe added, enigmatically.

At this point, Ben-Menashe abruptly changed subjects. He mentioned that Hugh was on good terms with Nick Davies, and claimed that Hugh, Davies and Robert Maxwell met regularly in Maxwell's office atop the *Daily Mirror* headquarters in High Holborn. Apropos of nothing at all, Ben-Menashe reiterated the claim in his book that the CIA had killed Maxwell. It would not be the last time that Ben-Menashe adopted a position that seemed designed to protect Israeli interests.

I confess I was beginning to like Ari. He was a charming host, a friendly chap, and had an attractive wife gracing the space beside him. What was not to like? Besides, I have an affinity for rogues. And Ari was clearly one of those. However, for all his entertainment value, I had no reason to trust Ari further than I could throw him. And so I took much of what he was saying with a massive grain of salt.

In particular, I remained intrigued by Ari's clandestine support of Israel's point of view. Sure, Ari would regularly criticize Israel. He would state with finality that there would never be peace in the Middle East, because Israel did not want peace, it wanted victory. And yet, Ari was careful always to deflect the more serious charges about Israel's covert activities away from its Intelligence Services – his former employers. And thus it was the CIA, not Mossad, that had killed Maxwell.

Then again, just when a listener might believe that Ari had overreached credulity, he would softly toss away a morsel of information that had about it an uncanny ring of truth. Little scraps that could only be known by someone who was truly connected.

Hugh had not been a great TV watcher. He liked to read, and preferred that his children did the same. However, I hate to read, and would rather that someone else spoon feed me my input. Preferably inconsequential mush. So it was that years ago, when Hugh was still alive, I had found myself one evening with Hugh's kids, watching a program, where the host guided us around a fancy room, and we had to guess to whom it belonged.

The room on this occasion was a vast office, in chrome, grey and black. Money and high-tech screamed from every surface, from the electronic window blinds, to the thick shag on the floor. And from the bank of TV screens arrayed behind the desk, to the multitude of expensive communication toys lined up around the edges of the same desk.

Hugh had been in another part of his home. Halfway through the program, he wandered in, fixed himself a scotch, glanced at the TV screen and, on his way out, stated casually, "Oh, that's Robert Maxwell's office." At the time, I couldn't for the life of me think what Hugh would be doing with a staunch supporter of the Labour Party. Clearly, arms-dealing and money-laundering easily crossed political boundaries.

Ari offered no further information about the relationship between Maxwell and Hugh. At least not on this occasion. In fact, we were just about done for the evening. On his way to driving me to a nearby hotel, however, Ari did mention that Hugh's girlfriend knew all about his arms-dealing activities.

***

Bright and early the following morning, I caught a taxi to Ari's townhouse. Haya and Ari's mother had gone shopping, leaving us alone to talk further. The townhouse itself was expensive and elegant. Obviously, Ari had done well from his clandestine endeavors in the '80s. However, for all its luxury, Ari's home felt unlived in: white leather furniture and chrome tables, but no homely knick-knacks or family photos.

Again, Ari wasted no time in getting down to business. He dove straight in on the subject of Mark Thatcher. Ari told me that he and "others" had been trying to nail Mark Thatcher for some time for his involvement in arms sales to Iraq. The impression I gained was that they were less interested in Mark than his *mother*. All that they had lacked was proof, in the form of the money trail, to Mark. And I had, unwittingly, supplied that.

Examination by Ari and the "others" of Hugh's activities and interests, even an admittedly cursory one, had revealed that he had been a business partner of Mark Thatcher's; that the business was arms sales to Iraq; and that Hugh had been responsible for laundering the proceeds back to Thatcher in Texas. Ari and his "friends" were in possession of Hugh's name for some time (a list, once again, was mentioned; I did not find out whether it was the same one or not), but they had not considered pursuing a possible connection until I turned up on the scene with my information.

I was curious as to who "others" and "friends" were. I raised this with Ari. I said that, on the one hand, I found it difficult to believe that it could be the Israelis, after they left him to rot in an American jail for a year. Yet, on the other hand, the agenda he seemed to be pursuing bore all the fingerprints of one the right-wingers in Israeli intelligence might want a "rogue stooge" to pursue, if they were so inclined. Indeed, exactly the sort of shenanigans Ostrovsky had been asked by the left-wing, as their "loose cannon," to thwart.

Ari's retort was a model of enigma. With a wry smile, he said, "'They' got pissed off at me because my revelations [about Bush Senior and his SSG/CPPG] removed their ability to blackmail Bush. I'm trying to make 'them' less pissed off at me." He was, however, still unwilling to be drawn on the identity of "they" or "them."

We quickly returned to the subject of Hugh and money. Ari alleged that, in addition to sending the arms sales' proceeds to Texas, Hugh had also sent the money stolen from his Clients' Account. The money had gone by a roundabout route, which included a trust account in Jersey, some lawyer in Bermuda, and another lawyer by the name of "Rebecca Parsons." She resided either in Reading, England or in Dallas, Texas. Ari was fuzzy on this point. But he was crystal clear about the fact that Rebecca had had an affair with Hugh.

Rebecca had also acted for Mark Thatcher, and was known to his sister, Carol. Ari didn't say what happened to the affair, but he did say that, at one point, Hugh had tried to get his money back from Rebecca, and she had refused to return it. This, Ari claimed, somewhat confusing me, may have been why Hugh had committed suicide.

In the middle of his presentation, Ari was called away to the telephone. When he came back, he seemed rather agitated, and he quickly brought the session to an end. He said he would need more time to make further inquiries, and asked if I would, in the meantime, suspend my own investigation so that we would not be stepping on each other's toes. As he bade me farewell at the front door, Ari, looking quite distracted, mumbled something about being in touch within a couple of weeks to report on progress.

***

I left Ari's townhouse and Montreal with my head spinning from the new directions appearing in my investigation. Whether as a renegade, or acting as a deep "sleeper" for Israeli Intelligence, Ari's allegations about interference in Britain's political affairs were startling, to say the least.

A couple of weeks stretched out into a couple of months. I went to stay with my mother in Grand Rapids, Michigan. She was in poor health. Then, not unlike Reggie, Ari's mellifluous voice suddenly re-appeared in my life without warning. I taped the conversation. Which was just as well, because it made no more sense to me then, than it does now, reading it all these years later:

B-M: "Your friend is being checked. And something may be coming out. I was in your homeland after I saw you. A lot of people are interested in your friend. Raised quite a bit of interest. Let's see what we can come up with. From the point of view of your friend, your trip was probably the best thing that you did. It started off a whole ... thing. And we shall see what happens. But, what's interesting about it is that one person I talked to right away turned off. As soon as he heard his name, he didn't want to deal with it. He warned me off. Well known person. [Pause] Very, very well known person. [Pause]"

G: [Goodness, was Ari scared? Because he sounded almost incoherent. Or was it just another Ari act? I decided to affect boredom, and see what happened.] "Well. I shall look forward to your telling me what you can, when you can."

B-M: "You're still around?"

G: "Yes." [Short and sweet]

B-M: "Good. I hope you'll be around for the next month or two. There will be a lot of this coming out." [Pause]

G: [Yawn] "Well. Let me know what happens."

B-M: "Definitely. On your behalf, I stirred a lot of shit."

G: "Well. Keep in touch." [Look. If you've got something to say, then spit it out.]

B-M: "I will. I'll not contact you for a while. I'll call in about a week or so." [Sigh]

***

At the end of 1994, Ari invited me to Montreal once more. He said he had proof to give me. Though I was skeptical, Ari promised me that I would come away with substantive evidence. So, I went.

This time, there were no champagne suppers in his townhouse. We met in my small hotel room. And Ari never took off his raincoat. It was all very John le Carré. But in every other respect, Ari did not disappoint.

Ari stated that, in the two years before his death, Hugh had transferred at least $12 million, from bank accounts under his control in England, through a bank account in the tax haven of

Jersey, to bank accounts under the control of Mark Thatcher in Houston, Texas.

This was the "seed money" for Mark's fortune, the phenomenon no one had been able to explain. This is what Ari and his friends had been able to piece together when I brought my information to them.

At some stage of the process, Ari continued, Hugh had become greedy. He wanted more money. Either he asked for it, or he just took it. Whatever, his associates had become unhappy with him, and they had killed him.

I decided to indulge in a bit of game-playing myself. I mentioned that Ari had always indicated that his knowledge of Hugh's activities had been obtained third hand. Ari smiled sweetly, as if in agreement. "Yet," I continued, "I know that you knew Hugh personally." Ari's smile froze on his face.

"And how would you know that?" he asked, his voice ever so gently beginning to freeze over. Oops. Maybe just a little too much of a push. Ah well, I'd started, so I'd finish.

"Since you were in business with Nick Davies [Ora Limited]," I stated, with a casualness that redefined the expression "forced," "and since you have already admitted that Davies was well known to Hugh, it follows that you must have met Hugh when he was alive."

The steel in Ari's eyes softened slightly from cold blue to a warmer ... silverish ... sort of ... look ... I wasn't the slightest bit interested in his eyes. I was concentrating on just one thing: exactly how many bones could I possibly save jumping from a window on the sixteenth floor?

"Ah, yes," purred Ari, after what seemed an eternity, "But he wasn't using his real name."

Ari made to leave, but not before announcing that Lord Justice Scott was due to report very soon, and that his report would deal with Hugh. All I had to do was wait. Sigh again.

***

The Scott Report on Arms Sales to Iraq (1996) was a whitewash. In blinding contrast to all of the testimony, Scott had concluded that there had been no illegal arms sales to Iraq from the UK. More to the point, there was no mention of Hugh, Mark Thatcher or any deal involving GEC engines and SCUD-B missiles. So much for my waiting three years at Ari's behest.

**

While with my mother, I had entered alcohol rehab. I then returned to Georgia, but to its northern mountains, there to heal – and continue the adventure.

So, Scott was a bust. It was time to try and get a hold of a copy of the other report: the Carratu Report. I tracked down Geoff Hughes, who had left the employ of Carratu, although he insisted that his departure had nothing to do with Hugh's investigation. He didn't sound nervous. He sounded terrified. He didn't have a copy of the Carratu Report. He claimed he had been asked to return even his notes for the report. He couldn't remember a thing. Who was I? Who was he? Good-bye.

I'm being a tad unkind. Geoff did at least take the time to say, on the record, that his investigation was not so definitive (through no fault of his own) that he could totally rule out the possibility of my allegations concerning Iraq having some basis in fact. Geoff always did have a stranglehold on syntax.

The bottom line with Geoff was that he did not recall telling me anything about Iraq and Mark Thatcher in 1995. Nor would he now. But. His investigation had been brought to an abrupt halt by the Law Society when his inquiries hit Atlanta. So, he could not say that his investigation had been "complete."

Next, the administrators of Hugh's Estate: They were rude, obnoxious and unhelpful. No way would they ever let me see the Carratu Report. Last gasp, the Law Society: They were pleasant, eager ... and unhelpful. Another "No" to my request to see the Carratu Report. They did, however, produce a letter stating that there were strong suggestions that Hugh had engaged in moneylaundering activities and export fraud in North America and Africa.

I tried Reggie one more time. He was sober, but still pretty scared about the whole situation. He affected boredom, and said he was not prepared to talk about Hugh's intelligence activities any more. Reggie did, however, let slip that British intelligence had never really been interested in finding out why Hugh had died; they were solely concerned with finding the money. What was it with that money?

Before leaving the subject, Reggie did muse for a moment. "You know," he said softly, as he did when he thought he was passing on something of import, "instead of looking at the '80s, you might look at the '70s. Everyone from the '80s has been 'got at.' The doors have been closed. Go back to when it all began. To the people he was with then."

Reggie then enthusiastically changed the subject, becoming much more animated when I told him where I was, and that I hoped to form a band to play my music. "Oh, really," he chirped, if a plummy upper-class accent can actually chirp. "The Land of the Banjo," he exclaimed. Suddenly, there was silence on the line, until I heard perfect bluegrass being plucked ever so furiously in the background.

After a few minutes, a breathless Reggie came back on the line to tell me that he'd trained on the mandolin; but he'd picked up the banjo, since they involved essentially the same techniques; and could he possibly be in the band? He promised to wear his kilt. I'm in the middle of a serious investigation, which is fast falling apart, and I'm surrounded by nutcases. I sighed. And I promised.

Then, somehow, we got onto the subject of the movie version of the story. Again, I was back in "Alice in Wonderland." Like one of that book's stranger characters, Reggie became quite the pompous marionette. He was very proud of his Equity card, and he wanted to be sure that I would use his full and proper stage name. Sniff.

I was almost impressed, until he broke down, and wondered excitedly if he could be played by Roger Moore? I left him with the threat that he'd be played by Stephen Fry unless he became more cooperative. I felt sure that Seymour Hersh never had to put up with this. Nor John Pilger.

Well. Drat and blast. I'd been convinced the past three years that, when Ari's imposed waiting period was over, if all else failed, one or other of these leads would provide the final key to unraveling the mystery. And yet here I was empty-handed. Ever the optimist, my sister, Maggi told me that I should use the hiatus to start writing the book. But I wanted to sulk for a while first.

***

I put down my pen, and rubbed my eyes. Always stop when you have a little more left in you. That way you'll have a place to start in the morning. Hemingway used to say that. Though I think it had more to do with finding an excuse to start drinking at five o'clock in the afternoon than with literary finesse. Whatever. I could associate with either reason.

I left my apartment and wandered lazily to the edge of the parking lot and stood there, my hands in my pockets, soaking up the early evening ambience. It was high summer, and the air retained a shimmering memory of its earlier heat; the sickly-sweet smell of pine sap still warm in my nostrils. My mind, already tired, was swiftly coaxed into a numbing, humming trance.

My gaze drew itself slowly upwards; so that it met the slowly emerging moonface, smiling and glowing a vibrant orange in silent tribute to the dimming sunset. My thoughts, unconnected and disconnected by the easy rhythm of the evening, drifted nowhere and everywhere.

The air, cool and soothing on my skin, was alive with the furious chatter of crickets. The piney woods, lit up like Christmas trees with winking firebugs, reflected the preternatural brilliance of the stars carpeting the Southern night sky.

My solitude was interrupted by Clint, a precocious 17-year-old high school student, who lived next door with his mother. He'd been working up the nerve to ask me what my book was about. Lazily, I gave him the 30-second version. His immediate response: "Well, did the police ever catch the guy who took the money from Hugh, and did that person kill him?"

I was slow from the evening's heat. I asked Clint to explain, without taking too much notice. "Well, you told me this Hugh character stole £5 million ($7.5 million) over two years, didn't spend it, and turns up dead. So, someone stole the money from him, which is why he didn't run away with it, and the guy who did it probably killed him to shut him up."

Something snapped in my head. Inadvertently or no, Clint had spurred me to something so simple and so obvious that I had difficulty understanding why I had not seen it in the previous eight years. Possibly because I too was simple and obvious? So much for the frantically "tidy" mind, and the overarching powers of calculation. I headed back into my apartment to grab my pad and pen.

We had been told that Hugh had been killed in order to stop him from using the stolen money for his operation. But. As Clint had pointed out, if Hugh was dead, why was the money still out there? Why had it not, in fact, been stolen?

Perhaps the "bad guys" had not known about the money? But sure they did. That's why everyone and his uncle were bent over backwards looking for it. Unless. Unless, we were talking about two different pots of money.

We had already come across much larger caches of missing money. Caches of a size that would make it worthwhile for the likes of British intelligence and Ari Ben-Menashe to spend their time looking for them.

What if it was these caches that formed the basis of Hugh's operation, and what if it was these same caches that everyone was looking for? Not Hugh's stolen money. What if, in fact, no one knew anything about Hugh's stolen money?

What if Hugh had only started stealing his clients' money in 1987, to use as a "Runaway Fund," because something was going horribly wrong with the operation? And what if he had simply piggy-backed this stolen money on top of the larger caches of cash he was already laundering?

This would explain why the Law Society had come across larger amounts of money in the same bank accounts as the stolen money. It would also explain why they had then shut down the Carratu investigation with such unseemly haste. It would further explain why those people, whose larger caches were missing, could do nothing to recover them: they had no idea, when Hugh died, that their money was all mixed up with other money, which would then become the subject of a Law Society investigation. No wonder they spent so much of their remaining funds putting me under surveillance. But man, were they going to be disappointed.

After a deal of thinking, I came up with some new twists for my rolling scenario: Hugh had become involved in something that was much larger, and possibly much "uglier," than I had previously imagined. This would have been about 1984. Whether "official," "quasi-official," or utterly rogue, this "something" at least garnered Hugh some sort of "protection," which was what had kept the Law Society off his back. At least, at first.

Something went wrong – very possibly the fact that Hugh was caught creaming off the top. He needed a way out. In January 1987, I was with Hugh when he learned that he had again been de-selected from a safe Conservative Parliamentary seat. We were on our own in his office, and I remember the scene vividly, because it was the first – and only – time I had ever seen fear in Hugh's eyes.

In the early days of the British and then the American intelligence services, most of the recruits were selected from the ranks of "Gentlemen." This was true across the rest of Europe, and into Russia also. Intelligence was a "Game" for Gentlemen, and the Game was played according to "Gentlemen's Rules." You didn't shoot people in the back. You didn't take out your counterpart when they were on home soil. If you had an "asset," who then achieved high political office, you backed off.

Could it have been that, aside from simple political ambition, Hugh had seen the possibility of election to Parliament in 1987 as his best way of avoiding the fallout from the mess he had got into with his covert "something"? Did he believe that in some way the Gentlemen's Rules would apply to him once he was seen as a potential government minister? And could it have been that, when the door to that exit strategy was closed, he devised another? Involving the stealing of his clients' money to create a Runaway Fund?

If so, Hugh was certainly in good spirits from the moment he began the stealing in April 1987, all the way through until the early part of the summer of 1988. Had something changed? And if so, what?

What if Hugh's innate greed had caused him simply to put too many fingers into too many pies? What if he had spent the better part of 1987 and 1988, with his glib tongue and his gilded sense of invincibility, simply promising everyone everything, while delivering nothing, in a vain attempt to keep everyone happy, while he continued with his exit plans?

What if, by the beginning of the summer of 1988, too many of the parties had simply become too pissed with waiting for so long? Or perhaps, one or more had discovered the exit plans, and realized that Hugh had no intention of honoring anything? What if Hugh's attempts at making himself indispensable had only had the effect of finally convincing certain parties just how "dispensable" he truly was? Maybe the pressure was increased? Maybe a bank account or two suddenly became unavailable?

The possibilities are endless. What is certain is the fact that, at the beginning of the summer of 1988, Hugh suddenly changed from Mr. Happy-Go-Lucky to a very stressed and very unwell individual. Also, according to Martin Pratt, he also became frantic about earning money. Large amounts. Any way that he could. This was the period when Hugh began to speculate furiously with the shares of Ferranti, a British defense electronics giant. Did he have some 'inside' information that allowed him to earn large sums on the daily fluctuations in the share price?

Then, at the end of the summer of 1988, and again, with equal suddenness, Hugh just lost heart and hope. The furious activity ceased. He calmed down. It was as if he had become resigned to his fate. Maybe the summer had been unsuccessful? Maybe the threats had been re-directed from Hugh to his extended family, and he realized that the only way he could protect them was to "go" – and to go quietly, so as to avoid retribution against that extended family? Maybe the "protection" had been removed? Maybe that was why the Law Society, the police and National Westminster Bank all took their action against him on exactly the same day? Maybe there was a little persuasion? Maybe someone, somewhere was simply "cleaning house"?

***

All of which left me looking for that "something larger and uglier" that could have been Hugh's operation. I needed to reopen some inquiries, and begin a few more. In my trademark fashion – just getting in peoples' faces. *However dangerous the face.*

CHAPTER ELEVEN

Games With Ari

OUT OF THE BLUE, I called directory assistance for Atlanta, and miraculously obtained the telephone number for Christopher Drogoul, the former BNL branch manager in Atlanta who had personally overseen $5 billion in illegal loans to Iraq.

Christopher was the very definition of helpfulness. He recalled the name Hugh Simmonds, but not the exact context. Chris could, however, clearly remember the Atlanta BNL branch issuing a Letter of Credit to the Central Bank of Iraq in favor of GEC for a considerable sum of money. He thought maybe about $28 million, but he couldn't swear to that.

Chris' memory was also a little vague as to whether it was for engines or spare parts. But he believed it was to do with rockets of some sort. No matter. His lawyer in New York, Robert Simels, had all of the paperwork. Chris would call him, and have him root out the Letter of Credit.

I went one better, and called Robert Simels myself. Robert was the model of New York charm and grace. Unfortunately, all of the papers for the trial were in about 70 packing cases in the firm's warehouse. But hey. For a modest fee, he could get one of his assistants to rummage through them, to find the offending documentation.

***

I had spent the years 1993-1996 doing little to rock the boat, primarily so as not to get in the way of Ari. But I was also conscious that I wanted to get my "preliminary" research and investigation completed before I "tipped off " those closer to the action as to my intentions.

In all circumstances, I took the view that I'd pretty much exhausted anything that would pass as preliminary, and following my experience with Christopher Drogoul, decided it was now time to talk to a few more "horses' mouths." However, the approaches would have to be effected quickly and in a group, so as to prevent anyone from comparing stories.

First, I thought it wise to wolf down another huge helping of humble pie and go and talk to Ari again. I knew that the immediate chances of my flying up to Montreal were zero. So, instead, I crafted a questionnaire. It really was time to get some sort of verification for all that he had been telling me.

When I telephoned him to get a fax number, he exuded charm and helpfulness. But he was very nervous about transmitting any information to me other than face to face. He did not trust the security of anything electronic or postal. He certainly didn't want to discuss my questions through the telephone. He was very agitated at the thought that I might let a name or two slip. As a compromise, he agreed to let me give him a "preview" of one of the more innocuous questions.

Totally at random, I chose one asking for the name of the lawyer he mentioned in one of our earlier chats, in 1993. The lawyer he claimed had handled money transactions for those selling arms to Iraq, and had known Hugh and what he was up to. From his explosive reaction, you'd have thought that I'd asked for a night alone with Ari's wife. Which, of course, would have been very nice. But. Ari had a conniption. In fact, he had a whole litter of them.

He wanted to help me, he hissed dramatically. He understood I needed verification. But. He had to be very careful, he continued in his stage whisper, as if whispering was going to confuse a high-tech bugging device. This was all very sensitive. There was only a very small group of people involved in all of this. No more than 40. If Ari was to be inadvertent in the way he described a source, it would immediately be apparent to the "others" who'd been talking. It wasn't just a simple case of his giving me a name ... wheeze ... gasp...

I was very impressed with the performance. I gave him an 8 out of 10, a bouquet of fresh roses, and a series of free lessons with Sir John Gielgud. But what on earth was so important about this lawyer?

Before I could say anything, however, all was overwhelmed by the sound of scraping and scratching on the telephone. And then Haya was on the line. She sounded very angry. She wanted to know why I was trying to get her husband into danger.

I mumbled something utterly useless and forgettable, all the while wondering what it was that Hugh could possibly have been in involved with that had a decent woman thinking I could be a source of danger to her husband. A person who had worked with one of the most feared intelligence agencies in the world.

I had expected games with Ari, but Haya I thought was a straight shooter. Along with being cute, she appeared to be genuine and honest. And on this particular day, very scared. It was a reaction I was to get used to over the ensuing months and years. There were some more scraping sounds on the telephone, and Ari's honey-coated purr returned. He seemed to have recovered his poise.

In much calmer mode, Ari explained that the lawyer in question acted for a number of people in senior positions in the Conservative Party. It was through him that Ari had discovered much of what it was he knew about the connections between Hugh, Iraq and the Tories. This lawyer, in turn, had obtained his information from his clients.

Ari said that he would need to make a couple of telephone calls to determine if it would be possible for him to give me the sort of information I wanted. He would then call me back. To my surprise, on this occasion, he did.

Ari confirmed that he could make the verifying information available to me, but that he was not prepared to speak through the telephone, or to put anything in writing at that stage. In the absence of a face-to-face, he promised that, once I had a publisher, he would meet with me and the publisher.

It sounded a little like Ari wanting to be the center of attention again. But I was still mindful of Haya, so I shrugged my shoulders and thanked him. And then felt freed to continue with my own inquiries.

***

I dug out the *Sunday Times* articles on Mark Thatcher, and made contact with Keith Praeger, a senior agent with US Customs in Miami, Florida. Hell, yeah, said Keith, they were still interested in Mark Thatcher. And yes, they'd be interested in any information that I could give them. The one thing they'd always been missing was the money trail. How soon could I let them have some leads?

I confess I became a little cagey. I didn't want law enforcement officers trampling all over my sources until I'd finished with them. I explained this to Keith, who fully understood. He'd be waiting, just as soon as I was ready. In the meantime, I gave him Hugh's name, and the details of his theft and death, so that he had something to check out. See if he could find out something all on his own.

**

Next, I sent out a bunch of faxes to the great and the good in the UK, setting out the basic facts I had to date, and asking them if they'd care to comment.

Lord James Prior, Chairman of GEC (UK), was the first to respond to my fax. Lord Prior was a Cabinet Minister under Margaret Thatcher between 1979 and 1983. His letter exemplified the unparalleled contribution the Conservative Party has made to the art of dissemble in the past 200 years.

In my mind's eye, I could clearly see Prior dictating the letter. First, he shifted his rotund form gingerly to the left butt cheek, and very carefully remembered to forget everything; without actually denying anything. Then, ever so gently he shifted all of that weight to his right butt cheek, and threw in a little personal memento; just to show that he was sending a signal, so that the judge would be a tad more lenient during the sentencing phase of the corruption trial.

And so it was that he stated categorically and definitively, for all the world clearly to hear that … he found it difficult to believe that there was any foundation to my allegations. I, in turn, still find it difficult to believe that the Chairman of Britain's largest privately owned engineering company admitted to not knowing, beyond all doubt, whether or not some $28 million of his company's products had been sold illegally to an embargoed country.

An embargoed country that had just fought a military engagement with the Chairman's own country. In which, allegedly, the products might have been used to extend the range of missiles, at least one of which had been fired upon and had ostensibly killed civilians in the State of Israel. But then, perhaps I'm losing my sense of objectivity.

Prior's one saving grace, and given the context, it was almost comical, was that he ended his brief letter remembering that he had met with Hugh on a couple of occasions. Would that have been at the Sedgwick-upon-Thames Annual Ladies Knit 'n Barbeque? Or would that have been when he, Hugh, and the lads from "Shipping" were loading the warheads onto the flatbed?

**

Keith Praeger of US Customs had also been busy. He had a couple of "friends" from "former occupations" who were attached to the American Embassy in the "Mayfair Square Mile" of London. These friends had checked out Hugh. Keith was happy to report that he was now definitely interested.

He was eager to know if I had anything more he could get his teeth into? What the heck. I'd hit rock bottom with the Law Society. Keith was law enforcement after all. He knew how to be careful. I gave him chapter and verse on the Carratu investigation. Keith said he would look into it immediately.

He came back almost as immediately. Good news. A friend (another one) in the (London) Metropolitan Police Fraud Squad had an "in" at the Law Society (wonderful things networks), and he was going to use it to try and obtain a copy of the Carratu Report. Praeger told me that he would then effectively "take over" the unfinished investigation of Hugh's financial affairs. He was convinced my trail led through Simmonds to Mark Thatcher.

**

I received a bashful example of "oops-was-I-there?" from the Secretary to Sir Richard Scott's Inquiry. I had written asking if there had been any submissions, besides mine, relating to GEC (UK); deals for rocket engines; Hugh Simmonds; Ari Ben-Menashe; or Mark Thatcher.

The Secretary's reply stated only that there had been no other submissions about Simmonds. The other names seemed, oops, to have slipped his mind. And he stated, oops, that he was relying only on his memory.

I wrote back, commending him, oops, on his excellent memory, which appeared, oops, to have instant command of what had been some 80,000 documents that had been submitted. I then wondered if he would like now, oops, to perform a slightly more, oops, scientific search of the, oops, computerized indices. I never heard back. Oops.

***

John Simmonds wrote to tell me that Geoffrey Hughes had told him that Carratu had discovered that Hugh owed a large sum of money to an arms dealer; that the arms dealer had never made a claim against the Law Society; and that the arms dealer had stated that Hugh had expert knowledge of a handgun in general use by the British Security Services.

John added that he had spoken further with Hugh's mistress, Karen George, who was now prepared to state that Hugh had been involved in a complicated arms deal at the time of his death. On behalf of Margaret Thatcher. I ignored the vicious little voice on my shoulder that hissed that it might have saved me some eight years of blindly careening around the world, if I had been given this snippet from Karen at the beginning of the exercise – when she had been egging me on to get to the truth.

***

I made my own contact with US Customs Agent Praeger, from whom I had not heard in a while. He was sorry all over the place. The fact is that his hands were tied. There was loads he'd like to do, provided he wasn't seen to be doing anything.

It genuinely was not his fault. Reading between the lines, it would seem that US Custom's intelligence agent Aida Perez kind of jumped the gun back in 1994, when she had said the house was going to fall in on Mark Thatcher. I gathered that Mark's lawyers pretty much brought the house down on US Customs in Miami instead. As a consequence, we had a vicious circle: Keith couldn't be seen officially to be doing anything with potential connections to Thatcher, unless he had ironclad evidence. Which he couldn't get without being seen officially to be doing something with potential connections to Thatcher.

All he could do was cheer me on from the sidelines. Just as soon as I had the whole jigsaw puzzle, he'd be delighted to issue a warrant for Mark T. I felt genuinely sorry for Keith. Politics can be a bum rap. I wish I'd been able to get him that puzzle before he retired a couple of years later. I hope he's marlin fishing now, and naming every single one that doesn't get away, "Mark."

***

Which put me in the mood for getting playful with someone else. What the heck? I telephoned Mark Thatcher's lawyers in America, and came up with some cock and bull story about Mark and Hugh. How Hugh had left me a letter telling me to get in touch with Mark. It almost worked. I got as far as Mark's executive assistant, before someone – Mark? – smelled a rat. But Hugh's name had rung some sort of bell.

***

Even more fun was to be had with the British Prime Minister, who at that time was still John Major. Back in 1993, I had sent a letter to Major asking him if he was prepared to confirm if Hugh had been attached to any branch of the British intelligence services. Major's Principal Private Secretary (or PPS), one Alex Allan, who later on became Sir Alexander Claud Stuart Allan, KCB, and was appointed Chairman of the Joint Intelligence Committee and Head of Intelligence Assessment for Her Majesty's Government by Tony Blair. Anyways, Allan had written back to me personally in 1993 to say that it was the government's policy "neither to confirm nor to deny matters pertaining to national security and the intelligence services." Standard line, but I was intrigued by having heard from Allan personally.

The British Prime Minister's PPS is a curious animal. There really is no equivalent in American politics, where all of the White House staff are now political appointees. The PPS is a Civil Servant, albeit the most senior Civil Servant attached to the Prime Minister. The PM's PPS is almost always promoted to one of the most senior offices in the Civil Service or Foreign Service, like, for example, the Head of the Domestic Civil Service – a step above what Sir Clive Whitmore was – or, Chairman of the Joint Intelligence Committee (JIC).

I guess the nearest American equivalent to the PPS would have been Bush's Karl Rove, Clinton's George Stephanopoulos, Obama's Daniel Pfeiffer. So, imagine writing to the President about your concern over the UFOs hovering over your house every day, and a personal letter from Daniel Pfeiffer pops into your letter box a few days later. My letter to Major, followed by a personal response from Allan was that significant.

Hmm. I almost got it, but not quite. Let me try that a different way. There is one huge difference between a "Rove" and the PM's PPS. The latter is always what the position suggests: a Civil 'Servant.' The PM's PPS does not do his own bidding. He does not have his own correspondence. He is the factotum of the Prime Minister. He does what the Prime Minister says. And he only does what the Prime Minister says. He does not do anything off his own bat. So, when Allan wrote to me, it was only after Major had personally read my letter, and had then personally instructed his PPS to write to me. That's the point. I had definitely ruffled feathers. And not just once, but twice. Because I wrote back to Allan, to pursue an additional point, and he replied to me again. Personally, saying that he had nothing further to add. Which, in Civil Servant-speak, meant that the Prime Minister had nothing further to add. But hang on, it got better.

At the end of 1996, while I was faxing the rest of the world, I sent Major the same fax that I sent to everyone else, with exactly the same allegations about Hugh, Iraq and kickbacks to the Tories. Once more, Allan wrote back to me. Oh heck, by this time we have to be on first name terms. He's probably written me more letters than he's received Valentines. So. Once more, "Alex" wrote back to me.

On this occasion, he referred me back to his first letter of 1993. Oh what fun. We were now at the coy stage of our relationship. I dug out the first letter, and noted that, essentially, all it did was refer to national security and the intelligence services. So, tongue-in-cheek, I sent another letter to Alex, asking him if this meant that he could not comment about my allegations because of their national security implications? I also wondered if he had a particular yen for Chopin and Chinese take-out, on a moonlit evening?

Alex was already taken. For he replied almost immediately, saying he had nothing further to add. Again. Zounds. And gnashing of teeth. Rending of cloth. Rejected.

But I was not done. Oh no. I sent off a further missive. To be honest, I can't remember what it said, but I was having way too much fun, giving PM and PPS regular doses of PMS with my TNT. But then the fun stopped. For I got a telephone call. From a woman. Now, to be honest, I do not believe that I ever put my telephone number on any of the faxes that I sent. But then again, we were talking about the Prime Minister of Great Britain. In any event, this woman told me that she was John Major's personal Correspondence Secretary, and would I be so good as not to bother the nice Mr. Major and his PPS any more.

Well, first thing is, she sounded like John Major's Tea Lady, not his Correspondence Secretary. But you will be glad to know that I resisted the temptation to ask for a couple of lumps and some milk in mine. Thank you.

Second thing is, this was now becoming serious. Fun and games aside, I'd had a quick word with Reggie. He told me that this sort of thing just didn't happen. There were hordes of good-looking girls, who did nothing all day long but write standard nonsense replies to folks like me. He knew this, because he used to work with the Ministry of Defence in London, and he spent most of his day chatting up their correspondence girls. Clearly, I was onto something.

So. I told the woman that I was recording the conversation and would she mind repeating what she'd just said. And she did. She gave her name. She confirmed that she spoke with the authority of both the Prime Minister of Great Britain and his Principal Private Secretary, and they didn't wish to be bothered by me any more.

And again, I was confused. If there was no truth to anything that I was saying, why not just deny it? If there was truth, why not just ignore me? Or get one of the Garden Girls to send me an autographed photo? Why instead become involved in all these convoluted acrobatics, merely to go on record as saying, please leave us alone? And why use some of the most senior officials in No. 10 Downing Street to do this? Unless it was and it still remains the case that a Prime Minister, who had staked his claim to a place in history on the purity of his image as "Honest John," could not and/or would not be seen to deny or completely avoid something he knew to be true; he knew to be devastating; and which he believed might one day come back to haunt him, and stain history's perception of him?

Then again, I might simply have been on a sugar-high.

*＊＊

Thwarted, I sent a briefing about my exchanges with John Major and Alex Allan to George Foulkes M.P., who was, at that time, New Labour's Frontbench Spokesman on Overseas Aid, and who was also still their point man on Iraq.

I telephoned George's Parliamentary Assistant, Nick, about a couple of weeks later to be told that Foulkes was so excited that he hadn't even bothered to wait to talk to me before Tabling a Question for John Major at Prime Minister's Question Time.

Anyone who is an aficionado of C-Span, particularly at 9:00 P.M., on Sunday evening, will know that Prime Minister's Question Time is the half-hour period, staged twice a week, when Members of Parliament have the opportunity to ask any question they like of the Prime Minister, while he is in the House of Commons.

I waited and I waited, eagerly scanning the newspapers and the Internet, but I read of no Question being Tabled. I tried telephoning Nick, but my calls were no longer being returned. Then, after the Christmas holiday, I received a letter from George. A "Dear Geoff" letter.

George wrote to tell me that he had spent the whole of the holiday season agonizing over my information, and had decided, reluctantly, that the Labour Party really didn't want to soil their hands or rock any boats with my allegations so close to a general election. I think his actual language was a tad more politically correct than that, but that was the upshot. Along with the very definite implication that the decision had been a group one. From higher up. But, to be fair, not in so many words. George was, after all, a politician. And a Scottish one at that.

No matter. In May the British general election of 1997 was upon us. And a good many boats were about to be severely rocked. A number of individuals, with close links to my investigation, would be left with seriously soiled hands. And the matters with which they were going to be soiled would be directly connected to Tory arms corruption – which would also later be implicated in the August 31, 1997, death of Diana, Princess of Wales.

Chapter Twelve

Diana, Arms Deals, Death

T HE GENTLEMAN attempting most of the soiling of the Conservative Party, after their devastating loss to New Labour in the British General Election on May 1, 1997, was none other than Mohammed al-Fayed, who had never forgiven the Tories for denying him British citizenship.

Even in his moment of crowning glory, with the tatters of the formerly invincible Conservative government lying at his feet, the warrior al-Fayed was not satisfied. He was recorded hither and thither, through any media outlet that would listen to him, promising to continue with his revelations of "sleaze," until the Tories were fully ground into the dust.

Of particular interest to me was al-Fayed's assertion that those revelations would include a complete rundown on all of the Tories' illicit arms deals in the '80s. As a famous British TV cop of yesteryear was fond of saying: "'ello, 'ello, 'ello; what do we 'ave 'ere?"

***

Now, as with Ari's allegations, I might have been prepared to ignore such apparent nonsense were it not for the fact that al-Fayed's claims found almost immediate corroboration from within the Conservative Party itself.

On the very evening of their election defeat, a damning statement was read from the steps of the Conservative headquarters by someone claiming to be a representative of the Tory Reform Group (TRG). This pressure group had become the resting ground of the left-wingers and "wets" in the Tory ranks, during Thatcher's triumphant right-wing reign.

Indeed, Thatcher was once seen at a Conservative Conference, storming up to the petrified young Chairman of TRG, all handbag and harridan. "What exactly, young man," she bellowed, "What exactly is it that you want to 'reform,' anyway?" The poor man was too stunned to respond, and without a backward glance, Thatcher swept onto other "shock and awe" engagements.

The TRG statement warned that any serious lurch to the right in the Party, resulting from the election defeat, would be met with a detailed exposition of what the right got up to in the '80s with respect to illicit arms sales. And there we were, back doing the "'ello, 'ello, 'ello" dance once again.

Finally, Tim Yeo, a former left-leaning Conservative Minister, announced that he was going to write a book about those alleged arms transgressions. He was later appointed Shadow Agriculture Secretary by the new Leader of the Conservative Party, William Hague, in his Shadow Cabinet.

Yeo remained in the Shadow Cabinet, under the two right-wing successors to Hague, right up to the General Election of 2005. I'm sure that Tim and Hugh would have found much in common on the subject of untrammeled ambition.

**

A couple of months after the election, the subject of Tories and illicit arms business hit the front pages again. Former Conservative rising star Jonathan Aitken met a sticky end when it was proven that he had lied in a libel action he brought against the *Guardian* newspaper. The newspaper had alleged that, in 1993, while serving as Minister for Defence Procurement, Aitken had had his hotel bill in Paris paid for by Said Ayas, a well-known bagman for the Saudi Arabian royal family in its arms purchases.

Aitken had been swearing up hill and down dale that his wife had paid the bill. Until the *Guardian* had proven that his wife was in Switzerland at the time. Big oops. Huge. Major league. End of political career. Divorce. Penury. And time in prison for perjury.

Aitken was an urbane right-wing Tory charmer. Not unlike Hugh. In fact, the two looked a lot alike. Aitken had finally made it into government in 1992, when John Major made him Minister for Defence Procurement – for which read, "Defense Sales."

The story was that Margaret Thatcher had refused Jonathan office for years because he'd dumped Mark's twin sister, Carol, in less than pleasant circumstances.

Now, Jonathan came to office with an enormous amount of baggage. He was reputed to have made his money as a partner in the asset management company of one Wafic Said. Wafic was another of those Middle Eastern cowboy businessmen, who loved the English lifestyle.

The thing of it was, to all intents and purposes, the only assets that Wafic and Jonny managed were the commissions, backhanders and kickbacks earned by them on behalf of the various members of the Saudi Royal Family.

Saudi Arabia is one big feudal candy store. It is all owned, lock, stock and barrel, by the Royal Family. And there's a lot of them. The bin Laden family (Osama too) are distant cousins. That's where he got all his money.

The country is divided between all the family members. Both on an activity basis and on a geographical basis. So Prince Fred, Second Cousin to the Ayatollah Harry and his wife, the Sultaness Germaine, might get the southern Province of Ali-Babadom, and the sardine fishing industry. What happens then is that every single time there is any sort of governmental financial transaction (generally a construction or supplies contract) involving one or the other, Prince Fred gets a kickback.

But there is no way that Prince Fred can be seen to be soiling his hands with such filthy lucre. Heavens no. So. He has a "bagman." Two of them in fact. One, from the country originating the services; and the other working out of the Middle East. Got to help the local brothers.

Now, Jonny and Wafic were respectively the British and the Middle Eastern bagmen for the biggest "bananas" on the fruit tree. Oh yes. And Said Ayas was the Middle Eastern bagman for the Saudi Minister of Defense.

Take a trip back with me, on the magic carpet of history, to the dark days of the Carter Presidency. His Director of CIA, Admiral Stansfield Turner, is ripping the guts out of the covert wing of the intelligence services. The big men of the CIA are worried. And the sheep are terrified. Something has to be done.

Some bright spark from Analysis comes up with an idea. Produce a fake Presidential Briefing. Convince Carter that the Soviet Union is going to run out of oil in the middle of the '80s. And that they will then almost certainly invade the Middle East, beginning in the East, and then working their way round to the rich pickings of Saudi Arabia.

Kind of what George Bush Junior did. But going in the other direction. Carter falls for it. Has a shrieking fit. And immediately demands that Congress agrees to huge arms sale packages to Saudi Arabia.

Then we have the "October Surprise," and Grand Pop Reagan comes to power. The CIA admits, oops, it made a mistake. Grand Pop nods, winks, chuckles and gets shot. And Bush Senior takes over foreign policy.

For all sorts of reasons, including the fact that Congress finally decides it doesn't like them, the US sales to Saudi Arabia wither a bit in the early '80s. At which point, enter the British, who pick up the slack, and effectively become the personal supplier of arms to the richest Royal Family the world has ever known. And these playboys want some expensive toys.

So. When we say that Jonny and Wafic were acting as bagmen for British arms sales to Saudi Arabia from the '80s on, we mean that they were making absolutely obscene amounts of money, for their principals and for themselves. And for others. For both were intimately involved with the Savoy Mafia. Why on earth shouldn't the British companies and individuals responsible for the arms sales also share in the candy?

It is believed that Wafic and Jonny were major brokers in the initial Al Yamamah arms deal between Great Britain and Saudi Arabia. The way it worked was this: the deal was a "rolling contract." The parties (the British and Saudi governments, and the brokers) agreed to an overall figure for the deal. Al Yamamah I was $35 billion. They then agreed on an amount for each year. Al Yamamah I was planned to "roll" for ten years.

Each year, the Saudis would produce a shopping list of what they wanted the British Santa to bring them at Christmas. British defense contractors would then submit bids to the British government, and "Santa" would award contracts accordingly.

When the services, goods, guns, missiles, ships, whatever, were subsequently supplied, the Saudi government would pay money over to the British government. The British government banks with the Bank of England. The major chunk of the money would go into a visible Bank of England account, and would then be disbursed by the government to the appropriate defense contractors.

Meanwhile, there was a less visible Bank of England account, into which commissions would be deposited, on an accruing basis.

On average, that bank account has been accruing at the rate of $300 million a year, every year, since 1985. It was the job of Wafic and Jonny then to carve up those commissions among their Saudi principals, the "other" British people, the Savoy Mafia and themselves – everyone who made Al Yamamah a possibility.

Wafic was a great chum of Denis and Mark Thatcher. Apparently, there is a famous picture of Margaret and Denis in a "family" shot with Bush Senior and Barbara, at the Bushes' luxury condo in Houston. Margaret and Denis bought a unit in the same complex, at Bush's suggestion. The Thatchers were in Texas visiting Mark, Diane and the kids, and they are in the photo too. As is Wafic, and his ravishing young wife.

So, why would John Major ask a crook to join his Government? Maybe it was all just coincidence? Maybe it was coincidence that Jonny was close to the Saudi Royal Family, and had a history of doing shady arms deals with them? Maybe it was coincidence that, less than a year after being appointed Minister for Defence Procurement/Sales, Jonny pulled off a negotiating coup with his Saudi buddies, signing them up for Al Yamamah II? And maybe it was mere coincidence that, at much the same time, the Conservative Party's general election (1992) overdraft of some $30 million simply disappeared?

Whatever the case, no sooner had the applause subsided than Jonny found himself rewarded with appointment to the position of Chief Secretary to the Treasury, a place at the Cabinet Table, and the general assumption that he was now Major's successor-in-place.

The allegations about the hotel bill surfaced in the *Guardian* in 1995, with the information being supplied by none other than Mohammed al-Fayed – who just happened to own the hotel in question, the Ritz, in Paris.

At the time, Jonny did what everyone concurred was the honorable thing: he resigned his Government post, and vowed to fight to the bitter end to restore his reputation. In mid-1997 the fight ended with egg being liberally smeared all over his face.

However, while everyone and his Auntie were busy falling over themselves with delight at the fall of yet another Tory icon, no one seemed to be paying the slightest attention to what I believed was the truly important question: Just what was Jonny, the Minister for Defence Procurement, doing meeting with Said Ayas, a meeting that Jonny himself deemed so suspicious that he had to lie about its circumstances?

It didn't seem to cross anyone else's mind that Jonny was most probably discussing with his co-bagman how exactly they were going to carve up the commissions from Al Yamamah II – details so obviously "delicate" that it required discussion away from any official ballyhoo. I mean. Why on earth would Jonny rule himself out of the illicit largesse just because he'd become a government minister? But then again, most of the media also missed the fact that Jonny's partner in crime, Wafic Said, had his own room in the Ritz that same weekend. The libel laws in Great Britain are draconian, and are heavily weighted in favor of the entity allegedly libeled. A particularly nasty device, used with much effect against less than well-off defendants, is a clever little item known as "aggravated damages."

Once a Libel Writ has been issued, if further alleged libel takes place, punitive damages can be levied for the further aggravation. This device is supposed to stop retaliation by the libeler against the libeled, as a "punishment" for issuing the Writ. However, over the years, it has become a favorite instrument of the rich and guilty, in their usually successful attempts to muzzle honest accusation.

It occurred to me that the reason Richard Norton-Taylor, then a leading investigative journalist with the London Guardian newspaper, and to whom I had sent a packet of information, did not pursue my story is that, since it dealt with matters already the subject of Jonny's Libel Writ against Norton-Taylor's newspaper, his editors may have been worried about aggravated damages.

Al-Fayed was, of course, beside himself with joy. Not only had the offending event occurred in his hotel, but he had been able to get the Guardian story going in the first place, with his invaluable inside information about Jonny's meeting.

More than that. Al-Fayed had then been able to apply the coup de grace personally. For it was he who had supplied the trial with the Ritz Hotel fax that had proven that Jonny's wife was in Switzerland, and not in Paris. Tubby little Fayed bobbed and weaved around London, in merriment and mirth, rubbing his hands in glee, just like Danny de Vito as the Penguin in *Batman Returns*.

Along with the bobbing, and just before the weaving, al-Fayed was also trumpeting to the press that he would now hammer the nail well and truly into the coffin of the Conservative Party, with total exposure of the Tories' remaining dirty dealings with respect to Al Yamamah. I put two and two together, and wondered whether he was in a position to do this because those dealings had also occurred in the Ritz Hotel?

I wrote a letter to al-Fayed, setting out my reasoning, and asking him if he'd happened to come across Hugh in his hotel, up to no good. Not really expecting al-Fayed to respond, I got a little "familiar" in the letter, and commended him on his courage in speaking out so boldly about arms merchants, who probably wouldn't be too happy at his threats to expose them, along with right-wing Tories.

Less than a month later, in the middle of the night of August 31, 1997, his son Dodi was killed in mysterious circumstances in a car crash in Paris, as he was traveling from the Ritz Hotel back to his apartment. Also killed in the crash was his girlfriend. With him. In the back seat of his Mercedes.

The girlfriend was Diana, Princess of Wales.

***

There is apparently an old saying in the Middle East, where retribution and feuds are more commonplace than on the loneliest hilltops of Tennessee: if you want to hurt someone, then hurt the one they love. And if there is a message to be conveyed, then send it with as much of an exclamation point as possible.

The only major nation not to suffer regular hostage-taking in Lebanon in the '80s was the Soviet Union. This is because, when the first two Russians were kidnapped, the KGB went out, found a couple of foot-soldiers of the Islamic militia responsible, and delivered them to the doorstep of the militia's headquarters, bound and tied, with their balls in their mouths. The two hostages were freed within the hour. No more Russians were ever taken.

There could have been no more poignant an exclamation point for Mohammed al-Fayed than the death of Diana. It proved to him the utter ruthlessness of those conveying the message. They were simply unmoved by the enormity of any "collateral damage."

To this day, Mohammed al-Fayed has not uttered a single word more about arms deals, arms merchants, arms middlemen, the Ritz Hotel or the Conservative Party. He has four young children by his second marriage.

***

The Lebanese hostage-takers got involved in a game where they thought they had established the rules. Only to come across people who played by different rules. Or no rules.

Mohammed al-Fayed interfered in a game, where he did not understand the rules. Or he knew them, and then broke them. Or he incurred the wrath of people, who ultimately were prepared shamelessly to toss the rule book aside.

I believe that Hugh Simmonds arrogantly and recklessly became involved in a game whose rules he thought he could bend. Or he thought he could con other people into thinking he was abiding by them, when in fact he was breaking them. And those people, at the end of the day, just didn't give a fig what the heck Hugh was doing about any rules in any event. They just wanted their money.

Ari was right. Everything changed in the '80s. Money became "King." Everything became subordinate to money. As it still is. Money is power. People don't like having their power taken away. They will do whatever they have to do to protect it. And at the end of the day, they won't allow rules to get in the way.

***

Meanwhile, all was not well in British intelligence. People were resigning. People were talking. About all sorts of shady goings-on. In both MI5 and MI6. We had one David Shayler, from MI5. And Richard Tomlinson, from MI6.

Now, it's a huge no-no for British government employees in sensitive parts of the bureaucracy to talk about their work in public. It breaches the Official Secrets Act, which all "sensitive" employees have to sign when they are hired. Hence, Reggie's initial reluctance to talk to me. Until someone decided it might be useful to have him talk to me.

Shayler became the more celebrated "whistle-blower," because he did a runner to France, and there held court with the press for some years. Eventually, he returned to Great Britain, did a little prison time, and disappeared into the countryside.

Tomlinson did his "thing" the other way round. He served prison time first. And then published his exposé. Which was a deal more explosive than anything Shayler had said. In particular, Tomlinson had some interesting input on Diana's crash.

Tomlinson agreed with Shayler that the core of British intelligence had become rotten, beginning in the '80s. But he went one further. He went on record to say that British intelligence actively engaged in assassinations around the world. Among other startling accusations, he insisted that the circumstances of Diana and Dodi's death bore a remarkable resemblance to a plan MI6 had been working on to "take out" Slobodan Milosevic of Serbia, in 1992.

Tomlinson also confirmed that the Ritz in Paris had had a reputation as a "safe haven" for arms deals and secret meetings between competing intelligence agencies, ever since the Second World War. That last point got me thinking. Surely, al-Fayed would have known this when he bought the place? Indeed, maybe it's why he was so interested in it? Al-Fayed had a background in illicit arms dealing with Adnan Khashoggi, a Saudi tycoon who had brokered arms deals between the US and Saudi Arabia. He would have been deemed an "acceptable" owner by its "shady" patrons. So long as he continued the tradition of confidentiality.

What, I was wondering, might those same patrons have thought when al-Fayed was reported all over the British press, promising to betray those very confidences he might have been expected to maintain?

Tomlinson also raised the suggestion that Henri Paul (Diana and Dodi's personal chauffeur, who was also killed in the Paris tunnel) was a paid informant for a number of intelligence agencies, including MI6. This would make sense. Your average intelligence agency would probably think nothing of playing both ends against the middle. Demanding "confidentiality" from the owner, and then bribing the staff to spy on the other guys.

It was therefore no surprise that later in 1997 it was reported that one of Paul's bank accounts had been found to have had about $150,000 tucked into it shortly before the crash. Mind you, wasn't it Ari who had told me that bank accounts could be played with?

Tomlinson also revealed that Paris had been awash with British agents the weekend of the crash, including the Director of the Security Service, MI5.

But the information that caught my attention most acutely was that relating to "Mickey Finns." I have to be honest, my notes indicate that this information came from Tomlinson's allegations, but I cannot swear to that fact. I wrote to Tomlinson, but he never responded.

In any event, the information that I scribbled down, because it fascinated me so much, was that there are knock-out drugs, which agents slip into drinks. That in itself is not so surprising. What stunned me was the claim that one of the primary features of the drugs is that they also raise blood-alcohol readings to incredible levels, for very short periods of time. The consequence is that immediate testing suggests that the black-out is the result merely of alcohol. So, no further tests are conducted; tests which might otherwise find traces of the drugs.

***

At about this time in Georgia USA, the rather rustic computer that I was using in Clayton had a fatal spasm. I took it down the hill to the one computer service store in the whole of Rabun County. It was owned by a fifty-something Egyptian expatriate by the name of Rezzac. Coincidence is an extraordinary animal that will leap up, and bite you in the soft nether regions the very moment you stop paying attention.

Rezzac had been born and raised in the same small town in Egypt as Mohammed Fayed: Mattria, between Alexandria and Port Said, close to the Suez Canal. According to Rezzac, Mohammed was close to the local British Forces, which, it being the '50s, were still stationed in Egypt, along with the French. Mohammed was known by all to be a regular smuggler of hashish from Israel into Egypt. Which suggests that his was a name most probably also known to the Israelis.

Rezzac said that Mohammed also "did some kind of dirty work for British Military Intelligence. He was 'looked after' by them." In 1956, the British, the French and the Israelis got up to all sorts of "dirty work" in Egypt, when they launched military action, in an attempt to topple the nationalistic leader of Egypt, Gamel Nasser, and wrest back control of the Suez Canal from him.

The whole sorry adventure came to a messy end when the Americans pulled the plug, refusing to condone the military action. This led to what is known in British history books as "The Suez Crisis." The Conservative Prime Minister at the time was forced to resign. It also effectively spelled the end of the British Empire as a serious global contender.

Just to backtrack a bit, it is now known that in the years before 1956, the Israelis themselves were undertaking some "dirty work" of their own in Egypt. During a three-week period in July 1954, several terrorist bombs were set off – at the United States Information Agency offices in Cairo and Alexandria, at a British-owned theater, and at the central post office in Cairo.

An attempt to firebomb a cinema in Alexandria failed when the bomb went off in the pocket of one of the perpetrators. That, in turn, led to the discovery that the terrorists were not anti-Western Egyptians, but were instead Israeli spies, bent on souring the warming relationship between Egypt and the United States, in what came to be known as the "Lavon Affair." Little wonder that two years later the Americans stuck it back to the Israelis, and their British and French partners.

Let's assume that British Military Intelligence had established in Egypt a network of people, like Mohammed Fayed, whom they "looked after." What happened to them when the British were forced to leave after 1956? The British could hardly hand them over to the Egyptian authorities. They would have been excoriated as "collaborators" and spies, and no potential asset would ever trust British intelligence again. The French were out of the question, because they were being forced to leave as well. But. You don't just let a good network go to waste. It's way too valuable. So, you find a "friend" somewhere to hand it to. Who else was left? Doesn't sense suggest that the only remaining option was the Israelis?

Is it beyond the realm of fantasy to suggest that this network, including Mohammed, was handed over, lock, stock and barrel, to Israeli intelligence? An intelligence service that might already have been well acquainted with some of its members? Say, the ones smuggling hashish from Israel into Egypt? Maybe the Israelis had been "running" them for some time, in collaboration with the British and the French, while they, the Israelis, were up to all their other "dirty work" in Egypt?

If one sees this conjecture through to the end, it is entirely conceivable that Mohammed Fayed simply got caught up in the Israeli net. It would have been way too easy to use blackmail to keep him ensnared. In fact, the more he would have become involved with illicit Arab arms deals, the more valuable he would have been to the Israelis.

Shift forward to the '80s. There is much suggestion that al-Fayed (as he had now decided to call himself) was heavily involved, throughout the early '80s, in the illicit arms trade with Iran, out of London. Well, who wasn't? Then came the famous "tilt" by the West, and by Bush and Thatcher in particular, towards Iraq. And the Israelis got pissed. In 1987, Ari was dispatched by Yitzhak Shamir to do whatever was necessary to put a plug in the arms pipeline to Iraq.

I had already heard from Ari that this included targeting right-wing Tories, both in Government and on the rise (Mellor and Simmonds), who might have had a pro-Arab leaning, and who might also have been centrally involved in the pipeline to Iraq.

Now, who else at that time was taking aim at right-wing Tories? None other than Mohammed al-Fayed, who had declared himself dedicated to exposing the shenanigans of the Tory right-wing, and who had already claimed the individual scalps of Aitken and Neil Hamilton, (who had been forced to resign as a Junior Minister in Major's Government, after al-Fayed had revealed that he had improperly paid Hamilton to ask formal questions on al-Fayed's behalf in the House of Commons) along with the defeat of Major's Government.

Was this mere co-incidence, or was it that al-Fayed continued to be an "asset" of Israeli intelligence at the end of the '80s and the beginning of the '90s to upend any and all right-wing Tories, particularly those engaged in the illicit sale of military technology to Iraq?

***

I was contacted indirectly by Philip Dumville, who had been the Conservative Agent for the Beaconsfield Parliamentary Constituency at the time of Hugh's death. He wanted to let me know that the doctor who had signed Hugh's Death Certificate was none other than The Right Honourable Liam Fox, MP, former Secretary of State for Defence in the UK's LibCon Coalition Government of 2010-2015, and a well-known cheerleader for Israel.

I was so dumbstruck that I decided to take a breather by collecting my mail. Sister Maggi had sent me another article from England. Huge allegations, all over the front page of the most recent *Sunday*

Times in London, about the Iranian Hashemi brothers and Margaret Thatcher. One of Cyrus Hashemi's older brothers, Jamshid, was being charged in Great Britain with fraud over a non-existent commodity deal. Jamshid was attempting to use what was becoming a common defense in the '90s – namely, that the government knew all about it. Yet, with Jamshid, there was a suspicious ring of truth. Hence, the *Sunday Times* article.

Jamshid, like his brothers, had a long history of involvement with both the CIA and MI6, infiltrating Iranian circles, and using the cover of illegal arms deals to filter useful information back to his intelligence masters on both sides of the Atlantic. Indeed, in the end, Jamshid was convicted, but Judge Andrew Collins granted Jamshid leniency, because of the "valuable information" he had given British intelligence.

But this wasn't what had caught everyone's attention. It was Jamshid's allegation that, in the '80s, he and his brothers had paid the Conservative Party some $120,000 to have a meeting with Margaret Thatcher, then still the Prime Minister. The thing of it was that the Party wasn't denying the money, and Thatcher wasn't denying the meeting. They were merely denying the connection, and were strenuously refuting any allegation that illicit arms deals had been discussed at the private meeting.

Thing is, no one had suggested that illicit arms deals may have been discussed at the meeting. Except for those denying the fact.

***

Finally, I received in the post reading material of a different kind: a book I had ordered, and written by Simon Regan. The book was primarily about Diana, but it contained information that would spark a whole new line of inquiry in my investigation – and much to my surprise, all manner of interesting verification of the meat of Ari's claims about the Conservative Party, the Thatchers, and Hugh.

CHAPTER THIRTEEN

Thatcher And Arms Kickbacks

SCALLYWAG WAS AN independent investigative journal founded in the '90s by Simon Regan, a bit of an outcast journalist who wrote for the *Guardian* from time to time. *Scallywag* liked to present itself as the scourge of the Establishment, but most of the flagellation seemed to be at the expense of Major's Conservative government. A fact which most observers attributed to the rumor that *Scallywag* was financed, in the main, by Mohammed al-Fayed.

Both Regan and *Scallywag* had first come to public notice with their exposé of activities at certain Boys' Homes in Wales. Regan alleged that there was a pedophile ring that plundered these homes. And that the residents were taken to London, where they were "provided" to a secret network of homosexuals.. The suggestion, none too squeamishly advanced by Regan, was that the pedophile ring most probably extended to leading figures within the Conservative Party.

Regan's well-researched articles eventually forced an inquiry, and several damning claims were upheld. But nothing much else happened, a paralysis that Regan felt was preordained given the links to the Conservative Party, and the operation of what he described as insidious Freemasonic interference in the original police investigations. Regan has been vindicated with the explosion all over Britain's quality newspapers of the very same allegations, in the wake of the Jimmy Savile child molestation scandal.

I was always on the lookout for possible assistance with my own investigation, and notwithstanding the ghostly presence of al-Fayed in the background, I felt that it might be worth a shot having a closer look at Regan. What finally made up my mind was the news that Regan had written a "stunning" book about the death of Diana. So I wrote to him.

***

It became clear from our first e-mail exchanges that neither one of us was convinced of the bona fides of the other. I was concerned over his links to al-Fayed. He was troubled by the fact that I might be an intelligence stooge, writing to him so totally out of the blue.

Regan assured me that his connection to al-Fayed had been severed, that it had always been at arm's length, and that it had only been about cash. Apparently, he became happier with me. We moved from e-mail to snail mail, neither of us being particularly comfortable with computers.

He encouraged me, without much explanation, to read the back copies of *Scallywag*, which were available on the Internet. In the meantime, he waded through a 5,000-word briefing of mine, which I had originally prepared for journalist Richard Norton-Taylor.

On Regan's website, I discovered a series of articles discussing the Conservatives' innovative fund-raising techniques in the '80s, and about $300 million sitting in secret offshore bank accounts, some under the personal control of Margaret Thatcher.

Regan went to some lengths to explain to me the distinction between "Party" accounts that were under Thatcher's control to avoid the scrutiny of Party "puritans," and accounts that were under Thatcher's control because they were for her personal use.

Regan was now very chipper about my investigation. He wanted the opportunity to fashion my briefing into a potential magazine article, then to assist me with the writing of my book. He sought nothing in return. He simply wanted to "get" the people he felt had "got" his half-brother (who had died in mysterious circumstances in northern Cyprus, Regan believed at the hand of enforcers operating for the illicit Tory arms trade).

I was not about to turn away any help. Particularly someone who knew the corridors of publishing in Great Britain. It didn't matter that Regan bore with him some doubts that had been raised about his credibility. Heck, here was I, talking to Ari, when I wasn't talking to myself. I hardly stood out as a beacon of universal respectability. Besides, I warmed to Simon's genuine interest and concern. Plus, he was the first person, aside from my twin sister and a close friend in the mountains of north Georgia, actually to gush about my findings.

We agreed that he would first meet with Maggi, in England, so that we could both add human faces and feelings to the paper and electronic bonds that had been formed. In the meantime, he urged me to contact a good friend of his, Kevin Cahill, who had also labored on the Tory "fund-raising" issue.

***

Before I had spoken with Cahill, I heard from one of the "puritans" to whom Simon had made reference: John Strafford had been the Chairman of the Beaconsfield Conservative Association when I had served as its Vice Chairman.

Hugh, Peter Smith, (former Treasurer and then Vice President of the Beaconsfield Constituency Conservative Association in the '80's, former International Chair of PricewaterhouseCoopers, and currently Chair of Savills, the largest property services company in the world), John, and I – plus many others of a like mind – had worked long and hard to enable Beaconsfield to achieve its high-flying status as a fund-raising powerhouse for the Tories.

In case there is any confusion, I'm talking here about Beaconsfield's legitimate status as a Party fund-raiser; not the quite separate shenanigans set out in this book by which Hugh and others in Beaconsfield may have contributed substantially, yet illicitly, to the fortunes of the Conservative Party.

After Hugh's death, John had gone on to succeed Hugh as Treasurer of the Wessex Area of the Conservative Party. And that position, as with Hugh, had led to John's membership of the secretive Conservative National Board of Finance.

John had not been the friendliest of souls towards me after the early revelations of Hugh's defalcation. But he had come across an early website of mine, on which I had set out a summary of my information to date, particularly those allegations concerning the funneling of large amounts of "secret" money into the coffers of the Tory Party in the '80s. John's subsequent e-mails in 1998 were a deal sight friendlier than he had been in 1988.

John was a Chartered Accountant by profession, and his e-mails were a model of professionalism. He had things he wanted to say, but his loyalties still lay with the Party, with which he had been involved his whole political life.

John would not directly answer my question as to whether or not he had come across any evidence of "secret" offshore accounts while he was on the Conservative Board of Finance. All he would say is that upon completion of his term as Treasurer he had immediately set up his own organization calling for more democracy in the Conservative Party.

In particular, he wanted the National Accounts of the Conservative Party to be placed under the control of a National Treasurer – all the accounts. And he stressed that the Treasurer should be elected by grass-roots Tory members, and that the Treasurer should make all of those accounts fully open to the membership. Beyond that, John wished me well, asked me to keep in touch, and suggested that I draw my own conclusions.

***

Kevin Cahill was an independent journalist who financed his own investigations by his research work for the *Sunday Times* Rich List – the annual list of the richest people in Great Britain. Apparently he also used the contacts he made to gather information for his own investigations.

In 1993, Cahill had written a series of long articles detailing the full history of "secret" Tory fund-raising, going all the way back to Winston Churchill. Originally, there were a number of what were called "River Associations" (named after Britain's largest rivers), through which "secret" donations were funneled. More often than not, these were donations from abroad, which might prove embarrassing to Party leaders.

In the '80s, what had been a "cottage industry" became serious business. This started under the Tory Party Treasurership of Lord Boardman (the NatWest Chairman who had ordered Hugh's bank accounts to be foreclosed) in the early '80s, and continued in earnest with Alistair McAlpine. In his autobiography, *Once a Jolly Bagman: Memoirs*, McAlpine (later Lord McAlpine) laid claim to having raised some $225 million for the Tories between 1979 and 1989. Barely a fraction of this appeared in any of the heavily abbreviated National Accounts produced after the audit each year by Peter Smith and his friends at Coopers & Lybrand, (which merged in 1998 with Price Waterhouse, to form PricewaterhouseCoopers).

Money was coming in from all over the place: from shipping tycoons in Hong Kong to banking overlords in Indonesia. The River

Associations were dramatically expanded into a complex network of international money-laundering entities, all fronted by the Party's legitimate banking arrangements with the Royal Bank of Scotland.

I gently wondered where this money-laundering expertise might have been garnered. It wasn't just a case of opening a bank account in Switzerland. And McAlpine had no background to suggest that the planning was all his. A thought made all the more relevant by the suggestions that bank accounts under the control of McAlpine had themselves been used, not only for the Party's own money-laundering, but as a piggy-back vehicle for other peoples' funds as well. A mirror reflection of allegations made by the Law Society about Hugh's "financial arrangements." Was it mere co-incidence that Hugh, as a member of the Conservative National Board of Finance, would have met regularly with McAlpine, who served as Chairman of the National Board?

Kevin took Simon Regan's explanation of "personal" bank accounts a stage further. He stated that there was no such thing as "The Conservative Party." There were Conservative Constituency Associations, which were stand-alone legal units. They then had their own umbrella group, the National Union of Conservative Associations.

These Constituency Associations chose their own Conservative candidates, who were subsequently elected Members of Parliament. The latter, in turn, agreed to take a common Conservative Whip in Parliament. The same was true of the unelected Conservative peers in the House of Lords. These MPs then chose a leader, who was recognized by the other component parts of the "Party" as their "Leader" also. In recent years, the specific rules have changed, but the principle is the same.

However, in the '80s, there was still no "National Party." Only the above loose arrangements, leading up to an acknowledged individual Leader. That Leader had a support staff, which was collectively known as Conservative Central Office. That "Office" had its headquarters on the edge of the "Mayfair Square Mile," a short distance from Parliament.

Central Office served all of the component parts of the Party, but it was still the Leader's personal Office. The Leader appointed the staff, and all of the Central Office and National Party bank accounts were in his/her name. So, if you were Jamshid Hashemi, you didn't make a check out to "The Conservative Party," you made a check out to "Margaret Thatcher, as Leader of the Conservative Party." And when she ceased to be Leader, it became "John Major, as Leader of the Conservative Party." And so on. And that's where the fun had begun.

***

My sister met with Regan in a cozy pub in central London. Simon Regan was in his fifties, and bore an uncanny resemblance to one of those seedy characters made famous by the British actor, Sir Michael Gambon. Lower middle-class; all worn blazer and comfy cardigan. Never without a tie. But equally, never without a glass of scotch in his right hand, and a cigarette dangling from his mouth. Maggi had taken to him instantly, and reported that he was thoroughly genuine and charming.

Simon's next letter to me was even more joyful than the first few had been. He had not initially picked up on the significance of my thoughts about illicit Tory arms dealing and the Mark Thatcher connection.

Simon said that it was well known that large amounts of the "secret" monies that had been raised by the Tories in the '80s, had come from arms dealings. But no one in the mainstream media had been able to find any money trail. Simon, on the other hand, said he had evidence that the trail led through Mark, and then back to the Conservatives, and ultimately to Margaret Thatcher.

Apparently, Mark had been chosen as the money pipeline precisely because no one "sensible" would think that matters of such importance would be entrusted to such a "clown." And Simon, on the basis of his information, had become convinced that they hadn't. Simon knew that Mark had expert money-laundering advice – he just couldn't locate the individual; he was too "well-hidden." The more Simon learned about Hugh, his past, his skills, and his singular importance within the Conservative Party, and to Margaret Thatcher, the more Simon came to believe that the adviser was not now "well-hidden"; he was dead. It was, and it always had been, Hugh.

Simon's information was the "two" that when added to Ari's "two" became the "four" I had been looking for: Simon said he had evidence that Mark was the secret pipeline to Margaret Thatcher and the Conservative Party of illicit profits from international arms sales. Ari had evidence that Hugh was, in turn, the secret pipeline of those profits to Mark. Had I discovered the entirety of the missing money trail? The proof of arms corruption at senior levels of the British Conservative Party, proof for which foreign law enforcement, foreign intelligence services, and a slew of journalists had been searching for over a decade. My, my I suddenly felt very unsafe all over again.

More to the point, I now had information that strongly suggested that Hugh had not been acting as a "rogue" in his nefarious shenanigans. Rather, he had been an essential link in the conduit of corrupt money to Margaret Thatcher and the Conservative Party. And in all the circumstances related so far in this book, and unearthed during my investigation, it is inconceivable that Hugh was acting other than at the express request of the British Prime Minister of the day, namely Margaret Thatcher.

Two questions, more than any other, continued to bug me: Why on earth would one of the most successful British Prime Ministers of all time risk her place in history for a few bucks; and why on earth would Hugh Simmonds risk his life to help her?

It was because of these questions that Simon became more anxious than ever to help me with further research for, and then the writing of my book. Kevin Cahill, Simon Regan, and I forged a three-way arrangement: Kevin would help with the research; I would provide Kevin with all of my information; and Simon would pull it all together, and do the bulk of the actual writing. Notwithstanding Simon's protestations, I always envisaged any ensuing credit as being shared three ways.

Alas, this was not to be. I never heard from Simon again. In 2000, I discovered why. Simon had become very ill and had then died. In the short time that I knew him, Simon was a good friend. He is sorely missed.

***

A couple of years later, on November 25, 2001, to be precise, there was an article in the Sunday Times headlined, "Arms bribe: police block £100 million [$150 million] fund."

> More than £100 million hidden in a Jersey [semi-autonomous small island, part of Great Britain, and situated close to the northern coast of France] trust has been frozen by

detectives investigating allegations that British arms companies paid financial sweeteners to help win lucrative defence contracts in the Middle East.

In what is believed to be Britain's biggest commercial bribery inquiry, police and legal officials have frozen assets in a trust fund controlled by a senior member of the ruling family in the Gulf State of Qatar [the base for joint US/UK operations in the Second Gulf War].

Judicial sources say the money is alleged to be the proceeds of commissions paid by arms firms to win contracts for military equipment worth hundreds of millions of pounds during the 1990s. British, German and Italian companies are all said to have made payments in the "cash-for-contracts" affair.

Yesterday, BAE [British Aerospace] Systems, Britain's biggest defence firm, confirmed it was co-operating with the inquiry. But Phil Soucy, its spokesman, insisted: "We are not the object of this inquiry and we would refute any allegations of corruption or any other wrongdoing."

The bank accounts belonging to the trust are now run by Standard Chartered Grindlays Trust Corporation.

Sources close to the investigation claim that payments were made into the trust in return for securing government contracts, including the purchase of military equipment such as aircraft. The money – which some sources suggest may be up to £230 million – was used to buy property around the world.

Britain has close ties with Qatar. The state's emir visited Tony Blair for talks at Downing Street two years ago.

Because of its excessive secrecy and tax-free status, Jersey has proved popular with wealthy individuals seeking to hide the source of their money.

Although its banking sector has been more strictly regulated in recent years, money laundering, tax dodgers and drug barons have all used offshore accounts in the Channel Islands to hide criminal profits.

Last March £100 million pounds linked to General Sani Abucha, the former Nigerian dictator, was uncovered by Jersey regulators. They found bank accounts used by Abacha's associates at five island financial institutions.

The nice Press Officer from the Law Society was prepared to confirm to me in 1996 that money associated with Hugh's bank accounts had been traced back to Nigeria.

Certainly in the '80s, and while Hugh was with Wedlake Bell, the latter firm had maintained offices on the island of Jersey. I believe on Grenville Street in St. Helier.

***

When next I spoke with Kevin Cahill, he confirmed what Simon had said about Mark Thatcher. Indeed, some of Simon's information had been unearthed during Kevin's research. Kevin suggested that I read a book called *Thatcher's Gold*, which was all about Mark's finances. And which, interestingly, had been co-authored by Paul Halloran, whom I had had a brief phone conversation with when I first tried to get the media interested in Hugh's story.

By the by, I raised with Kevin my own suspicions that there had been deliberate political destabilization efforts in Great Britain in the '80s and '90s, with the intention of securing a Thatcherite succession of the Leadership of the Conservative Party. Oh man. I opened the floodgates. The first thing that Kevin did was to fax me a bunch of information, including organization charts, to back up what he was about to tell me.

Kevin began recounting conversations he had had with a former senior Cabinet Minister who had served under both Major and Thatcher. This well-known Cabinet Minister had described a serious plan by right-wing businessman and politician Sir James Goldsmith to take over the Conservative Party after the fall of Thatcher.

Kevin considered Goldsmith to be one of a new breed of parvenu British businessmen, who amassed and wielded power not by adhering to the rules and conventions that had cemented the British Establishment in the past, but with money, lots of it. And very little of it from legitimate sources. In particular, Kevin was convinced that Goldsmith was heavily involved with Tory arms dealing.

Kevin suggested that I read a novel published in 1993 by John le Carré, called *The Night Manager*. The book described an unholy alliance between the head of Britain's Secret Service and a sleazy businessman, who could have been one of any number of real-life sleazy billionaires operating in British business in the '80s.

Kevin explained that le Carré had originally written it as non-fiction, intending to expose the corruption that had overtaken MI6 in the '80s, when Britain's Foreign Intelligence Service had decided to put aside "service" and go into business for itself. Primarily, the arms and money-laundering business.

MI6 had become overrun by people who were no longer gentlemen, and who had no appreciation of Gentlemen's Rules or the concept of duty and loyalty.

When John Major was elected Thatcher's successor in 1990, everyone thought that they would be dealing with a Leader and Prime Minister of like mind. According to Kevin, Major had met with a delegation of the "Grey Men" of his Party the weekend before the succession became final. They shared with a stunned and decent John Major the full extent of the corruption in the Tory Party, the intelligence services, and his new government in general.

The Grey Men had not expected Major's reaction. In the space of a couple of years, he set up: the Scott Inquiry, which the Grey Men feared would expose all of their illicit arms dealing; the Nolan Commission into Standards in Public Life, which set as its first priority a thorough review of all party financing; and a further government commission, which sought to overhaul corporate governance, in particular the secrecy surrounding many of the financial decisions made in board meetings in Great Britain – the mandarins of Tory Finance saw the possibility that their donations would be decimated, since so many of those corporate donations were made only on the basis that they remained secret.

The next thing we knew: Goldsmith was planning to oust John Major and take over the Conservative Party with his money; John Le Carre was planning to write in his nonfiction book that Goldsmith and others were in cahoots with the head of MI6; and I was seeing signs in Great Britain of a destabilization technique, in popular use by intelligence agencies and potentially aimed at undermining the institutions of the British establishment.

Kevin told me that in le Carré's final version of his book the fictional character "Roper" was Goldsmith, and "Darker" was Braden Camp, reputed to be Chief of MI6 at that time.

Goldsmith had eventually been rebuffed by whatever powers-that-be, and had gone off in 1994 to form the Referendum Party, along with McAlpine and one Paul Sykes, another rich right-wing British businessman.

Goldsmith died of cancer shortly after the 1997 general election, and the Referendum Party was disbanded.

One twist I was beginning to formulate in my mind was that any "campaign" against Major may not have been so much about bringing Thatcher back to power, as it was about keeping secret what Thatcher had been doing in the '80s.

I hadn't laughed at Kevin's suggestions. And he didn't laugh at mine. But then, Kevin hadn't yet finished – although here is where I cannot name names due to the draconian libel laws in Great Britain.

Kevin stated that Goldsmith's plan, although doomed by his ultimate death, bears an uncanny resemblance to activity engaged in since Goldsmith's death by a gentleman, formerly a Treasurer of the Conservative Party and currently a very powerful figure within Conservative politics. This activity appears to be funded, at least in part, by the $300 million in arms slush money sitting in those offshore bank accounts. Perhaps not surprisingly, the gentleman in question was a very close friend of the Thatcher family, not least Margaret's husband, Denis.

What is not clear is what might be the ultimate purpose of the gentleman's well-funded machinations. A continuation of right-wing Thatcherite leadership at the top of the Conservative Party and in any Conservative-led British Government? Keeping mouths closed about the arms shenanigans of the '80s? A resuscitation of the lucrative pipeline of arms commissions under the current Conservative-led UK LibCon Coalition Government of 2010-2015? Or, perhaps, the entrenching of a more secret, darker, and more wide-ranging agenda, begun in the '80s?

What is clear is that the gentleman has enormous influence in Conservative politics, and, if any part of these suggestions is true, then that influence has proven to be, and continues to be, a poisonous toxin at the heart of the British body politic. And it is one that explains so much of what has seemed to be unexplainable about decisions made by British governments from the '80s up to the present.

***

At this point, there was a regular exchange of information between Kevin and me. I was working on a list of names for him. Anyone and anything I could remember being associated with Hugh, to give Kevin a starting database of leads for him to take his inquiries wherever they might go.

Then one day, Kevin telephoned to say that he'd been approached by a "person of credibility," who had told him, in no uncertain terms, to drop all interest in me and Hugh. Kevin seemed quite matter of fact about relaying the conversation to me. Not in the slightest bit worried. But I never heard from him again.

***

At this time, I had a rather useless but friendly conversation with Reggie, who told me that I would be unlikely to pry any more information out of folk about the present. Too dangerous. But I could do worse than have a look at Hugh's early political career and work forwards. Why was it that all involved felt that it was amusing constantly to talk to me in riddles?

Well. What I did know was that Hugh's early political career was intimately intertwined with the shenanigans of the loony, pseudo-paramilitary right of British politics. What I did not know was that a gentle wander through those days would lead to a character who would dump me headfirst back into the arms corruption of the '80s.

Clever Reggie.

Chapter Fourteen

Arms And Thatcher's Rise To Power

I N THE LATE '60s, Hugh was in his early twenties and had recently graduated from Merchant Taylor's School. Not quite Eton, but very swank anyway. According to Hugh and Reggie, this was the time that Hugh had been "recruited." He had then spent time in Czechoslovakia and perhaps on the seafront at Marseilles.

Hugh's father told me that it was his understanding that Hugh worked at a RadioShack in West London, at this time. Indeed, Hugh had shown me a house that he had rented during this period, in the Kensington part of West London. But was this ruse merely a cover for Hugh's real activities? According to Hugh, he was a part of the real "Austin Powers" set: intelligence work by day, and "Swinging London" by night. Czechoslovakia during the week – and parties on the French Riviera on the weekend, with Mick Jagger and Bianca. Meanwhile, I was still at school. And all I wanted to be was a farmer.

And so, we moved into the '70s. It was an unsettled time politically, and, as it turned out, it presented Hugh an opportunity to make a name for himself among those on the right.

Conservative Prime Minister Edward Heath had won election on a set of right-wing principles, and then had pretty much abandoned them. Right-wingers accused Heath of developing cold feet and converting to socialism. Heath's supporters countered by saying he had simply grown a conscience.

Regardless, in 1972, an open rebellion erupted within the ranks of Conservative Parliamentarians against the left-leaning Heath. Ministers resigned. Ordinary members made clear to the leadership that they would not support the Conservative government on votes that pursued a socialistic agenda, or sought to take Great Britain down a path towards a federal Europe.

Two of the leaders of the Conservative Rebellion were Enoch Powell, a former Conservative cabinet minister, and Ronald Bell, the then Member of Parliament for Beaconsfield. I would come to know Ronald Bell quite well, when later I served for seven years as the Chairman of the Beaconsfield Young Conservatives, and as a Vice Chairman of the Senior Conservative Association. Small of stature, his right-wing views and quiet manner belied his sharp mind and quick wit. In 1972, however, his protégé was the then chairman of the YCs, one Hugh Simmonds.

Heath reacted brutally to the challenge of his underlings. Secretly, he instructed his Conservative Central Office to run heavy-weight candidates against each of the rebelling parliamentarians during the process that, in England, was the equivalent of a primary. In Beaconsfield, the young and dashing Michael Heseltine was given the task of "deselecting" Ronald Bell.

These fights quickly became causes celebre, although the tactics used nowhere near matched the perceived majesty of the purpose. In this regard, Hugh established himself as king. No stone was left unturned in Hugh's efforts to save Ronald Bell his parliamentary seat.

New members were bused into meetings; headquarters and safes were broken into; and all manner of negative stories were spread, wherever they would do the most damage. Ronald Bell defeated Michael Heseltine, and Hugh made a name for himself as a right-wing "dirty tricks" meister par excellence.

Hugh lost no time in building on his newfound intra-party fame. While establishing an elective record in local politics in Beaconsfield, he also set up camp on the national scene.

If you want proof positive of Hugh's burgeoning influence at that time in right-wing politics closely associated with Margaret Thatcher, you need look no further than the fight against the European Referendum three years later, in 1975.

By that time, Labour Prime Minister Harold Wilson had returned to power, and Thatcher had ousted Heath as Leader of the Conservative Party.

Wilson had agreed to allow the British public to vote on continued membership of the European Economic Community (EEC), by way of a National Referendum.

With his growing reputation as a political organizer and public speaker, Hugh was invited to join the National Committee of the "No" organization, campaigning against continued membership of the EEC. He found himself alongside the likes of Enoch Powell, Michael Foot (later Leader of the Labour Party) and Tony Benn (a long-serving Labour Cabinet Minister) – all while Hugh was at the tender age of 27.

Throughout this period many on the right genuinely believed they were fighting for the very soul of Britain's continued independence and freedom.

Besides the EEC referendum (where the "yes" vote ending up winning), Wilson's government had given extraordinary powers to the trade unions. In 1976, the Labour Party printed its Annual Program, which pretty much laid the groundwork for transforming Great Britain into a Communist junkie. The right felt something needed to be done to protect the nation from the leftist threat. It could not be abandoned to the well-cushioned denizens in Parliament.

Ugly right-wing talk began a-brewing in the gentlemen's clubs of London, in particular the Reform Club – a favorite haunt of senior intelligence officers. In the same Gaming Club that Hugh frequented on Curzon Street, in the Mayfair Square Mile, Lord Lucan (later made famous when he murdered his children's nanny) preached to his friends about the better aspects of *Mein Kampf*.

The remnants of the pro-Hitler gentry from the Second World War silently joined forces with the organizing talents of the New Right and created new entities, ostensibly to "protect" Great Britain from socialism and communism: parapolitical, far-right groups, like the Freedom Association. Along with the parapolitical came the paramilitary. David Stirling, formerly a senior officer in the SAS, formed his own private army, GB75.

Extra-legal activity was condoned in the intelligence services.

And even the mainstream Conservative Party, in the form of its right-leaning faction the Monday Club, got into the action. Intelligence officers freely offered their views and advice at Monday Club meetings.

The frenzy eventually settled down into three lines of approach:

First, strenuous organizing activity on the right of the Conservative Party, to re-align it more aggressively against socialism – and Europe.

Second, aggressive moves by neo-political groups to actively counter socialism and break the stranglehold of trade unions.

Third, and much more discreetly, assistance from right-wing elements in the intelligence services: advice; illicit destablizing psychological operations in the political arena; and other more direct action.

It was no accident that Margaret Thatcher, the newly crowned darling of the Tory right, found herself surrounded in her ascent by many with intelligence connections: Airey Neave and Ian Gow, to name but two.

The right-wing truly believed itself to be at war with International Socialist Terror – just as much the UK and the US now perceive themselves to be in a War on Terror. And this attitude informed and infused everything that Margaret Thatcher did in her march to power – and then in her exercise of it.

It was a heyday for these right-wing groups.

***

And Hugh was heavily involved in most of them, as they organized against socialism, communism and Europe. Some of these were quite "safe," while others were way out on the fringe, as is made clear in the best narrative on the "loony right" and its allies in the '70s: a splendid book called *Smear! Wilson and the Secret State* by Stephen Dorril and Robin Ramsay.

Hugh even created a few groups of his own. The most successful was the Selsdon Group. (The name was a pointed reference to Edward Heath's previous nickname. Heath won the 1970 British general election running on a right-wing manifesto that emerged from a brainstorming session held at the Selsdon Park Hotel in the run-up to the election. He became known as "Selsdon Man" – at least until 1972 when he abandoned those policies lock, stock and barrel.)

Hugh was the founding treasurer of the Selsdon Group, which established itself as the primary guardian of right-wing libertarian laissez-faire free-market economic philosophy in the Conservative party throughout the '70s and '80s (and I know that my description will have certain purists up in arms). It was to a private meeting of Selsdon Group leaders that Margaret Thatcher first announced her intention to challenge Heath for the Leadership of the Conservative Party in 1975. It was also from this group that Thatcher drew early inspiration for her speeches – from Hugh, as well as from the likes of John O'Sullivan and Frank Johnson, well-known writers for London's *Daily Telegraph*.

Notwithstanding Heath's disastrous policies, the Tory party has always placed a premium on loyalty. Leaders chose to leave; they were not forced. And if it became necessary, finally, to "bend" a leader's ear, it was done quietly, by the "Grey Men." It was still considered heresy openly to challenge the sitting leader. But this is what Margaret Thatcher did in 1975, and she faced an uphill battle. It was for this reason that she relied so heavily on groups like those with which Hugh was involved – to provide her with the logistics necessary to challenge the Conservative Central Office power base, which was still under Heath's control.

First order of business for Margaret Thatcher after her election as Leader of the Conservative party was Europe. The Conservative party had suffered egregiously as a consequence of the bruising battle over Europe. A major effort would be needed to heal the wounds and move on. The party turned to Hugh, who recognized that this was his chance to enter the mainstream of the party. I was with him as he toiled day and night to rally the rag-tag bunch of Tory individuals and organizations who had fought valiantly against Europe. The message was simple: That fight is over; it's time to join forces, defeat the socialists and win the upcoming general and European elections. As far as the latter was concerned, it didn't matter whether you liked the European institution or not, if there were elective positions up for grabs, they needed to be filled with Conservative trousers.

The focal point for all this effort was a private meeting of the Conservative party's Central Council, and a heavily stage-managed "debate" on the issue of Europe and its elections. This debate was held in mid-1978. Hugh was slated to give the keynote speech. He and I worked on it for two weeks. The idea was that every major anti-Europe individual and organization would then take the podium and give their support to the consensus language that Hugh and I had crafted. Douglas (now Lord) Hurd, the leading Conservative pro-European, and the man chosen by Thatcher to expound the party's views on Europe publicly, would then offer a gracious closing speech. The device, although Soviet-like in its organization, was a complete success. Wounds closed, the party pulled together, the Tories won all of the British seats up for grabs in the European elections.

And the peace that Simmonds and Hurd had negotiated on Europe lasted until Margaret Thatcher was deposed as Prime Minister and leader of the Conservative party, in 1990.

***

Slap bang in the middle of all of this fascinating navel-gazing – it was about 1997 as I was putting together this history of Hugh – one of the more prominent former Monday Club members suddenly hit the headlines in the UK. One Gerald James, who was also reputedly involved with the Savoy Mafia, through his Chairmanship of Astra Holdings. Astra had been one of Britain's leading arms suppliers in the '80s, until it came under heavy Government investigation for alleged illegal arms sales.

Astra owned BMARC, which was accused of being deeply engaged in the supply of military technology to Iraq (and, with admirable lack of bias, to Iran, also). Astra had also bought PRB, a Belgium gunpowder manufacturer, from Société Générale Belgique, one of the largest companies in the world. Either Société or PRB, in turn, had a stake in Space Research Corporation, the corporate vehicle of the Canadian weapons scientist Gerald Bull.

James had finally had enough of being whipping boy for the sins of the Conservative party in the '80s, especially as they related to illicit arms activity, and he had decided to commit his version of events to paper. In the form of a headline-stirring book, *In the Public Interest*, a copy of which my sister Maggi sent me for my birthday.

James was brutal in his description of the arms backdoor operated on behalf of Margaret Thatcher and her Conservative government in the '80s. And in the process, provided the conclusive context for Hugh's activities and ultimate death, the search for which context had been the trigger for my own investigation in the first place.

CHAPTER FIFTEEN

Astra And Thatcher's Arms 'Backdoor'

G ERALD JAMES was a Chartered Accountant by profession. In the early '80s, he had become involved with Astra, a struggling company, which at that time was best known for making fireworks.

James was brought on board to turn the company around. Yet, he wasn't terribly interested in fireworks. What he saw was the opportunity offered by the fact that a fireworks company already possessed most of the work place conditions and licenses necessary to be an arms manufacturer. James was intent on fashioning Astra into one of Britain's leading defense contractors.

One of the first things I noticed about James was the similarity of his approach and Ari's in the writing of their books. They both told their stories in a disingenuous manner, which would have the reader constantly believe that the narrators were disinterested observers, standing by watching all this heavy stuff just happening around them. What they failed to share was the fact that, more often than not, they were the ones making it all happen.

I was aware of James' association with the active right in the '70s; and, in particular, his membership of The Monday Club. He made no secret of his delight in Thatcher's accession to the Leadership of the Conservative party, and then, to the office of prime minister. He seemed happy to be associated with all that he described as occurring within Astra. Until it all started blowing up in his face. Excuse the pun. But nevertheless, it gave me a fascinating perspective on the direction my thoughts were taking.

As Chairman, James built up Astra rapidly through the '80s, by way of acquisition of existing defense companies. Between 1986 and 1989, Astra was transformed from a small group specializing in fireworks and military pyrotechnics, with assets of $2 million and an annual turnover of $8.3 million, to an international manufacturer of armaments and ammunition and other defense related products, with net assets at March 31, 1989, of $78 million and an annual turnover of $142 million.

James focused particularly on explosives and ammunition companies, and that is why he bought the likes of PRB, the Belgian ammunition specialist, which was closely linked to Gerald Bull. Another company was BMARC, where he made Jonathan Aitken a director, at the latter's insistence. In his book, James is careful not to claim for himself all the credit for Astra's phenomenal growth. He had a lot of under-the-table help.

First, Thatcher's Government bent over backwards to supply him with all of the licenses and export credit guarantees that he needed. Even when the rules needed to be bent. Then, there was the active networking of the Savoy Mafia, rustling up contracts.

Finally, James found himself the newest member of another secretive arms network: The Parlor Club. This was a Europe-wide cabal of the heads of all of the major arms companies in Europe. They met on a regular basis to carve up arms deals around the world. No one saw any reason to lose out on mindless competition when there were enough goodies for everyone in the global arms' "gold rush" of the '80s.

In return for all of this lucrative "glad-handing" on behalf of Astra, all James had to do was play ball. And that meant looking the other way as the government used Astra to carry out its "backdoor" arms deals.

When Thatcher came to power, Britain ranked fairly low on the list of the world's exporters of arms. Thatcher was determined to see Britain move up that list. The two keys to this were continuity of supply and finance.

You sell the most arms to the people who use them, or who feel the most insecure. And these are generally dictators in the Third World, and the countries they have their eye on suppressing or invading. More often that not, since these entities are usually in a state of conflict, international arms' embargoes are in place, and the "boy scout" countries have to withdraw from supplying them.

In the '80s, under Thatcher, Britain sent out a message, loud and clear: we are open for business; all hours; whatever the conditions.

If an embargo is in place, just use the backdoor. And Astra became the primary "back door."

James describes in his book how Astra warehouses were regularly used as stopping off points for arms on their way to Iraq. He also confirms the cross-Atlantic arrangement, whereby companies, on both sides of the ocean, got around their own domestic restrictions on trading with the likes of Iraq and Iran, by using a subsidiary on the other side of the pond.

As for finance, and notwithstanding her much proclaimed disdain for public subsidy, Thatcher opened the government check book (associated with the Export Credit Guarantee Program) for the newly burgeoning arms industry. It was like a President Day's Sale at the pre-owned car lot, gone wild.

Thatcher tramped the world, drumming up arms business. There was no state visit too grand or pompous that could not wait while she hawked some wares on the side. Bad credit rating? No matter. No money? No problem. Bad payment history? Who cares. Not likely to be in power long? Let's throw you in a nice villa in exile.

The shakiest of arms deals were done. On the basis of commercial letters of credit, which everyone knew would never be honored. And all of which were underwritten by the government's Export Credit Guarantee program. The reason? Because Thatcher took the view that the expense was worth the investment in building up Britain's arms manufacturing base, its sales network, and its list of recurring clients.

James had done his figures. In the '80s, the revenues from the oil fields, discovered around Britain's shores in the '70s, finally came on tap for the government. To the tune of between $10 billion and $15 billion a year. James reckoned that, through the decade of the '80s, almost all of this money, each and every year, went down the tubes, on fulfilling Export Credit Guarantees that had gone sour. Some President's Day Sale.

Clever man James. Knew a lot. Perhaps too much? By the end of the '80s, Britain had secured its spot as the "Number Two" arms exporter world-wide. Just behind the United States. The two major clients of the '80s, Iran and Iraq, were no longer at war. It was time to "clean house."

That's when Astra's acquistion of PRB suddenly went sour. The next thing James knew, Astra was under investigation by the Department of Trade and Industry. The final report was so damning that Astra was closed down, and the component parts sold off.

Of course, being sold off didn't mean they stopped functioning; they just did it more quietly, under different ownership. But that was small comfort to James, because he was no longer the owner. He'd gone from practicing how to thank the Queen for his knighthood, to being an industry pariah – overnight.

He tried to talk to the media. But that did no good. James details in his book how one journalist, to whom he was feeding information, died in mysterious circumstances in a road accident.

Before cutting off contact with me, Kevin Cahill had passed on some of my information to Gerald James.

At the time, we exchanged a few telephone calls and letters. Gerald always sounded kind of distracted.

Gerald had immediately recalled Hugh, from their mutual membership of The Monday Club in the '70s. Gerald was not a part of what he described as "the Simmonds' Set." These were a group of hyperactive fanatics, who included intense, right-wing political types and intense, right-wing intelligence officers.

Gerald told me that he had always assumed that Hugh was one of an increasing number of young activists, who straddled the fence between intelligence and the Tory party, because of Hugh's close relationship with Bee Carthew, a veteran far-right activist and former wartime intelligence agent. Gerald also confirmed that he had, for the same reasons, naturally concluded that Hugh was himself an intelligence officer.

Gerald agreed with my feeling that I might best be able to track down what Hugh had been up to in the '80s by tracing forward from his contacts in the '70s. Gerald agreed to undertake some inquiries of his own, and then get back to me.

When he did, he was the most animated I recall him being. He confirmed that the trail involving Hugh all the way from the '70s was proving very fruitful. For starters, Gerald had found definite connections between Hugh, dickey arms matters and: Tiny Rowland, Lonrho and sanctions-busting in Africa in the '70s; a former Conservative Secretary of State for Defence; and a company called Anglo-Israeli Shipping. Like everyone I'd spoken to before (Ari, Simon, Keith, et al) once Gerald began looking closely at Hugh, he found connections to political arms money-laundering that had gone undetected before.

Gerald said that he didn't have time to explain further. He had more leads to follow and would be back in touch. He sounded quite energized, almost breathless. It was as if I had given him some sort of renewed hope for payback. But this was much about the same time that Kevin stopped communicating with me. And although I have tried from my end on a number of occasions since then, Gerald has never made contact with me again.

Before I even had opportunity to register disappointment, I came across an article in an English newspaper, which led me to believe that I may have discovered "the lawyer," with the shady Conservative connections, the mention of whom had caused Ari so much grief. And Haya to be so fearful. And it was very clear why Haya had been so scared.

CHAPTER SIXTEEN

UK as Covert Military Operative for US

THE ARTICLE IN QUESTION also put all of Gerald James' information into context. The article stated that a London solicitor, called Michael Rogers, had just been jailed for stealing a client's money. The client was Dodi Fayed. But that is not what had caught my attention.

The article described Rogers' plush offices in the Mayfair Square Mile; his business dealings with Mohammed al-Fayed [who had a townhouse just round the corner, on Park Lane]; his services for Robert Maxwell; his representation of a number of senior Tories, including Sir Gordon Reece, Margaret Thatcher's close adviser; and the fact that Rogers had acted for Jamshid Hashemi.

Apparently Sir Gordon had instructed Rogers to post bond for Hashemi, when the latter had first been arrested and charged with selling arms illegally to Iran. Sir Gordon was essentially Thatcher's hairdresser, speech coach, and "walker." He would not have dreamed of doing something like this unless it was at her specific direction.

Had I inadvertently uncovered Ari's "lawyer," and with him, discovered a major missing piece of the jigsaw puzzle?

***

But let's pause long enough to catch breath: We had a large number of the players in the '80s' arms game we have been describing all hanging around in the Mayfair Square Mile, and all seemingly connected to each other through a lawyer. Surely this was all too much simply to be a coincidence?

The one minor surprise, to be honest, was al-Fayed. I knew he had been involved with illicit arms dealing with the Saudi business-man Adnan Khashoggi, but I had not previously read of any direct link, either to the Iran arms deals of the '80s, or to Margaret Thatcher. I had been forced to focus on more indirect connections. I checked a few sources, and elicited two further *Observer* articles through the trusty Guardianlies.com website.

They described a secret trip in October 1984 by Margaret Thatcher's son, Mark, to see the Sultan of Brunei regarding a contract to build a £600 million university complex in Brunei. The articles contended that Mark Thatcher traveled to the oil-rich kingdom with Mohamed al-Fayed, on al-Fayed's private jet.

From the *Observer*, January 12, 1986:

"Mark Thatcher visited Brunei with Mohammed Fayed from 24-26 October 1984, traveling via Singapore on the Egyptian's private Gulf Stream jet. Their names appeared on the Royal Guest Immigration Register. The visit has also been confirmed to The Observer by a senior official of the Brunei Government.

"According to a report last week, Mark Thatcher was introduced to the Sultan of Brunei by a letter from the Finance Minister of Oman. It is believed that he was representing a Gulf construction company with an interest in a £600 million university complex in Brunei."

At the time of the trip, al-Fayed was competing with R.W. "Tiny" Rowland, Chief Executive of Lonrho, to take over the British department store group House of Fraser, which included Harrods. After the trip, the British government essentially locked Rowland out, allowing al-Fayed to buy House of Fraser.

The *Observer* article went on to say that Rowland "wrote furiously to the Prime Minister:"

"Why have you had anything whatsoever to do with Mohammed Fayed? ... We have a natural right to know why [the House of Fraser decision was made]. In contrast with Mohammed Fayed, Lonrho is a very large British company with 60,000 shareholders, against whose bid no good grounds of objection were ever made, but whose offer was put under restraints, which unbelievably were continued at the behest of your Minister, (Norman Tebbit), even after the clearance of the Monopolies Commission. The damage suffered by our company was devastating, when you gave this man, who boasted to me that he has never paid income tax anywhere in the world, what you denied to a long-established, international-ly known, public company which employs 150,000 people world-wide, and which has annually published its accounts for 75 years."

When Fayed made his £615 million bid for House of Fraser, it was unclear to many City observers who he was, or where he de-rived his funds.

The article also suggests al-Fayed may have obtained a good deal of his funds from the Sultan.

A followup article in the *Observer* (May 18, 1986) said that in January following Mark Thatcher's trip to Brunei, "The Sultan and Mohammed Fayed met Mrs. Thatcher at Downing Street. Brunei then transferred five billion dollars from the US to relieve the Brit-ish Sterling crisis.

"In April, Fayed arranged for Mrs. Thatcher to meet the Sultan at his sumptuous palace in Brunei."

***

So, all at once, we find al-Fayed in bed, not only with Mrs. Thatcher, but also with her son. Who was heavily engaged in both the Savoy Mafia, and all sorts of illicit arms dealing in the '80s. With coun-tries including the likes of Iraq. Plus, we have al-Fayed, through his lawyer, connected to many of the other players involved with arms sales to Iran in the early '80s. And with his main London town-house conveniently located just round the corner in Park Lane.

Is it safe to conclude that we now have a better understanding of how al-Fayed and Ari were able to know so much about what the Tories were up to in the '80s? And perhaps, more to the point, a clearer perception of how Ari knew what Hugh was doing? I found myself drifting off into one of those moods, where I saw new pat-terns emerging in the bigger scenario.

***

It's the beginning of the '80s. Everyone's in town, and in much the same place: the Mayfair Square Mile. Rogers is slap bang in the middle. The American Embassy is off to one side. Various US mer-cenaries, plus Les Aspin, and a bunch of others connected to SSG/CPPG or "The Enterprise," are staying a few streets along, in the

Portman Hotel. Al-Fayed is down the road, on Park Lane. Where you'll also find the main London branch of BCCI. And across the street is the Iranian Bank Melli.

A block or so away, all in a line, are London's famous gentlemen's clubs. Including the Reform Club. These clubs are not to be confused with the American version of "gentlemen's club:" there's just "Old Boys" in the London Clubs; not dirty-minded "Good 'Ol Boys." Over on the Thames is Tory headquarters. And just a tad downstream is the "Best Gentleman's Club in London," also known as Parliament. Meanwhile, we have Ari, Hugh, Maxwell, Oliver North, the Hashemi's and a few others popping in and out of the Mayfair Square Mile, all through this period.

It's all very cozy. Everyone knows everyone else. And everyone's in Swinging London to play "The Biggest Arms Game in Town." Namely, Iran. Heck. The Biggest Arms Game in the World, at least, in the early part of the '80s. Before it began also to include Iraq in earnest. And everyone's on the same team. Everyone's goal is identical: to sell as much military hardware as possible to Iran, and to make pot-loads of money.

First, it's the Israelis. Then, the Americans want to do their big "thank you" number to the Iranians, for the October Surprise. The Yanks get bitten by the money bug, and decide to get more permanently involved. Then, it's all about releasing hostages, cuddling up to Iran, and helping the Contras. It's all good stuff. No one minds. So long as the money remains good. Until 1984, and the first ripples of discord appear.

The Americans are getting a bit itchy about the Israelis. The Iranians don't mind the Israelis too much, until they start beating up on their Shiite Muslim brothers in Hezbollah, in Lebanon. And then, the Americans start having their own problems in Lebanon with Muslims; what with hostages and exploding Marine Barracks, and all. So, the Americans decide to back off using the Israelis as partners – just for a while.

The Israelis are a little miffed. But they shrug their shoulders. They're going to do their own thing anyway. But then, the Americans develop even more problems. Congress is getting antsy. Enforcing oversight. Wants to know what's going on. Oh no! The '70s all over again. So, the Yanks need a surrogate to pick up the slack. Hello. Enter the British.

Now, Margaret and company have been doing their own thing, getting the British economy back in order, and trying to expand their domestic military machine. They have wonderful six-month "Arms Fair" in 1982, known to the rest of the world as "The Falklands War." But they are now looking for other opportunities. Why? Ah. Good question.

**

The socialists had pretty much left the UK bankrupt at the end of the '70s. Industry had been destroyed by nationalization and by giving the trade unions too much power. Those companies that were still in private hands had been crippled by taxation and over-subsidy, which left them unproductive and uncompetitive.

The economy had stalled. Income from taxation was way down. Public expenditure, particularly that for dramatically increasing unemployment, was off the meter. So too was inflation. The deficit was so large, no commercial bank would lend the government any more money. The Labour Chancellor of the Exchequer had had to stand in line, cap in hand, behind Third World countries, to get loans from the International Monetary Fund.

Everything and everyone in Great Britain had run out of money. The country, the people, the trades unions, the economy, the government, the military and the intelligence services. Maggie and her troupe were doing what they could. They were cutting public spending; getting inflation under control; de-regulating left, right, and center; and removing the unhealthy support structure for British industry. In due course, the deficit would disappear; taxes would be cut; and the new "enterprise economy" would be in place. But in the meantime, what little was left of the manufacturing base was collapsing.

British industry had been so weakened by the socialists that, when the support structures were removed, it wasn't strong enough to step up to the plate, and compete with the rest of the world. That is why Maggie was hell bent on building up the arms industry. To have something to replace the lost manufacturing base. And the Falklands War had allowed Great Britain to showcase the full range of weaponry and military technology it had to sell. But Britain needed ongoing showcases, and it required money for its own military. Plus, the intelligence services needed

165

money. And the Tory party wasn't going to say no to a dollar or two, either.

So. Maggie Thatcher hit on the idea of pimping out Great Britain Ltd. to America. Or more specifically, to her best mate, Ronald Reagan, his Vice President George Bush, and his SSG/CPPG. Lock, stock and barrel. In the '80s, Britain became the global surrogate for America's military and intelligence adventures. Wherever and whenever the price was right.

All of a sudden, Bush and his SSG/CPPG were being forced by Congressional oversight to be a little more circumspect about their covert, and often illicit, global activities. So, they asked the British to step in. And the British were happy to comply. Whether it was arms deals, military action, intelligence gathering, or a bit of covert operation, it didn't matter. Whatever was needed, the British were there. Provided the price was right. And assuming there was a little something for the Tory party to put in its own back pocket.

John Loftus and Mark Aarons in their book *The Secret War Against the Jews* describe how Britain, its special forces and its intelligence services were much more involved in the '80s in Lebanon, Central America, and Iran than anyone had previously known. And slap bang in the middle of all the plotting we find our old friend Les Aspin.

Another problem that the Americans had was with assassination. There had been, since the purges of the '70s, a presidential prohibition on American-sponsored assassination. Simple, the British did it instead. In Lebanon and Afghanistan, among other places.

For centuries, Afghanistan, and its fabled Khyber Pass, had been seen as "The Gateway" between the Middle East and the rest of Asia. Wielding influence in that country had become all important in the power struggles in the region, power plays that had been given the glorified title of "The Great Game." The British, the Russians, the Turks had all fought over this stretch of land in the centuries leading up to the First World War. The military chess game had become the stuff of romance and legend, memorably captured in the writings of British author Rudyard Kipling.

In the 20th Century, and into the 21st, Afghanistan once again became a focal point for military conflict. In 1979, the Soviet Union invaded Afghanistan, and placed a 100,000-man army of occupation within its borders. Carter and then Reagan were none too happy, but were prevented by Congress from direct interference in Afghanistan itself. The CIA had to comfort itself with setting up training bases for the anti-Soviet Muslim mujahideen in Pakistan.

Eventually, the Soviets had had enough, and in 1989, they withdrew, leaving the country to the Muslim mujahideen.

What was not generally known was the extent of the hands-on British role in the anti-Soviet effort; a role which played no small part in eventually persuading the Soviets to withdraw from Afghanistan. In his book, *Charlie Wilson's War*, George Crile continues the tradition of romantic writing about the ongoing military struggles in Afghanistan, with his lush descriptions of the heroic exploits of Texas Congressman Charles Wilson in aiding the Muslim mujahideen. Wilson was a major factor in ensuring that the program of support for the Muslim mujahideen became the single largest military support operation ever undertaken by the CIA.

Crile describes the extraordinary spectacle of the CIA joining forces with the Israelis to provide weaponry to both Muslim Pakistan and the Muslim mujahideen, in order to fight the Soviets, whom the CIA and the Israelis clearly regarded at that time as a greater threat than Islamic radicals.

However, due to the restrictions imposed by congressional oversight, the US effort was limited only to support. They could not assist the Muslim mujahideen within the borders of Afghanistan. But the British, with their long tradition of involvement in this area, most certainly could. And did. For the right price.

As a first move, Britain stepped in with its own efforts to provide the Muslim mujahideen with arms and ammunition. The British arms pipeline began with deals in Marbella, and a supply line that meandered back through Palestinian quartermasters in Yugoslavia and Czechoslovakia.

More important than mere support, British special forces and their intelligence counterparts were able to run amok in the mountains of Afghanistan. Something the Americans and the Israelis could not do. And run amok the British most certainly did.

They secured supply lines deep into Soviet-held territory. They lent invaluable assistance to the Muslim mujahideen in the efforts of the latter to harry the Soviets with bombings and rocket attacks. And there being no British prohibition on assassination, they proved themselves none too squeamish about taking out the odd dozen Soviets or so while they happened to be on the scene.

In addition to the "official" government interventions of the Americans and the British, a plethora of private "aid" agencies, think tanks and other odd-bod outfits joined the fray, with the ostensible aim of helping the Afghans to liberate their nation from the clutches of the Soviet invaders.

It was the usual story: nice looking humanitarian organization up front; donations going to buy weapons and ammunition by the backdoor, when no-one was looking.

Hugh had ties to two of these groups: Afghan Aid (UK) and Radio Free Kabul of London.

Afghan Aid was set up by Romy Fullerton in Peshawar, Pakistan, where the main Muslim mujahideen camps were. The main sponsor and funder was Viscount Cranbourne, who also represented a UK Parliamentary Constituency in the same Wessex Area of which Hugh was the Conservative Party Treasurer.

Radio Free Kabul was formed almost immediately after the Soviet invasion of Afghanistan by Lord Nicholas Bethell, a former Lord-in-Waiting to Queen Elizabeth II. A career British intelligence official, with a specialization in Iranian and Arab affairs, Lord Bethell had served in the Middle East and Soviet sections of MI6. In 1981, Lord Bethell accompanied Margaret Thatcher on a tour of the United States, dedicated to drumming up support for the mujahideen. Thatcher and Lord Bethell met more than 60 Congressmen and Senators and aided in organizing the Committee for a Free Afghanistan, the de facto US arm of Radio Free Kabul.

One of the members of the Board of Radio Free Kabul was Ray Whitney, OBE. Ray was a former British Intelligence official who had for years run the disinformation operations unit of the Foreign Office, the Information Research Department. I had served on the campaign to get Ray elected as Conservative MP for High Wycombe in the important by-election of 1977. So had Hugh. No wonder the two of them had been so friendly.

This new role of Great Britain Ltd., as global surrogate for the Great Satan, became pretty much fixed in stone during the '80s. The money was simply too good. One unfortunate consequence of this corruption was that Britain became firmly established, not only as a troubleshooter for American "state terror," but also as an unofficial "Offshore Trading Haven for all Global Terror," both state and factional.

Great Britain was still an open society, with ease of entry and exit; no restriction on movement; relative freedom of speech and political assembly; and the ability to raise and move funds quickly and without the interference of international exchange controls. London in particular had, over the years, become a "safe haven" for political refugees. However, as we have seen, with the political often came the paramilitary.

Whereas in the past, the British security services might have sought to crack down on any nascent paramilitary activity and its proponents, now they either turned a blind eye, or even worse, actively encouraged it.

On the one hand, there was money to be made acting as a trading exchange for all the needs of the modern terrorist or freedom fighter. On the other hand, with its own nefarious activities around the world on behalf of the Americans, the British security services sometimes needed their own "surrogates." And a readily available cesspool of fully-equipped "pirates" made for a useful pool of talent.

Beyond this, since London already had the commodities and financial expertise to be one of the world's leading exchange centers for everything from oil to foreign exchange to stocks and shares, why not for terror also? This was the '80s. Money was king. Nothing else mattered.

The upshot was that the very country the Tories were entrusted with protecting was transformed into a global quartermaster to all manner of wider terror networks, countries and factions: from the likes of "The Enterprise" and the "International Terror Network," to Osama bin Laden, al-Qaeda, and Saddam Hussein. London became and remains an international bazaar for mercenaries, terrorists, pariah regimes and nascent coups d'etat. You need a government overthrown, a ship hijacked, an illegal arms deal negotiated, London is the place to get your "business" organized and financed.

Another and in many ways sadder consequence was that, with the very best of intentions, namely saving the economy of Great Britain Ltd., and ostensibly to protect a society that had a glorious tradition of not needing the same rules (such as a written constitution) as other less secure nations, Margaret Thatcher made scrap-paper of the few rules that did still apply in Great Britain.

She was so assiduous in behaving as if the normal rules of conduct did not apply to her and her government, that she made a mockery of the very rule of law, which she so vocally championed.

As a result, she effectively turned Great Britain into a country, which has become lawless in its activities at the highest level.

***

Meanwhile, back in 1984, Britain was only just beginning its role as America's new global surrogate. And the Israelis, who were feeling a tad the jilted lover, were none too happy. But they pretty much kept it under their hat, and got on with their own arms-supplying and money-making ventures. Sometimes in competition with the British, and sometimes not.

"The Team," in the Mayfair Square Mile, was essentially still working together helping Iran, because Iraq continued to have the upper hand in its fight with Iran, and because everyone needed Iran's help to free their hostages in Lebanon.

True, one or two parties had begun the process of playing both sides, and were now supplying Iraq as well as Iran with military equipment and technology. But that was because the money was good. And the Israelis didn't seem to mind all that much – at least, not at that point.

Indeed, the Israelis appeared to be quite happy teaming up with the Christian Lebanese militias, in order to give a bloody nose to Hezbollah and the other Muslim Lebanese militias. And everyone knew that the other primary benefactor of the Lebanese Christians was none other than Iraq. So, strange bedfellows all round.

On the home front, it being 1984, Hugh was still smarting from his temporary political setback – his deselection as Conservative candidate for the safe Conservative parliamentary seat of South West Cambridge – and was starting to hurt for money. He'd wound down his law practice in anticipation of being an MP. It was at this time, according to John Simmonds and Hugh's mistress Karen George, that Hugh became involved in complex arms dealing for Margaret Thatcher.

So, there was a slight ripple in the water, but overall, nothing too terrible. Until 1987.

***

By then, Iran was beginning to win its war with Iraq. Iran was hurling millions of its youngsters against the border with Iraq, in the hope that sheer numbers would overwhelm its mortal enemy. The fanatic Shiite Muslim leadership in Iran showed no signs of moderating its stance or its strategy, notwithstanding attempts to put a more secular face on its radicalism. The last thing the West wanted was that same leadership in control of Iraq's oil reserves. While at the same time sitting perched ready to strike on the border of yet more oil reserves in Saudi Arabia.

The US had seen the percentage of its oil imports from Iraq increase from single digits in the early '80s to very nearly 25 percent by 1987. Plus everyone had become terminally tired of the hostage-taking by Iran's surrogates in Lebanon. Plus Iraq was becoming a better customer than Iran for arms. Which translated into more money. Plus Iraq was not making as much headway with its own domestic military industry as it would like, and so its hunger for military technology seemed to be insatiable. Plus Iraq was just beginning to get serious about using its WMDs to stop the Iranian Tide; and WMDs, not withstanding their illegality, were a definite money-spinner. Plus … well … any one of a dozen other inexcusable but highly remunerative, reasons the arms industry in the West cared to come up with. And so began the famous US-UK "tilt" in both government policy and arms sales towards Iraq.

At which point, the Israelis cracked. From their own experience over the decades, Iraq had always proven to be more of a threat to them than Iran. Plus, the Israelis weren't selling any weapons to Iraq, so a "tilt" towards Iraq didn't do them any good. On this occasion, the Israelis did more than just blow off steam.

Ari, who was by now the Counter-Terrorism Adviser to Yitzhak Shamir, the Israeli Prime Minister, was instructed to do whatever was necessary to put a plug in the now-burgeoning Iraqi arms pipeline. As luck would have it, Ari was in the perfect position to plug the Iraq "game," because: he knew all the players and where to find them; he knew what they were doing, and he knew how to "get" to them. After all, he'd spent the best part of the '80s "playing" the Iran game with them, in London's Mayfair Square Mile.

Ari knew about Maxwell in Eastern Europe. He knew about the Tories. He knew about Hugh. There was al-Fayed slicing up the Tories. And Ari was working during the period of time when Hugh, most likely under pressure, began to steal money from his Clients' Account.

We already know that the Israelis had become agitated with the British for supplanting them as America's favorite surrogate. Did this encourage Ari and his "friends" to set about their task with an extra degree of relish? Did this cause the British to retaliate? Did the British know about the Maxwell-monitored CIA and Likud arms funds in Eastern Europe? Did they know about them through Hugh? Had Hugh helped to set them up? Was Hugh using the same channels to funnel money to Bulgaria and Yugoslavia?

Was Maxwell asked by British Intelligence to mess with those funds in his care? Was he then double-crossed by the CIA? Or murdered by Mossad? Or was Hugh instructed by British intelligence to mess with the funds? Was he told to steal the funds, or some part of them? Did he, perhaps, just steal some part of them for himself?

Did this aggravate the Israelis even more? Or the CIA? Was this why Reggie was so fearful of the CIA? Did this give rise to the somewhat esoteric "alliances," that Reggie had so cryptically referred to as operating in Eastern Europe, in the immediate aftermath of the collapse of Communism in that region?

Did Ari, the Israelis, the CIA, even the Knights of Malta, or, indeed, all four retaliate in kind against Hugh? Was that the cause of the increased pressure on Hugh in the summer of 1988? Or did British intelligence discover that Hugh was two-timing them, and were they the ones applying the pressure to Hugh?

Am I getting the most amazing migraine? Are you? Sigh.

***

Whatever the case, the next important period was the summer of 1988. The Iranians and the Iraqis declared a ceasefire. The arms pipeline to the Iranians pretty much dried up overnight. But not so the pipeline to the Iraqis. All of the arguments for its original expansion in 1987 now held true for its continuation past 1988.

This went beyond the pale for the Israelis, who raised the stakes to new heights. This was when they started sending assassination squads into Western Europe and Great Britain. And on the subject of killing, there was one thing on which the superiors of all of the former Iran arms game players were agreed – it was time to "clean house."

Senior players from the US, Israel and Britain died in mysterious circumstances, were imprisoned, or were discredited in other ways. Ari went to prison in America for a while. Oliver North and company were convicted and then pardoned. Gerald James lost his company and his Knighthood. And Hugh turned up gassed in a small car near his and my home town in England.

I felt once again a question nagging at the back of my mind. Something out of place. And once again, it was at first too faint for me to hear.

What I heard much more clearly were searing questions I had for Reggie and Ari concerning Hugh's role in my Thatcher arms scenario. I didn't care if they didn't want to speak to me. I wanted some answers from them. Perhaps it was my anger that encouraged them? Or perhaps I was beginning to strike a little too close to home? In any event, on this occasion, they both had much more to contribute on what exactly had been Hugh's precise role in my arms scenario. And how that role had also sealed his fate.

CHAPTER SEVENTEEN

Maggie's Hammer

I N 1991, I BOUGHT a book called *Open Verdict*, written by Tony Collins, a former Editor of Britain's *Computer News* magazine.

It detailed the mysterious deaths between 1982 and 1988 of a long list of low-level employees, who had been associated with British defense contractors, especially in the field of US defense electronics and particularly associated with Marconi, which was later bought by GEC (UK).

Collins came up with a hypothesis, which I slightly adapted, in light of what I had been learning. What if the CIA or others had defense-related projects that they wished to keep "invisible" from congressional oversight? What if the British government, in pursuit of its newfound role as global surrogate-for-hire to America, agreed to piggy-back these "black" projects onto legitimate and "visible" British "Star Wars" projects?

The scientists working on the black projects, and the administrative staff rendering them support, would be unaware of anything untoward. Indeed, perhaps to lend even greater cover to the projects' invisibility, maybe the British Government dispensed with the need for staff working on the black projects to sign the UK Official Secrets Act (standard practice for all staff working on sensitive matters – to prevent an Edward Snowden)?

A problem then would be you couldn't tell the staff not to talk about what they'd been handling. While, at the same time, you couldn't have them wandering down to the local pub and gabbing, because you didn't know what media or foreign intelligence services might be staked out there, to pick up precisely those sorts of morsels. So, you needed to "clean house," without it looking like "house-cleaning." And you needed someone deep, dark, and secret to do the cleaning. There were episodes in *Open Verdict*, concerning deaths in Bristol in 1986, which disturbed me. I remembered that in 1986 Hugh and I had traveled to Bristol, ostensibly to attend some esoteric regional Conservative Conference. The thing was that we'd never attended regional conferences before. They were a waste of time. But we did spend a lot of time on Clifton Suspension Bridge, from which one of those who later died would "fall." And Hugh had sent me back to the office on my own a day early.

As eerie as this was, it was nothing compared to the chills that danced a merry tattoo up and down my spine when I read the next few passages:

In the case of the "lady in the lake," as it became known, the shortfall of forensic evidence was not only conspicuous, it was embarrassing. The search for the woman's murderer seemed to get little further than a dispute between the family and the authorities over whether indeed she was murdered. Her death occurred on the night of Good Friday, April 17, 1987. It was an Easter bank holiday weekend and, for Thames Valley Police, the beginning of what had seemed at first to be a routine murder investigation. It was an inquiry which would end inconclusively six months later, leaving behind a series of unanswered questions over not only the death but the direction of the subsequent investigation.

Early on the evening of Saturday, April 18, 1987, physiotherapist Marjorie Arnold, out walking her Alsatian dog, saw the body of a woman lying near the edge of Taplow Lake, a popular sailing and fishing spot close to the homes of celebrities such as Terry Wogan, Michael Parkinson, Ernie Wise, and Frank Bough [and about an hour's drive from Hugh's home]. It was also 150 yards from a manned police checkpoint on the A4. [Highway route in UK from London to Bristol.]

Mrs. Arnold stopped a motorist and together they pulled the body ashore. The dead woman seemed about 20 years old and was wearing blue jeans, a red T-shirt and a quilted, sleeveless jacket. She had been gagged with a blue scarf, a noose was tied around her neck, her ankles were secured with a tow rope and her wrists were tied behind her back. She had been face down in eighteen inches of water for an indeterminate period.

Shani Warren's seemingly immaculate black Vauxhall Cavalier car was found parked in the lay-by adjoining the lake. It was later found to have a faulty gearbox which prevented it being driven away in first or second gear. Some of the car's contents were strewn around the grass, as if someone had been looking for something. Her handbag and some keys were missing.

Within a day of the body's discovery a high-ranking police officer spoke of suicide. Six months later that view was officially confirmed. A pathologist employed by the Home Office declared that Shani had tried to strangle herself, gagged herself, bound her ankles, tied her hands behind her back and hopped in stiletto heels into the shallow water where she drowned…

Against a background of the family's vociferous rejections of the suicide theory, a noticeable lack of evidence, and a growing disbelief among the public that Shani had killed herself, the police went on the BBC television program "Crimewatch" and announced that they were treating the case as murder and to make an appeal for witnesses…

The police's attitude to the whole investigation was curious. It did not take a person of exceptional perception to notice that they had no overwhelming desire to find a murderer. For example as soon as "Crimewatch" had finished, a reporter rang one of the numbers given and asked for further details of Shani's car. The reporter did not identify himself and, as far as the police were concerned, could have been an eyewitness.

A policewoman answered the telephone politely, listened to the question, went away to find the answer and returned within two minutes with the information. After this there was an embarrassing silence while the reporter waited for the policewoman to ask why the information was being sought, who was seeking it and whether the caller had information about the murder…

The BBC said that after its "Crimewatch" program 100 viewers rang with possible leads. One was certain she saw Shani in the lay-by and also remembered seeing a well-dressed man and another car, possibly green, perhaps a BMW…

But Mrs. Elsie Warren told the South Buckinghamshire coroner, John Roberts [who also acted as coroner for Hugh's death, the following year], that Shani had never shown any sign of contemplating death…

The only person believed to have seen a woman resembling Shani's description at the lakeside on Good Friday evening was nursing sister Mrs. Sandra Organ from Kettering, Northamptonshire, who had responded to the police appeal on "Crimewatch." She said her daughter had called "hello" to a woman carrying dustbin liners. She said the woman turned, smiled and waved to them.

Mrs. Organ noticed a well-dressed man about 200 yards away. "There was a man standing looking on, wearing a smart suit," she said. "He was in his late 30s or early 40s." She said the man had been driving an expensive dark green car – probably a BMW. Police have been unable to trace the man or the car.

***

Hugh bought for himself a limited edition, dark green BMW 6 Series Mark M in 1985.

After reading this book, I went down to a very large BMW distributor in Slough. I saw a standard BMW 6 series sedan – about the only model of BMW which, at that time, a passing onlooker would have reasonably described as "expensive," as in possibly large and "expensive." The sedans were painted a rather dusty green color. Hardly a color that would stand out.

I then asked to see photographs of the 6 Series Mark M. This was the limited edition sports coupe version of the 6 series, sufficiently "limited" that they did not have a model hanging around in their showroom. As I recalled, the coupe had severely more distinctive lines and was painted a much darker, and more noticeable green, than the sedan.

The salesman confirmed that the limited edition coupe had come out only in the middle of the '80s. And that only a handful had been sold each year in the whole of southern England. Which conformed with my recollection of why Hugh had bought one in 1985: because he was a show-off, and he wanted to have one of the first of a model that few other people would be driving.

It occurred to me that my "detective" work had not taken all that much effort. And that if the police had been truly interested in finding "the car" back in 1987, then it should not have taken them long to link the "expensive dark green...BMW" to a very limited ownership of "expensive dark green...BMW" 6 Series Mark Ms.

And that showing photographs of the limited number of owners to the likes of nursing sister Mrs. Sandra Organ may have elicited the information that the "well-dressed" man "wearing a smart suit," and "in his late 30s or early 40s," was indeed Hugh Simmonds, former Mayor of a town just seven miles away, who was rarely seen in other than a tailored three-piece suit, and who celebrated his 40th birthday the following year, the same year in which he himself died in mysterious circumstances.

***

I hadn't forgotten that Reggie had told me that he didn't want to talk about Hugh's clandestine activities any more, but I needed some answers to this one. Reggie was all charm as he answered the telephone. He had a new girlfriend. He'd also had his own problems because the girlfriend's previous boyfriend had become a little jealous, setting fire to Reggie's car, and causing the whole affair to make the front pages of the nation's tabloids. There were many such times when I seriously wondered if I was conducting an investigation, or had merely become a bystander in a particularly zany reality show. Reggie's gurgling and gushing came to an abrupt halt as I read to him the above passages. After some moments of silence, he sighed deeply, and in a very quiet voice said, "Geoff, your mate was trained to kill. That's what he did."

Reggie then lightened the mood a hair's breadth by adding, "Of course, the bugger would never listen to me when I told him that he had to be inconspicuous. Not everyone, I told him, not everyone wears bloody three-piece suits when they do this sort of thing. It will be your downfall. I did warn him..."

Had it been Hugh's downfall? Had he been inconspicuous just once too often for his "masters" any longer to entertain?

Reggie then reminded me of an episode that I had told him about when we had been together at the RAC Club in Glasgow. I had completely forgotten the incident. It had been in about 1978, when I was living on my own in a ground-floor apartment in Beaconsfield.

Hugh had come banging on the door at about 3 o'clock in the morning. He looked awful: pale, ashen, and shaking. This was not your usual Hugh. He made straight for the Scotch bottle; I can't remember that he even bothered with a glass. I asked him what was wrong. He didn't reply until he'd had a hefty swig or two of the amber.

Then, he looked at me a moment before speaking. His eyes were watery and out of focus. "There is no James Bond," he said very quietly, with a voice as dead as I'd ever heard, "there's no one fancy out there, wandering around, with a license to do whatever the hell he wants. It's all very bureaucratic. Very British. Something goes wrong, and someone has to be bumped off, then there's someone 'senior' on the scene to give the 'OK.' That's my job. Except this evening it all went wrong. And I had to do it myself. That's now my job, too." And then he'd got up, and gone home.

I hadn't thought much about the episode at the time. Just put it down to Hugh's overactive hyperbole. In fact, I'd felt nervous even telling Reggie about it in Glasgow. Particularly, when his only reaction then had been to look embarrassed. The reason for that embarrassment was now much more clear.

Was it the case that, in the '80s, while Thatcher was pimping out Great Britain Ltd. to America as its military and intelligence whore, Hugh had been acting as whore for the whore?

Was that the role for which he had been enrolled by Thatcher back in 1984? Someone in the right place at the wrong time? Someone known personally to Thatcher; someone with a desperate desire to get somewhere fast; someone at loose ends; someone with all the right contacts and background; someone who could be trusted to stay quiet; someone who could straddle all the interfaces and act as both a political and intelligence troubleshooter? And most important of all, someone who, at the end of the day, was eminently deniable and expendable? Because it would be too easy for folks to believe that vainglorious, ambitious, grandstanding, corner-cutting, reckless Hugh had turned victory into defeat just once too often?

Was it indeed the case that Hugh had never been acting on his own, as some kind of "rogue operative"? But rather that he was very much the "insider"? One of the most closely held secrets? A "dirty tricks meister," acting for and available to any one of the entities then building the new Great Britain Ltd.? To do the "dirty work" that no one else wanted to do? Acting for the Conservative party. And its government? For the military? For defense contractors? For the intelligence services? For the Savoy Mafia?

Whatever "Dirty Little Job" needed doing? Arranging a highly secret arms deal? The one that led to Margaret Thatcher's very private bank account? Her very own "retirement fund"? The one deal, the one money trail that no one could ever be allowed to find? A little money-laundering here? Looking after the boy Mark there? Taking care of Tory kickbacks everywhere else? Or Maxwell's slush funds? In Eastern Europe? Yugoslavia? And Bulgaria?

The final twist was that, before he went "offline," Kevin Cahill had remarked, in a moment that re-defined "coincidence," that he knew *Open Verdict* author Tony Collins personally. Kevin had been the Deputy Editor of *Computer News* back in the '80s, when it had first commissioned Tony Collins to pursue the story of the strange defense-related deaths. The last thing Kevin had promised was that he would put Tony in touch with me. And then Kevin had gone "off the air."

And in the context of *Open Verdict*, I couldn't help but wonder if Hugh's dirty tricks in the '80s might have included cleaning house, not so much to protect national security any more, as much as to protect other peoples' dirty little secrets? And that maybe, in a final twist of irony, Hugh himself had simply been "cleaned" away? In which regard, it was difficult not to notice that the last defense contractor employee mentioned in *Open Verdict* had died in September 1988. Two months before Hugh was found dead. The two of them in almost identical circumstances – gassed in their own cars in a local beauty spot.

I ran all of this by Ari.

***

Ari's initial reaction was the same as Reggie's. He went very quiet for some moments. Then his old sing-song voice was back. But slower and more deliberate than usual. Almost as if Ari were choosing his words carefully. For the benefit of someone leaning over his shoulder. Listening. Figuratively speaking – of course.

"Ah, the '80s," Ari exhaled gently, "you know, when you get to the end of a period like that, you often have "dirty laundry," that you need to clean up. I was dirty laundry for a while. That's why I was in jail. But then, I had some friends..."

He paused for a moment. As if looking for the right word. "Your friend," Ari continued at last, "had run out of 'friends.' He'd pissed off too many people. He was trying to please too many people at the same time. Plus, he'd got greedy. And he knew too much. It doesn't serve any purpose to talk about who might have wanted him dead. Or, did he die this way, or that way. He was simply on too many peoples' Dirty Laundry lists. He was going to have to go, sooner or later. One way or another."

***

So, at the conclusion of the '90s, facing the onset of a new millennium, I was looking back at the closing stages of the '80s, and this is where I appeared to be:

Margaret Thatcher and the Tories had inherited a country that was bankrupt. Their solution had been to turn the country into Great Britain Ltd., transforming its industrial base into an export-driven military-technology powerhouse.

Continuity of export sales required an illegitimate but officially-sanctioned "back-door," which in turn needed money to keep the hinges greased, and a "doorman" to arrange that money, clear away any human problems, and generally be responsible for keeping that back-door open.

We weren't just talking about the odd grand or two, every couple of years. The back-door would only stay open – over a period of time and through changes in Government administration – if both the civil service and the political establishment were systemically, hugely, and regularly corrupted.

It was appreciated that arms commissions and profits, on their own, might not be sufficient to maintain that systemic corruption. So, the Tories set up "piggy banks," in a variety of offshore accounts, which could be dipped into by senior and trusted individuals during dry periods, when the arms business was slow. The setting-up and the maintenance of these piggy banks were essential elements of the job description of that same doorman. That doorman, or doormen, needed to have the right skills, the right political and intelligence connections, and the right attitude – let's not get squeamish now, I mean a "killer" instinct. But more than this, the individuals needed to be utterly trustworthy and eminently expendable.

Enter Hugh: the dirty tricks meister. The guy who kept the arms back-door open for Margaret Thatcher. Her very own doorman. But it wasn't just the arms back-door that needed looking after. An unfortunate consequence of the systemic corruption was that

Great Britain Ltd. also became the offshore trading haven for the world's terror activity. It was inevitable. You could hardly ask law enforcement to interfere, but there had to be some measure of control and so it fell to the doormen to keep some semblance of order.

Meanwhile, with all this lolly floating around, free from public gaze, why shouldn't those responsible make some money on the side? Including politicians. Including Margaret Thatcher. Safely tucked away in those Swiss bank accounts. The ones holding some $300 million. All it required was someone trustworthy. Who could set up an invisible pipeline. Via an individual no one would suspect – Mark Thatcher. Someone who could ultimately be denied. As Hugh has been. Someone who ultimately would not be missed when he died. Before his time. In mysterious circumstances.

What caused Hugh's death? Clearly, something went wrong. Maybe he got too greedy? Maybe he was double-crossed? Maybe he had too many fingers in too many pies? Or maybe it was just time to clean house? And he was too dangerous to leave alive? What I can say is that I believe that, as with Margaret Thatcher, Hugh became involved, not just for the money, but because he too believed his activities were for a "higher purpose."

***

OK. Great adventure. But what do we actually know? Well. We know that Hugh died, in mysterious circumstances. And that before his death, he stole at least £5 million from his clients. We know that Carratu found at least £10 million more, which Hugh had been laundering for other individuals or entities. And that Geoff Hughes later intimated that the laundered amount could have been as much as £100 million. All of which kind of blows a hole in the official version, which was that Hugh stole the money for himself, spent it, and then took the coward's way out. Clearly, we need to find another explanation – along with some folks missing £100 million and loose change.

What do we find, as we wander the world asking pointed questions of the wrong people? We find Reggie, telling us that Hugh was MI6; was before his death engaged in some sort of intelligence-associated operation, which somehow involved the stolen money; where some associates took a dim view of Hugh and what he was doing, and somehow rendered the operation inoperable; thereby necessitating an exit by Hugh. It looks like Hugh may have considered a runner. Was possibly dissuaded by threats to his family. And so, took his own life (maybe). Without leaving any incriminating information, which might have brought retaliation down upon his family. Which absence of info also left a whole bunch of money unavailable to a whole bunch of people who were none too happy about it – and who thought I knew where it was (and is).

We find Ari, bouncing back and forth with his different explanations as to how Hugh died, the conflicting nature of which explanations most probably arose from the fact that Ari had had a hand in Hugh's death. But nonetheless sharing with us the fact that Hugh, through the combination of his unique qualities (MI6, senior Conservative, money-launderer, and close ally of Margaret Thatcher), was ideally placed to become a member of an elite group around Thatcher, who arranged illegal arms deals, and then laundered the illicit profits and commissions back to senior figures in the Conservative party.

In this regard, we have Ari telling us that Hugh was arranging a deal to sell GEC (UK) engines to Iraq, a deal confirmed by the gentleman responsible for its financing, Christopher Drogoul, former manager of the Atlanta branch of BNL. We have Ari confirming that Hugh was in business with Mark Thatcher, and that Hugh had been chosen to mind the money trail to Mark, so that the poor clod wouldn't lose the money, expose it, or spend it on overpriced candy. And we have Ari describing a series of money transfers from Hugh to Mark, between 1984 and 1988, totaling some £8 million – one key component of the invisible money trail to the Thatchers, which trail had previously eluded journalists, law enforcement agencies, and intelligence operations alike.

We have Simon Regan and Kevin Cahill providing another key component. Namely, their confirmation that they were in possession of evidence of the money trail from Mark to Margaret. Together with knowledge of bank accounts in Switzerland in the name of Margaret Thatcher and containing some £200 million, much of it coming from illicit arms dealing.

Finally, we have Ari and Gerald James making the point that troublesome loose ends were eliminated. We have Reggie telling us that Hugh was trained to kill. And we have strong circumstantial evidence of Hugh's presence at the scene of at least one such elimination. Suggesting that Hugh's usefulness to Margaret Thatcher and her "elite group" extended well beyond babysitting and money-laundering.

Fine. So if we have all of this, why was Margaret Thatcher never prosecuted? Well, as the old saying goes: knowing something isn't the same as being able to prove it. The proof was always Hugh. Who was not using his own name, according to Ari. Who generally kept most information in his head (that one's from my own knowledge). And most importantly, was dead. Indeed, as I have set out the facts time and again, all manner of involved parties have checked their own data and readily confirmed that, well blimey, Hugh fit the bill. But it ain't proof. And look at what happened to those who tried to get close to the proof. Geoff Hughes' leads took him to Atlanta and Dallas, destinations that figured large when we addressed Hugh's illegal arms dealing. At which point Geoff's investigation was shut down by the Law Society, a fact confirmed by the Chairman of Carratu International. Was someone worried about Geoff coming across the individuals to whom that £100 million belonged? A little research of my own elicited the information that one of the members of the Law Society committee formed to oversee Carratu's investigation of Hugh had previously been appointed OBE, with no explanation given. Which, as was explained to me by Reggie, generally meant it had been for intelligence activity.

Keith Praeger, special agent with US Customs in Miami, genuinely believed there was an arms money trail leading to Mark Thatcher, but Keith had previously been unable to finger the money-launderer. He desperately wanted to investigate Hugh's circumstances, and to take over the Carratu investigation, as he was convinced Hugh was the most likely candidate. But Keith had been muzzled. Had the formidable Thatcher legal machine been brought to bear? Along with pressure from the Bush White House?

Various journalists, at first willing to help with my investigations, were warned off. As I had been. And when I approached senior members of the British political establishment to confirm the allegations about Hugh, they fell over themselves, like so many Keystone Cops, in their determined haste to avoid answering any questions about Hugh, arms deals, the Conservative party, or the two Thatchers.

I had myself attempted to obtain written documentation confirming the SCUD-B missile deal from the US Government, but had been thwarted. Drogoul's New York lawyer, Robert Simels, had confirmed his own memory of the deal to me. And that he had this memory because he had seen the actual Letter of Credit. As he explained, he saw it among the papers received from the FBI by way of formal discovery in Drogoul's criminal trial. All of those papers having been previously seized by the FBI from Drogoul's office. This made the document a part of government papers, in the public domain, and therefore available to the public. So. I began a three-year process of trying to obtain a copy through the Freedom of Information Act.

Well. For three years, the US government, under the Presidency of Bush Junior, moved those papers from this department to that, each time requiring a new FOIA application by me. Eventually, I ran out of country. Literally. The papers were returned to BNL in Italy, where they remain beyond my reach.

Is it too late now? Heck no. The one thing about cumbersome, intrusive, overbearing bureaucracies, private or public, is that they like to hang onto records. It's really quite simple. The UK and US governments should re-open an investigation into the circumstances of Hugh's death, using this book as the starting point for those to be questioned. Oh. And requiring that those same governments open all their own files on Hugh and the two Thatchers, as well.

But why bother with re-opening an investigation? This all happened back in the '80s. Surely it has no relevance now? Let's get one thing clear. This book is not an attempt to sully the reputation of Margaret Thatcher. For better or worse, I am proud of many of the accomplishments of the Conservative governments 1979-1997. As to the rest, not so proud.

No. I did not set out to write a political exposé. I began my investigation because the circumstances of the death of my best friend, the father of two young daughters, did not make sense. I continued that investigation, even when it became dangerous, because I was uncovering proof that my friend was not a simple crook. And I am writing this book now for one reason and one reason only: His family deserve to know the truth about Hugh, and the rest of us deserve to know the truth about those we elect to trust.

The fact is that, whatever we may think of Margaret Thatcher, there is strong reason to believe that arms corruption in the British body politic did not end with the demise of the Conservative administration in 1997. It likely continues, even today. And the best way to expose it is to use this book, and a re-opened investigation of the circumstances of Hugh's defalcation and death, as the startting point of a roadmap to reveal the continuing culprits.

Epilogue

DID ARMS CORRUPTION continue into the administrations of New Labour after their first election victory in 1997, and then into the LibCon Coalition government headed by David Cameron between 2010 and 2015? Did both New Labour and Cameron's government choose to continue Britain's new and sleazy, but highly remunerative, role as America's deeply covert global hired gun? There are enough worrying footprints to suggest that they did – on both counts.

***

In 1997, Tony Blair became Prime Minister of Great Britain, at the head of his New Labour government. I wrote to him. And eventually, I received a response from a civil servant in Blair's New Labour Foreign Office.

It was signed by a "Mr. D. Walters," which brought with it many flashbacks of my days at a British boarding school, where no one had a first name, just an initial. It was "D's" opinion that, in respect of my inquiries about illegal arms sales to Iraq, and the alleged attendant political kickbacks, the new British government had "nothing to add to your correspondence with [the] previous Prime Minister."

But there was more to this response than immediately meets the eye. Thatcher and her gang may have trampled roughshod over many of the rules and conventions previously governing the British establishment, but one, for certain, remained. I know this, because I still see reference to it all the time in the British media.

When a new administration takes power, there is a convention that they do not rummage through the "dirty laundry" of the previous government, exposing all their dirty little secrets. The reasoning is that, if this convention did not exist, no one at a senior level in government would ever engage in open debate in the sometimes unseemly but equally necessary exercise of executive power, for fear of being ratted on by the successor administration.

A corollary to this convention is another, which states that, if a minister of one administration wishes to make reference to correspondence of a predecessor minister, either himself or through one of his civil servants, then that civil servant must through his own minister gain the express permission of that minister's predecessor.

Put more simply, "D" had to go to his minister to get permission to refer to the previous administration's correspondence with me. That New Labour Minister, upon seeing that the previous correspondence had been with the former Prime Minister's PPS, would have known that the previous correspondence would have, in fact, been issued at the specific request of the previous Prime Minister, namely John Major.

Therefore, the New Labour Minister would have passed on my request to the new Prime Minister, namely Tony Blair, and his PPS. Tony Blair would then have had formally to request of John Major his permission to refer to Major's PPS's correspondence with me. Once obtained, that permission would then have made its way from Tony Blair, through his PPS, to the New Labour Minister, to "D," allowing "D" to refer to "your correspondence with [the] previous Prime Minister."

That is the convention. That is the only way that it could have worked. And it raised, once again, in my mind, all those questions about what it could have been that Hugh had been involved in that required, not only that his own political party keep it quiet, but also the opposing political party, who, in every other respect, had shown themselves only too willing to expose all manner of corruption associated with arms sales, and, in particular, those which had been illegal and had involved Iraq.

Was there some truth at the heart of what Hugh had been doing that was so "awful" that even New Labour realized that, to expose it, would undermine the entirety of the British body politic? Could that something be the fact that Margaret Thatcher herself had succumbed to corruption? And that Hugh's GEC deal was part of that trail of corruption?

Plus the notion that, in order to protect the wider arms backdoor, the private illegal arms sales, the trail of corruption to her and others in the Conservative party, Thatcher would have instructed Hugh and others to engage in whatever activity was necessary to effect such protection, including state-sanctioned murder?

Was it the fact that New Labour realized that exposure would underline the fact that they had not done a proper job of "opposition," and that the public would form the view that they were complicit by their silence? Much as we now believe that the Democrats never really properly castigated Reagan for Iran-Contra, because they had been complicit in covering up many of the attendant operations themselves?

The Democrats may have been happy to see neo-communism opposed on the American continent. But, by the time they understood that the entirety of the process also included massive corruption in Lebanon and Iran, was it too late to make a noise?

Or was there something else to the somersaults that New Labour were performing, in order not to have to answer my questions? Did they have some newfound "investment" of their own in those matters, which I had yet to discover? And which, indeed, I was about to discover. Had Tony and New Labour decided that, since the process already existed, they wouldn't mind some of the candy, too?

**

Before I could formulate the proper thoughts in my mind, I received a further letter from another civil servant in New Labour's Ministry of Defence. This one stated, without shame, that it was the policy of the New Labour government to deny that the UK had ever engaged in illegal arms sales to Iraq.

I made a special trip to the public library in Clayton, Georgia, that day. I waited patiently in line until a computer was free. And I then spent three hours writing down the full names of each and every one of the some 160, out of some 350, New Labour Members of Parliament I calculated would have a screaming fit if they knew that "their" government was now pretending that there had never been any illegal UK arms sales to Iraq.

Was this a slip? An over-eager civil servant? Someone who still regretted the passing of the Tories, who, after all, may have been the only "masters" he'd ever known? Remember, by 1997, the Conservatives had been in power for 18 very long years. Or again, did this correspondence represent something more? Were New Labour doing some "house-cleaning" of their own? Did they have a secret agenda, to which we mere mortals were not privy? Was "clearing me out of the way" part of the preparation for something new and large, on a horizon the rest of us could not yet see or define? Bottom line: What the heck was going on? What was the deal?

***

One of the most colorful of Tony Blair's new team was undoubtedly the controversial figure of Peter (now Lord) Mandelson. He had already won for himself a place in the history books as the man who, along with Tony Blair and Gordon Brown, had transformed the Labour Party, from a socialist footnote of the '70s, into a powerhouse of politics, beginning in the '90s, and lasting into the 21st century.

That, in itself, was a pretty formidable record. Unfortunately, the tactics he used – a mixture of spin, bullying, and manipulation – won him as many enemies as friends, both within the Labour Party and the media. Even his greatest pal, Tony Blair, accepted that his friend was so widely disliked within the Party, that he once declared that his job would only be done when New Labour had "learned to love Peter."

That may have been a lost cause, and even Mandelson has since admitted that he probably made too many enemies at that time. But what truly astonished even those who despised him were the scandals with which he would become associated. No one expected him to be that careless or undisciplined in his personal dealings. But what became even more sinister was the alacrity with which Tony Blair allowed him to bounce back. Every time.

***

First up, in 1998, was the scandal of "The Loan." At the time, Mandelson was the Secretary of State for Trade in Blair's New Labour Cabinet. Mandelson's Department was the one responsible for overseeing the Government's Export Credit Guarantee Program.

On December 23 of that year, the *Guardian* newspaper, an unlikely left-wing source for an expose against a nominally left-wing government, printed details from a book by one Paul Routledge of a secret loan of £373,000 ($580,000) to Mandelson from his Ministerial colleague Geoffrey Robinson. The money had been used to buy an expensive house in Notting Hill, London. (Of course, I take a moment to collapse in helpless laughter at my description of £373,000 as "expensive." House price inflation in London since 1998 has been such that the same amount would be unlikely even to buy a toilet in that district today.)

Geoffrey Robinson was the man who as Paymaster General was literally in charge of the nation's checkbook with the Bank of England. It is perhaps an unfortunate irony that money was also the cause of Robinson's own personal political minefield. Hmm. Maybe it wasn't such an irony after all? In any event, Robinson's wealth had proven to be a double-edged sword for more within New Labour than just the accident-prone Mandelson.

Senior officials of the Party, among them Tony Blair, had been able to enjoy lavish favors at Robinson's expense, including holidays at his homes in Tuscany and the South of France, and meetings at his penthouse flat in London's Park Lane, on the border of the Mayfair Square Mile, just a sheep's nibble away from Robert Maxwell's lawyer, Michael Rogers, who was an attorney with all the "right" connections.

Welcome as those favors were to New Labour, many of the headlines associated with Robinson's largesse were to become much less welcome – the Mandelson home loan, undeclared interests in offshore trusts, corporate misgovernance, and an alleged financial deal with disgraced tycoon Robert Maxwell, to name but a few.

After national service in the intelligence corps, Robinson was recruited by the then Labour Prime Minister, Harold Wilson, as a researcher at Labour headquarters. In the days of Labour's fondness for nationalizing British industry, Robinson soon became involved in state-run industries, rising to become the financial controller of British Leyland and, at the age of 34, the chief executive of Jaguar Cars, then state-owned.

In 1976, Robinson entered the House of Commons, representing Coventry North West. His interests also took in ownership of the left-leaning *New Statesman* magazine, and a place on the board of Coventry City soccer club. Throughout the '80s, while

Labour was in opposition, Robinson was seen as an asset to a party that severely lacked business backers of any profile. He held frontbench positions, speaking for the Labour Party on trade, industry, and science.

However, almost from the moment that Robinson was made Paymaster General, straight after the 1997 General Election, his financial affairs came under tough scrutiny from the Tories.

Eventually they proved his undoing as a Minister, when details of the home loan deal he struck with Mandelson became public. Despite being small change to a man whose personal wealth at the time was estimated at around £30 million ($45 million), Robinson's £373,000 ($560,000) informal mortgage triggered both men's resignations in December 1998.

***

Much about this time, the *Sunday Times* leaked a report from the Department of Trade and Industry that was highly critical of the improper role of Coopers & Lybrand (before it became PricewaterhouseCoopers) in the management of The Mirror Group by Robert Maxwell, and the disappearance of the pension funds into Maxwell's back pocket.

The article made clear that Coopers & Lybrand had already been fined £3 million ($4.5 million), and had made civil settlement of some £67 million ($100 million).

A little later, there was publicity of an equally damaging nature about the failure of Price Waterhouse properly to give warning of the shaky nature of BCCI's finances to, among others, the Bank of England, which was at that time the body responsible for monitoring legal compliance by all banks within Great Britain.

As Senior Partner of the newly merged PricewaterhouseCoopers, and as the immediate past Chairman of Coopers & Lybrand, Peter Smith's name was all over the groveling press releases that accompanied these shameful exposures.

***

An "Insight" article in the *Sunday Times*, dated August 27, 2000 highlighted the links between Alan Duncan, then a Conservative

Opposition Trade Minister (and later a senior Minister in the International Aid Department of the UK LibCon Coalition Government, in which position he was responsible for financially vetting foreign countries for development aid and arms sales), and Sheikh Ahmed Farid, a well-known London-based Arab arms dealer. There was speculation about Duncan in the light of Aitken's role as a bagman for the Saudi Royal Family in their arms deals:

"One of Farid's key Westminster contacts is still Aitken, who was released from prison last January [1999], after his conviction for perjury in a 1997 High Court libel case.

Soon after his release from jail, Aitken introduced Farid to Kevin Maxwell, the son of the late Robert Maxwell, the disgraced media tycoon. Duncan is a close friend of Aitken and supported him during his recent troubles."

***

In 2001, Mandelson was hit by a flurry of scandals, which forced his second resignation from Tony Blair's Government.

First, there were allegations of his misconduct over a passport application by a couple of Indian brothers, the Hinduja's. These brothers were already the focus of some controversy, having been linked to charges of bribery in connection with an arms deal between the Indian Government and Bofors, a Swedish gun manufacturer.

The press was saying that Mandelson fast-tracked a passport application for the Hinduja's, in return for their financial support of the Millennium Dome, the huge white elephant in East London, for which Mandelson had originally been responsible. I checked my conversation with Ari, and there, sure enough, was a reference linking Hugh to money laundering for a couple of billionaire Indian brothers.

An interesting side issue appeared in connection with this last scandal. Apparently, the Hindujas had first applied for British passports back in 1990, much the same time as al-Fayed. And like the Egyptian, the Indian brothers had been refused. However, unlike al-Fayed, they bided their time, and struck it lucky with New Labour.

The rumors were that the brothers had been friendly with al-Fayed, and had counseled him to take their approach, namely to wait it out quietly. Which advice al-Fayed had clearly ignored, to his considerable cost.

Next up, there was some suggestion that Mandelson had improperly used his influence to assist with gaining planning permission for a chum of his, by the name of Wafic Said. Wait a minute. Could this be the same Wafic Said, who, as partner to Jonathan Aitken, had been the mastermind behind the Savoy Mafia, and the Al Yamamah arms deals with Saudi Arabia? Hello. One and the same. We were also told that Wafic was now very chummy with Charles Powell, former Foreign Policy Adviser to Margaret Thatcher (in which capacity he was present during the initial Al Yamamah negotiations in the '80s); brother of Blair's very own Chief of Staff Jonathan Powell; and a gentleman who was made a life peer by Tony Blair himself, in 2000. In fact, the friendship between Said and Powell extended to the former making the latter the new head of his asset management company, the position previously occupied by Aitken. Just to round out the connection with Al Yamamah, in 2003, Lord Powell was made a political adviser to the BAE Chairman.

It was also in 2001 that Geoffrey Robinson faced another controversy of his own, surrounding an alleged £200,000 ($300,000) deal, done with Robert Maxwell. Robinson claimed he never received the money, but as with so many figures associated with Maxwell in the '80s (and Robinson was – closely), there have been regular questions as to how Robinson made all of his money.

***

The fact is that, for reasons which have more to do with Britain's draconian libel laws than the truth, it would appear that Geoffrey Robinson was much more closely associated with Robert Maxwell than the mainstream media have been willing to admit. He was essentially seen by many as being Maxwell's "bagman," and the person who, after Maxwell's death, knew where most of the skeletons were hidden, which may be another reason for so little being exposed about him.

Maxwell was a mighty financial supporter of the Labour Party, not least in the '80s, and again, Robinson most probably knew the ins and outs of how that support operated. Certainly, he still seemed to be engaged in some form of active "support" even in the

'90s, when he helped out a senior Government Minister like Mandelson with a house loan.

There were rumors going back to the '80s that Maxwell performed some highly secret role for Margaret Thatcher. Certainly, Maxwell harbored a surprising affection and respect for the Lady who should have been his political opposite.

Maxwell had connections, through his solicitor, Michael Rogers, with many of the players involved in the British end of the Iranian arms pipeline in the early '80s. Perhaps Maxwell did more than just help Ari and the Israelis with their arms sales? Maybe Maxwell had a finger in the British pie, also? Either with the arm's deals themselves, or with the money laundering? And maybe Maxwell had help? From a "bagman"? Who maybe became the keymaster to the arms money that Maxwell left behind when he died?

Then, the Tories were out and New Labour was in. The British arms industry had, by this time, achieved second place in world arms exports. Leaving aside all questions of political affiliation, everyone in that private industry wanted the exporting to continue. At full tilt. Both the capitalists and the trade unions. After all, one in every five people employed in the UK was then (and now) associated, in some way, with the burgeoning arms industry.

That required that the same "front door/back door" approach to continuity of service be maintained. Meanwhile, the Al Yamamah series of arms deals with Saudi Arabia were still up and running. And hundreds of millions of pounds of illegal commissions were still pouring into secret bank accounts with the Bank of England, bank accounts now under the control of New Labour's new Paymaster General, Geoffrey Robinson. So, would New Labour have continued to support the arms industry, in every way, just like the Tories? And if they did, who would get the commissions and the other financial advantages going forward?

What if Tony Blair was painfully aware of the decisions that needed to be made? What if he knew that there was simply too much to lose if anything was exposed about the arms shenanigans of the '80s? That revelation would undermine the whole British body politic? What if he knew that his own party had, to some extent, shared in the illicit largesse?

What if Tony Blair had been approached by his own group of "Grey Men," and like Major, had been told the "awful truth"? What if he was given an ultimatum: if you want to achieve any success with your government, you leave defense, the military, and intelligence matters (not to mention arms sales) well alone; in return, the civil service will bend over backwards to fast-track any other legislation and initiatives that you care to bring forward?

Did Blair reflect upon the Wilson years, and recall what had happened when Wilson took on the defense establishment – and lost? Did Blair do a "Dirty Deal" with those Grey Men, to save his fledgling government? Did Blair look out at the nation, and realize that the arms industry was now a major fact of life in its affairs, and that there was no purpose in fighting it?

Certainly, Blair had uncanny success in negotiating the wiles of the civil service. Undoubtedly, his government drew heavy criticism from many of its own left-wing supporters, for its stance on matters relating to intelligence, foreign policy, and arms sales (not to mention the invasion of Afghanistan and Iraq). Blair actively sought the prosecution of both of the intelligence whistleblowers, Tomlinson and Shayler, to furious outcries from those in his own party, who declared that Blair was betraying the party's long fight against the innate and dangerous secrecy of the British establishment.

And Blair's government continued the tradition of the Tories in the '80s, of pursuing controversial arms deals with countries of dubious legitimacy. Perhaps most notorious were the series of arms sales negotiated with the Indonesian government, at the same time as that government was using the equipment violently to suppress the legitimate aspirations of the East Timorese.

What if it is the case that the whole seedy arms network that Margaret Thatcher put together in the '80s simply picked itself up, by its rather soiled petticoat, tiptoed gently around the 1997 general election, and deposited itself, ever so gracefully, into the beckoning arms of the New Labour Party?

What if Tony Blair, resigned to this Dirty Deal, but wishing to make sure that his own hands never became muddied by direct contact, turned the whole matter over to one of his closest buddies? A man who just happened now to be in charge of all Export Credit Guarantees, especially those relating to international arms deals? Someone who appeared to survive in political office, regardless of scandal? A man with his own connections to folk of arms background?

And what if this man teamed up with the person now in charge of the government's Bank of England checking accounts? The bank accounts still receiving some $300 million a year in illicit arms commissions. And what if this same person was the guy who might have retained his separate influence within the Labour Party as the pipeline of money from the Maxwell legacy to the Labour Party? An influence not unlike that of the aforementioned senior Conservative gentleman, with his keymaster role in connection with the $300 million offshore Tory arms slush funds?

And what if the Dirty Deal included some realization on everyone's part that, in order to send the strongest message to the world about the certainty of Britain's offer of continuity of arms service to its clients, it was necessary to have some sort of under-the-table, cross-party co-operation on the secret aspects of the arms industry? Would this account for the meeting between Aitken and Duncan? Would it also explain the apparently friendly dealings between Aitken, Charles Powell, Duncan and Wafic Said on one side and Mandelson, Robinson and Kevin Maxwell on the other?

Did this require of the Conservative party that it also keep its mouth shut, the door firmly shut on its archive of secrets, and a power structure in place that would be seen to be one that would continue the "dirty" arms dealings, as and when the Tories returned to power? Would this, in turn, explain the almost unseemly haste with which the two Conservative leadership "failures," William Hague and Iain Duncan-Smith, were dispatched, all with the open interference of Lady Thatcher herself? Would it account for one of the Thatcher "old guard," Michael Howard, eventually assuming the mantle of leadership in 2003, followed by one of his ambitious acolytes, David Cameron, in 2006?

***

Continuing the theme that this story never seems to end, in August 2004, Peter Mandelson sealed his reputation as the "comeback king" of British politics, with his appointment to one of the most powerful jobs in the European Union. As the European Union's Trade Commissioner, Mandelson represented all 25 EU nations in important trade negotiations around the world, a crucial role in the continuing moves towards globalization.

More remarkable even than Mandelson's staying power was the fact that it was reported at the time that Tony Blair was planning to bring his old friend back into the Cabinet, but was forced to drop the idea after stronger than expected opposition from Gordon Brown, the Chancellor of the Exchequer (and Blair's eventual, short-lived successor as Prime Minister), and Deputy Prime Minister, John Prescott.

Which was somewhat surprising, bearing in mind that, in 2008, Gordon Brown (later Prime Minister) himself re-appointed Mandelson to important positions within his Cabinet. The man just would not go away. Was this simply the natural consequence of a wealth of talent? Or did Mandelson have some other hold over the Labour Party specifically and the British body politic in general?

***

Meanwhile, much of the rest of what Thatcher wittingly or unwittingly set in motion also carried itself forward into the reign of Tony Blair and New Labour. Notwithstanding some half-hearted attempts at legislation, aimed at controlling the activities of terrorist organizations within Great Britain, the country still operated, under New Labour, as the primary Offshore Trading Haven for Global Terror. But why, you might very well ask? The answer is both simple and sad. And already stated. But worth repeating, since the primary and perhaps the saddest point is that the answer applies whatever your political affiliation in the modern Cool Britannia.

***

A fully-fledged and successful arms industry requires an ongoing back-door for illegal arms deals. This, in turn, necessitates that there be a network of "underground" services, on immediate tap: warehouses, false papers, personnel – and security.

Beginning with Thatcher's government, and continuing through Major's, into Blair's (and beyond), that need has been met with classic British efficiency, at all levels: from the corridors of power in Whitehall, to the oak-paneled offices of the City of London, to the darkest of back-alleys in Soho and Leicester Square.

Add to this the further climate of corruption that has accompanied Britain's continuing role as covert surrogate for America's agenda of state terror (otherwise known as the "War on Terror"). And London has become a full-service marketplace for all the accouterments of the modern "metro-terrorist": arms, explosives, mercenaries, money-laundering, and terrorist contacts.

Whether you are the CIA, MI6 or Mossad, or the "Enterprise" or Donald Rumsfeld's now-famous "off-the-books" operations; al-Qaeda, Islamic Jihad, or the Knights of some faction of the Priory of Sion. Whatever your name, whatever your need, you can obtain service from Great Britain Ltd. – the world's finest Offshore Trading Haven for Global Terror. They are open for business, to anyone and everyone – provided the price is right.

Of course, this is made all the easier by the fact that the UK is still a remarkably open society, that encourages full expression of political thought. The borders are open: not only to people, but also to the unfettered import and export of cash. London is the financial capital of the world. And Britain is an island, which sits within sight of the northern coast of France – an absolute dream for anyone wishing to bypass customs and immigration controls.

Is it any wonder that there are so many British connections to the worldwide bin Laden network; or that so much of 9/11 had its genesis in the UK? Are we truly surprised that second generation Pakistani immigrants, who, for all intents and purposes, should have been model products of Thatcher's "British Dream," and Blair's "Enterprise Society," were so easily able to manufacture and then to explode five bombs, with such devastating effect, on London's transport system, on 7/7?

Why then, didn't Tony Blair do something to stop the corrupt arms trade, and all of its insidious offshoots and nefarious consequences? The answer is that he couldn't. It was and remains too late. It was and remains too lucrative.

OK. But couldn't Blair at least have cleaned up some of the act, by refusing any longer to act as America's surrogate operative, in the export of its state terror? Not so fast. What makes anyone think Blair would have been allowed so casually to abandon that role? Again, it was – and still is – way too remunerative.

In addition, Blair had too much to lose by coming clean: He knew what was going on under Thatcher and Major, and yet he stayed quiet – he wanted power too badly. Once New Labour was in office, it continued, at best, to turn a blind eye to the ongoing shenanigans, because it wanted to stay in power.

More than this, Blair wanted a legacy. He had no interest in becoming a martyr. Which is what would have happened if he'd blown the whistle. Because he'd have been blowing the whistle on himself. One of the many issues that would have come under the media microscope would have been whether or not Blair benefited personally – and that is likely not the sort of scrutiny that Blair could have survived.

However, this is all moot. The fact is that Bush Junior never had any intention of allowing Blair to abandon Britain's role as America's surrogate. That is why the world witnessed the curious courtship between what it perceived, on the one hand, to be a gung-ho right-wing imperial President, and, on the other, a seemingly articulate, intelligent, left-wing Prime Minister. Bush knew where the skeletons were hidden, and he used them to blackmail Blair.

***

Blair might have got away scot-free, but for the investigative activities of the *Guardian* newspaper, which in turn triggered a full-blown investigation by Britain's Serious Fraud Office of bribes associated with the Al Yamamah arms deals. An investigation which was eventually stopped after direct intervention by Blair himself, due to complaints by the Saudi government.

In 2006, under pressure over his role in a completely different corruption scandal ('Cash-for-Peerages'), Blair announced he would stand down as Prime Minister and leader of New Labour in 2007, which he duly did. On my birthday, June 27. Gordon Brown became Prime Minister. Was by common agreement a disaster. And lost the general election in 2010. So, onto the LibCon Coalition government formed after the 2010 General Election.

***

All of the elements that existed during the Conservative governments between 1979 and 1997, and which led to the alleged corruption attached to the international arms dealing encouraged by those governments, were back in place for the LibCon government headed by David Cameron between 2010 and 2015.

There was a Conservative Prime Minister openly dedicated to expanding Britain's trade in arms. That trade still required a backdoor. And there was a new and expanded international network into which this backdoor trade could feed, spawned by the covert War on Terror. The Enterprise on steroids.

There were all manner of British-based banks caught up in scandals involving money-laundering. Britain's lead defense contractor was caught red-handed offering huge bribes in order to obtain arms contracts around the world, not least in the Middle East. And many of the same players who were names in the illicit '80s arms enterprise were back in positions of power in the Conservative-led coalition government and in the Conservative Party itself. Not least Alan Duncan, who was given the choice role of vetting all foreign countries for foreign aid and arms sales.

The *Sunday Times* reported that another old friend of ours, Wafic Said, arms commission pimp for the Tories in the '80s (and maybe thereafter for New Labour?), was once again helping to fund the Conservative party. Said had found a way around restrictions on donations by foreigners. He had his wife make enormous bids at Conservative auctions. In this way, Said managed to slip the Tories about £500,000 between 2004 and 2015. It was further reported that the Saids belonged to David Cameron's private Leaders Club, which was made up of individuals who donated more than £50,000 to the Conservative Party, and who were then rewarded with private dinners, lunches, and drinkies at Chequers, the Prime Minister's official country manor house.

What's more, Charles Powell's son, Hugh, formerly Head of the Foreign Office's security department, which oversaw the activities of BAE, became David Cameron's Deputy National Security Adviser. Small world, isn't it?

On May 7, 2015, David Cameron's Conservative Party was elected to a second term in office. But this time, with a small overall majority, and therefore, without the restraining influence of a coalition with the Liberal Democrats. Cameron's initial appointments to posts which have an important influence on arms sales suggest that the Tory arms bribe machine is about to swing back into full gear.

Use this book as a roadmap, follow the money, follow the names, and who knows what else might be unearthed?

Afterword

I didn't set out to write an exposé. My intention has always been merely to find the truth about Hugh for his family. I didn't know that the truth would be so hidden. I didn't know that I would have to travel halfway around the world to get the first few glimpses. But make no mistake, this book is only a start.

There is only so much one guy can do. It is for others now to fill the gaps. To take responsibility and open their files to let Hugh's family finally know what happened to him, and why.

This book does not pretend to be an academic tome. There are no footnotes. No references. No links. It is the simple, honest chronicle of my quest for the truth. The diary of a journey. A record of the conversations I have held. With the information offered, in good faith, to help me move to the next stage of that journey. Where I could not immediately understand the information proffered, I engaged in research. Not in any journalistically correct fashion. But in a manner efficiently sufficient to allow me to make sense of what I'd been told. No more. No less. Where possible, I have included in the rear of the book a list of the books I have read to such end.

Sometimes, I have been able to record the conversations I have held. Most of the time, I have relied on my legal training to take contemporaneous notes. Unfortunately, almost all of my belongings, including most of my papers and supporting materials for this book, were stolen in 1999 (nothing sinister; just a good friend gone wayward). Fortunately, I had already written the first two drafts of the book, and all of the important notes, tapes, and letter content had been transcribed to one or other of the two drafts – which drafts I kept with me.

Every single major name mentioned in my book has been contacted in writing and told of the circumstances in which they are named in my book. No malice attaches to their mention. I have only included names where it is vital to the important trail of circumstantial evidence, leading to the overall picture of what might have happened to Hugh. I have always been aware of the impact of mention. Sometimes, I have struggled. Only two people have ever contacted me to demand exclusion. In the case of the former, a well-known politician, I made further contact with my informant, who confirmed the words attributed to the politician. However, erring on the side of caution, I removed mention of that politician from my book. In the case of the second individual, mention was too significant for total exclusion. Besides, there is verifiable public confirmation of the matters attributed to that individual. However, again, with caution in mind, I considerably watered down reference.

So, why has it taken almost twenty-seven years for this story to move from Hugh's death in 1988 to publication of my chronicle in 2015? Hmm. Good question. I finished the first draft of the book in 1996. Immediately contacted a bunch of literary agents in London. Cast your mind back. Immediacy in those days meant fax and telephone. Just as immediately, I was introduced to the concept of the victorious rejection. It's not whether or not you have been rejected; it's how. So. I scored very well. Twenty-two initial indications of interest. Twenty-two ultimate rejections. But. One now very well-known agent insisted I stay in touch, as the re-writes improved my writing. I did. And he has always been very supportive. Mind you, though his opinion of my writing changed, he never did take me on as a client. But. Personal contact, highest level, first-name terms? Primo, primo rejection.

After that, first-name terms with the Managing Director of a leading firm of London literary agents. But no contract. A host of personally signed letters of rejection. Still pretty good. And one rude hang-up. OK. Not my fault. I wondered if she could get me an advance. She replied that was for me to negotiate. Which is why I wondered aloud if I really needed her at all. Click. None of the rejections were sinister. It was my first draft of anything ever. They wanted more meat and better writing.

Second draft in 1997. Followed by third in 1999. At which point, I was exhausted and dried up. I totally sympathized with the fellow who had written somewhere about the lonely, hate-filled ritual of writing. It might have been Hemingway. I loved the thinking. The planning. Hated the writing. It was agony. Never finding the right word. Despairing of my inability to channel thoughts into reflective words. Thrashing the Delete button like a manic road drill. Only to delight in the finished product. In any event, I couldn't write another word, or face contacting agents until 2004. When I had a hiatus between jobs, and found my fingers gliding over the keyboard ivories that hot sultry August in Texas.

In 2005, I attempted the rounds of US literary agents. They might not buy into the politics. But I wondered if the rollercoaster adventure might turn them on? Nope. This time, they loved the writing. They saw the relevance. I mean, who didn't know Thatcher? And there were loads of connections to the US. But I hadn't yet fleshed out the bigger picture of US-UK covert connivance. And it left an obvious hole. Well. Obvious now. At that point, they just felt something was missing. The book needed something to tie it all together. Suggestions were made that I try to get a newspaper involved in investigating. Why not? Well, because newspapers don't do that much investigating any more. Their counter-suggestion was that I write a book, which they could then serialize. Sigh.

Final re-write and self-edit in 2013, immediately after the death of Margaret Thatcher. Irons hot, and all that. Get it? Iron. Lady. Hot. OK. Forget it. Anyway, the final draft and edit rounded out the book. At least in my view. Got straight onto e-mail and shot a zinger to about seventy literary agents in London. She's dead. I've got a story. I was pretty much immediately whittled down to two agents. Both very interested. Both of whom insisted they wanted me to keep the book nonfiction. Both of whom were full of admiration for how much one man had accomplished. But both of whom were looking for more front-page tabloid evidence.

Which, of course, is the revolving conundrum. If one of my informants or sources had evidence immediately worthy of frontpage publication, why would they give it to me? And if they did, why would I need to write a book? All I wanted was truth for Hugh's family. If that was contained in some hard evidence, my work would be complete. Instead, I had painstakingly to create an audit trail of informed but circumstantial evidence, so as to paint a picture sufficiently different from the "official" story, that it would put pressure on the powers-that-be to come clean. All the while, being sure not to offend or defame anyone along the way. In any event, my two agents were hugely supportive. Scored nine out of ten on the quality rejection scale.

At which point enter TrineDay, which was recommended to me by a gentleman I had met in Chapel Hill, NC, when I was performing one of my early unpublished non-book readings. Whose owner, Kris, upon reading the section of the book in which Ari Ben-Menashe offered to provide me with evidence of his claims once I had a publisher, contacted me to say, well, here we are. What about that evidence?

So, early in 2015, I tracked down Ari. I hadn't communicated with him in almost twenty years. I had no idea what to expect. Even if he would remember me. Well, he returned my contact within 24 hours. I recorded the telephone call. And he was very straightforward. I will leave out all the extraneous pleasantries. He made it clear that the essence of his allegations to me held true. And that they were, in short, that, in the '80s (we never have discussed beyond the '80s – that may be a further book), to his knowledge, the Conservatives had been involved in selling arms to Iraq, the Labour Party in selling arms to Iran, through Robert Maxwell, and that Hugh had been a member of a group of lawyers who had arranged for the laundering of the illicit proceeds back to senior politicians in both political parties.

I didn't ask Ari for any more. Not because I didn't want to. Not because I didn't think he had more to offer (far from it; I think Ari has way more to say, and I believe that what he knows could be even more explosive). Nor because I felt that his statement was enough due diligence. I didn't ask for more because due diligence, by definition, has to be undertaken by the publisher. It is his independent confirmation that he can stand by the contents of the book he is publishing. In other words, due diligence is for his purposes, not mine. It must be undertaken by him, not me. To his satisfaction. Not mine. Nor yours.

I told Ari this. He knew it already, since he went through exactly the same process when he published his book. And he told me that. I gave him my publisher's telephone number. Contacted my publisher. And told them to do together whatever it is they needed to do. This book is now published. So, I am assuming my publisher was satisfied. Certainly, I sent him a further letter setting out what questions I might ask of Ari at this point, with respect very specifically to the allegations in this book.

Now, do I think that Ari knows more than he has set out in this book? Absolutely. Could I have pursued him for that further information? Of course. As I could all of the other leads in this book. Save for two things. First, the exercise at this stage is not investigation; it is publisher due diligence. We are not about creating new material (that is for a further book); it is about legitimizing what has already been written. Secondly, I am but one person. Without the resources of a newspaper, or a law enforcement agency. I have done as much as I can at this stage. For sure, I may have further conversations with Ari. But that will be a separate and a different project. For the moment, if anyone wants to ask Ari what else he knows, I will happily provide them with his public e-mail and telephone number.

More to the point, this book is only a beginning. It is, in effect, a challenge. To all those mentioned within it to come forward with all that they know. And to those in authority to open their own books, in order finally to bring truth to Hugh's family and to those of us who rightly expect the highest standards of behavior from those we entrust to govern us.

Documents

Solicitor who kept clients' £4m gassed himself in his car

By Mark Souster

A disgraced solicitor and failed Conservative parliamentary candidate killed himself the day a Law Society investigation into his affairs was due to begin, an inquest was told yesterday.

Hugh Simmonds, a former mayor of Beaconsfield, killed himself, rather than face being unmasked as a swindler who had defrauded clients out of at least £4 million.

Simmonds, aged 40, and a father of two, who became a CBE in 1985 for his work for the Conservative Party, committed suicide by gassing himself in his car, at Amersham, Buckinghamshire.

At the inquest at High Wycombe, Mr John Roberts, the coroner, returned a verdict that Simmonds, had committed suicide. "I am convinced he died of carbon monoxide poisoning", the coroner said.

After the hearing it was disclosed that hundreds of people may have lost large sums of money through Simmonds's business dealings.

Mr Geoffrey Green, a solicitor appointed to examine the affairs of Simmonds, said: "We do not know exactly how much money is missing but it is likely to run into millions.

"We are talking about money missing from property transactions, investment money missing, not redeeming mortgages and people left with two mortgages to pay. It looks like it has been going on over a 10-year period.

"His office account was £250,000 overdrawn and his client account, which should have been sacrosanct, was over £190,000 in debt."

Mr Green said Simmonds's financial affairs would take years to unravel.

"So far no one had been able to trace the missing money", he said.

Mr Green said Simmonds, of Stratton Road, Beaconsfield, Buckinghamshire, enjoyed the good life.

"He drove a Maserati, he had a very high-profile life and he was always seen at the best restaurants entertaining people".

The solicitor, who ran his practice from The Highway, Beaconsfield, was found dead in his beige Austin Metro car on November 15 last year a few miles from his home.

On the day of his death, the court was told a representative of the Law Society's Solicitors Complaints Bureau had been due to arrive at his office and examine his books.

Local police had also received complaints about Simmonds, who was twice dropped as parliamentary candidate for safe Conservative seats: once when the party in the rural seat of South-West Cambridgeshire discovered his wife was a member of the League Against Cruel Sports and the second time in Warrington when it was disclosed he had a mistress and an illegitimate son. Previously he had been beaten when contesting Leeds in 1979.

His wife Janet, aged 37, said she last saw her husband on November 14 when he helped their two children with their homework. She said he left the house at 4.30am the next morning and she assumed he was going to the office early.

She said she was aware that her husband had at one stage had an affair with an international horse breeder, Miss Karen George, but believed it had ended. She said that he had also been depressd about his political progress. She knew nothing of her husband's financial problems.

"He was fairly depressed about his lack of political progress and I think it played on his mind."

However Miss George, aged 32, told the inquest in a statement that the solicitor planned to marry her as soon as he was free.

Last night the Law Society said that claims against Simmonds totalled £3.8 million, which had been, or would be, met by the society, which in turn could claim against his estate.

Investigators believe much of the missing cash was transferred to foreign bank accounts.

P. Geoffrey Gilson
851 Tahoe Bluff
Apartment G
Roswell, Georgia 30076, USA
Tel. (404) 552-8143
Fax. (404) 993-5550

The Right Honourable John Major, M.P.
10 Downing Street
London
England

August 27, 1993

Dear Prime Minister,

Investigation into the death of Hugh Simmonds

I can understand how busy you must be in these troubled times, but I would appreciate it if you could find the time to give me a little assistance.

I attach a clipping from "The Times", dated March 21, 1989. I was for 14 years a close friend of Hugh Simmonds.

It is clear from the clipping that Simmonds was very active, at a fairly senior level, within the Conservative Party. Indeed, you "knew" him briefly - I was present when he took your call of congratulations upon his being selected as Prospective Parliamentary Candidate for Cambridge South-West.

For the past five years, I have been looking into the circumstances of the missing money and his death because many aspects of those circumstances do not seem to make sense.

Some time after his death, I met with a colleague of his (a Professor Reginald von Zugbach de Sugg) who claimed that he and Simmonds had at one time been associates in some aspect of British Intelligence and that that connection would throw considerable light on the circumstances of the missing money and his death. I did not and do not know whether to believe him, but he remains insistent.

I am aware of your desire for increased openness with regards to British Intelligence. In those circumstances, I thought I could do no worse than write to you and ask you to use your good offices to attempt to clear up this situation.

Could you, therefore, please obtain the answers to the following four questions?:-

1. Was Hugh Simmonds at any time involved in any way with any aspect of any institution of British Intelligence or British "special forces", whether military or civilian?

2. Was Reginald von Zugbach de Sugg at any time involved in any way with any institution of British Intelligence or British "special forces", whether military or civilian?

3. Were either Simmonds or von Zugbach at any time involved in any way with the Black Watch?

4. In 1985 Simmonds was appointed C.B.E. for public and political service. That was a civilian appointment. Is it true that he was presented with a military ribbon, along with the civilian ribbon, in recognition of his services to Intelligence?

Once again, I would be grateful for any help that you can give me and my efforts. Wishing you all the best with your problems.

Yours sincerely,

1O DOWNING STREET
LONDON SW1A 2AA

From the Principal Private Secretary   15 October 1993

Dear Mr Gilson

    Thank you for your letter of 27 August to the Prime Minister about the
death of Hugh Simmonds. Your letter was not received here until 21
September and I am afraid there has therefore been some delay in replying.

    It is the Government's policy to neither confirm or deny whether
individuals were involved with the security or intelligence services. I can
confirm however that there is no evidence that either Mr Simmonds or
Professor von Zugbach de Sugg were ever involved with the Black Watch.
There is no record that Mr Simmonds was ever presented with a military ribbon
to the CBE.

    I hope that this is of assistance.

Yours sincerely

Alex Allan

ALEX ALLAN

Mr. Geoffrey Gilson

P. Geoffrey Gilson
851 Tahoe Bluff
Apartment G
Roswell, Georgia 30076, USA
Tel. (404) 552-8143
Fax. (404) 993-5550

Alex Allan, Esq.
10 Downing Street
London
SW1A 2AA
England

Halloween, 1993

Dear Mr Allan,

Investigation into the death of Hugh Simmonds

Thank you for your letter of 15 October 1993.

I am very grateful for the time you spent putting together the answers. That said, in order to determine whether they are of assistance will require that you spend a little more time on my behalf.

The helpfulness of the answers depends very much on the answers to the following further questions:-

1. Does the fact that "there is no evidence that either Mr Simmonds or Professor von Zugbach de Sugg were ever involved with the Black Watch" preclude the fact that they may have been so involved?

2. Is it general practice to keep any form of "evidence" of individuals' involvement with the Black Watch for any period of time?

3. Are there any exceptions?

4. If it is the case that any form of "evidence" is maintain maintenance?

5. Is it the case that there is never any such "evidence"?

6. Is it the case that there is never any evidence if the individ is concerned, a civilian?

7. Is it the case that there is never any evidence if the indi connected with military or civilian intelligence or the spec

8. Is it the case that it is Government or military or intellige form of policy) that such "evidence" will not be released the existence of such evidence will not be acknowledged?

---

10 DOWNING STREET
LONDON SW1A 2AA

From the Principal Private Secretary   9 November 1993

Dear Mr Gilson

Thank you for your further letter of
31 October. I do not feel there is anything I can
usefully add to my earlier reply.

Yours sincerely

ALEX ALLAN

Mr Geoffrey Gilson

Contragate

Who will rat on mole?

THE US Senate's intelligence committee, currently grilling Robert Gates, President George Bush's CIA nominee for the second time, should begin with the two most obvious questions about Gates.

Why is Bush prepared to risk reopening the whole Contragate can of worms — wherein the president's own role bears little examination? And what, in short, does the Reagan-Bush axis that thrust Gates forward in 1987 owe to the obsequious Gates?

The answer may lie in the 1979-80 US presidential election campaign. Former President Carter has told the *Eye* that he believes there were two moles in his administration working for the Reagan-Bush camp. The first was almost certainly Donald Gregg, currently ambassador to South Korea. And many now believe the second, lesser agent, was Gates himself, first during his time on Carter's national security council and then in 1980 as executive assistant to CIA director-general Stansfield Turner.

Campaign strategy documents were undoubtedly leaked; but the most important contribution of the Reagan moles — almost certainly recruited by the conveniently deceased masterspy William Casey — was to keep the Republicans informed of the Carter team's efforts to negotiate the freedom of the American hostages in Teheran. This enabled Casey to do a deal with the mullahs that prevented Carter springing an "October Surprise" and winning reelection.

That sort of footwork seemed to convince Casey of Gates's potential. Under the former's stewardship of the CIA, Gates leapfrogged scores of peers to become head of the analytical section in 1982 before becoming the CIA's youngest ever deputy director at just 42 in 1986. The following year he was put forward as presidential nominee for the top job when Casey succumbed to a brain tumour.

Bush, it should be recalled, has a habit of becoming bogged down by nomination hearings when trying to look after those who have performed personal services. Remember John Tower? The man who was rewarded with a nomination for defence secretary after keeping Bush's name out of Congress's Contragate investigation was, however, not confirmed by Congress. Gates could go the same way.

The charge about Gates *vis-a-vis* Contragate and the CIA's role in it rests on the management ladder. Casey, Gates's boss, knew. Clair George, the man below Gates in the pecking order at No 3, has just been indicted by a federal grand jury for knowing and lying to Congress. How, it is argued, could Gates possibly not have known? After all, he's supposed to be an intelligence agent!

Gates, of course, did know. A simple check of his testimony to the Tower Commission shows that he admits being told of the illegal diversion of profits from Iranian arms sales (for US hostages) to the contras by CIA analyst Charles Allen on 1 October 1986. "I was startled by what he told me," Gates told the commission. "I told him I didn't want to hear any more about it."

Notes that Oliver North was forced to release during his trial show that he, Casey and Gates, had lunch on 9 October 1986. Gates has adopted an amazing defence even by his own standards: he says he didn't ask North about Allen's revelations. The meeting, he claims, concerned the legal, Congressionally-approved CIA programme to assist the contra rebels.

Not according to North. His notes show Casey concerned about "vulnerabilities if Richard Secord and Southern Air Transport (SAT) become public". Both Secord and SAT were at the heart of North's private support system.

Other records show that Gates knew about the arms for hostages concept before he became deputy director of the CIA. On 5 December 1985 Gates attended a CIA meeting where he was informed that US hostage Benjamin Weir had been released in exchange for "one plane load of arms" but that there had been "nothing for a second planeload". Gates was told that North was "arranging for five planeloads".

Gates has since described the arms-for-hostages deal as "an exchange of bona fides". But if that is not enough to persuade the intelligence committee that Gates has no judgement at all, his role in supplying arms to Iraq should. According to separate affidavits and dispositions from a former Israeli intelligence officer, Ari Ben Menashe, and an international arms dealer, Richard Babayan, Gates was pivotal in the supply of chemical agents and cluster bomb technology to Iraq.

Ben Menashe says he met Gates on several occasions to try to persuade him to halt the supply of such weapons to Iraq through third parties, in particular, the notorious Carlos Cardoen group in Chile. At one such meeting in Santiago, Chile, Gates told Ben Menashe Israel was just being "paranoid".

In the end, Israel resorted to the time-honoured method of bribery. Gates received two cheques totalling US$1.5m. Authorised by the Israeli government, the money was drawn from the National Westminster Bank, processed through the Discount Bank of Israel which ordered its representatives in the Cayman Islands, a Crown colony, to pay issue cheques to a senior CIA bagman, George Cave.

According to Ben Menashe, now described by US senator Alan Cranston as "a credible witness", the process was supervised by a part-time Mossad agent working in what was once the Street of Shame. The same "journalist" had also facilitated payments from Iran for the Hawk missiles and tank parts supplied for hostages.

So it is that even some of the most hardened professional liars at the CIA flinch at the idea of Gates becoming the US's top spy. "Gates? Deceitful, mendacious, smoothly corrupt," was the verdict of one veteran of the clandestine assassination programmes in Vietnam. No wonder Bush is convinced he's found the right man for the job.

THE SUNDAY TIMES

No 8,877   9 OCTOBER 1994 $4.75

Focus page 13

Revealed: Mark Thatcher's secret profit from £20 billion arms deal

MARK THATCHER made his multi-million-pound fortune by helping to fix the biggest arms deal of the century while his mother was prime minister.

He was part of a team of middlemen who earned a secret £20m commission for brokering the Al Yamamah agreement to supply British jet fighters, naval mine-hunters and semi-station to Saudi Arabia. Sources close to the deal say Thatcher's cut was £12m.

An investigation by The Sunday Times has uncovered transcripts of bugged telephone conversations between arms dealers and agents of the Saudi royal family in which Thatcher's role in the £20 billion deal is discussed. He is variously described as a man with "excellent connections"

and "influence with the government".

British officials directly involved in the negotiations, which took place in 1984, protested to Downing Street at what they saw as the "inappropriate" interference.

A senior civil servant, Sir Clive Whitmore, then permanent secretary at the Ministry of Defence and former private secretary to Margaret Thatcher, was sent to the prime minister to deliver what was termed a "wrath-warning" about the potentially disastrous consequences of her son's involvement. Mrs Thatcher, however, appears rattly ignored their protests and allowed her son to profit from the deal even though she was its principal signatory.

MPs will want to know whether her son's involvement compromised her under the protocol for ministerial behaviour. The Whitehall protocol, Questions of Procedure for Ministers, first published in 1992 but dating back to 1918, states that "ministers will want to see that no conflict arises, or appears to arise, between their private interests and their public duties".

It also says that "no minister or public servant should accept gifts, hospitality or services from anyone which would, or might appear to place him or her under an obligation. The same principle applies if gifts are offered to a member of their family".

Thatcher played a pivotal part in securing the Al Yamamah deal when she visited Riyadh, the Saudi capital, in April 1985 and met King Fahd, Michael Heseltine, then defence secretary, said her role "cannot be overstated" when he unveiled a memorandum of understanding with Prince Sultan Bin Abdul Aziz, the Saudi defence minister, in London the following September. This clinched the first part of the deal, involving Tornado strike aircraft and Hawk trainers.

The second instalment, involving Tornado jets, was struck by Saudi intelligence agents who were monitoring their bids by British and French, in mid-1988. United States to supply the Saudis own jets. The transcripts, and corroborating evidence found in secret documents, indicate that Mark has influential connections with the government and he has good information.

Thatcher first made his fortune. It has never been satisfactorily explained how Old Harrovian, a three-failed accountant and would-be racing driver, rapidly went from modest means when his mother became prime minister in 1979 to multimillionaire status a few years later.

In one conversation, an Arab man believed to be Adnan Khashoggi, the international arms dealer, tells a Saudi royal official: "It has to work today and I will confirm to him the money will never be more than $300m for sure and his group."

Khiewi, a Saudi first secretary at the United Nations who defected in May and was granted political asylum by the United States after revealing the Saudis' secret nuclear programme.

Khashoggi, involved in another bugged conversation, stepped out of the British deal in the early stages, switching over to help the French rival bid for the Saudi contract. Speaking about the negotiations for the first time last week, he confirmed that the successful Al Yamamah deal was brokered by Wafic Said, a Syrian millionaire working on behalf of British defence contractors, with the help of Thatcher.

"Wafic was using Mark for influence," Khashoggi said last week. "His value to Wafic was his name, of course, and that whenever Wafic needed a question answered, Mark could go directly to his mother for the answer."

Company sources involved in the deal have confirmed both Thatcher's role and the total amount of commission.

For some British officials, Thatcher's involvement was ethically wrong. "Mark Thatcher was an opportunist on a gravy train, scooping whatever money he could from these deals," said a former British Aerospace executive who played a central role. "He touted his name and position in relation to Margaret Thatcher."

The revelations could not come at a worse time for Mark Thatcher. His marriage to a Texan is reported to be in difficulty, one of his American companies has gone bankrupt, and he is due to be served with papers accusing him of "racketeering" in a civil case brought by a former business partner in Texas. In Dallas last night, Mark Thatcher refused to comment.

The Thatcher tapes   pages 6 and 7

INSIGHT

London Fashion Week opens in style

Tories split by bitter infighting

Saddam planned Kuwaiti attack for two weeks

THE SUNDAY TIMES 21/7/96.

Wedding day: Susanna's marriage enraged Zugbach's rival

Recovering: the Zugbachs are now on sick leave in German...

Stalker's hate mail stuns Scots campus

by Iain Martin

POLICE are investigating a campaign against a Scottish academic and his German wife allegedly involving poison-pen letters, phone-tapping and a car explosion.

Professor Reggie von Zugbach, an author, ex-army major and lecturer in management studies at Paisley University, is recovering with his wife Susanna in Düsseldorf after the nine-month ordeal. It is believed the incidents are the work of a love rival jealous of the couple's marriage.

After meeting Susanna a few times, the rival bombarded her with mail, flowers and threats for almost four years. He was outraged when the couple were married in December.

The threats increased, and in letters more than 100 pages long the rival told Susanna: "God has allowed you into this marriage with one purpose — namely to break you, because

there is no other way. My prophesy is this: I believe that your marriage will not survive. It will end with a catastrophe. You will be terribly injured."

The letter-writer cannot be named for legal reasons, but the affair has shocked academics. Police are also investigating an

incident last month when the Zugbachs' car caught fire. The couple say the blaze happened on the anniversary of the day the rival first met Susanna at a conference.

Last week Zugbach praised police handling of the incident. "I'm a military man with a high tolerance level, but it is the effect of this on my wife that upsets me. The police have done everything they can. I'm writing to the chief constable to

> *6 Your marriage will not survive. It will end with a catastrophe. You will be terribly injured 9*

thank him. But the whole thing is very worrying ..."

The saga began in 1992 at an academic conference in Canada when Susanna, a senior civil servant in the Rhineland state church, rejected an approach from a man she had just met.

She started to receive letters

at home in Germany, often over 50 pages long. She repeatedly stressed that she did not want to hear from him — but the letters became more threatening.

Zugbach met her in October 1995, at a society party to celebrate the 90th birthday of Lord Borthwick.

Three months later the couple were married in Germany, but the correspondence and threatening phone calls allegedly increased. Police are

understood to have agreed to monitor the calls to trace the caller.

Then last month the engine of Zugbach's car exploded outside Paisley University. It had been left unattended for a week as he is convinced that it was sabotaged. The police and fire brigade were called and the soldier managed to escape from the burning car with a bundle of his students' exam papers and his dog.

The couple are both on sick leave from their jobs. Zugbach plans to return to Scotland to teach.

Zugbach came to prominence in the world of management studies when his book Power and Prestige in the British Army, was published in 1988. It was critical of management structures within the services and it aroused the interest of senior officers in the Free army.

Police said yesterday ... had been questioned about incidents.

OFFICE FOR THE SUPERVISION OF SOLICITORS

VICTORIA COURT, 8 DORMER PLACE, LEAMINGTON SPA, WARWICKSHIRE CV32 5AE
TELEPHONE: 01926 820082 FACSIMILE: 01926 431435 DX 292320 LEAMINGTON SPA 4

OUR REFERENCE

P. Geoffrey Gilson

YOUR REFERENCE

Fax No: 001 706 782 1880

15 October 1996

Dear Geoffrey,

I have just returned from the Solicitors Annual Conference and received your list of questions regarding Hugh Simmonds and the Carratu International report.

Having read the report and your list of questions, I feel that there is little point in me answering each of the questions in turn. As I explained on the telephone, Carratu International were employed by the Law Society to carry out an asset tracing investigation. Their work looked at Hugh Simmonds' business interests and bank accounts and included investigations with staff of his practice and some business acquaintances. At no time did it include investigations with, or reference to, the individuals you listed in your fax to me. The report does not cover the issues you raise or touch on the allegations you have put to me both verbally or in writing. I understand that you have several theories about Hugh Simmonds' activities, but I have to tell you that none of these are in anyway substantiated by the Carratu investigation.

I realise that you will be upset with my answer and that you have hoped to confirm some of your suspicions with evidence from the report. I can only assure you that I am hiding nothing from you in stating quite categorically that such information does not appear in the report.

As far as your questions regarding the Law Society are concerned, I can summarise our involvement as follows. The Law Society employed Carratu to trace funds in order to recover amounts paid out by the Compensation Fund. Applications were made to the Fund; not all of those led to a grant and very little was made in the form of cost recovery. The Adjudication and Appeals Committee saw all information received from Carratu regarding Hugh Simmonds' activities and accounts and had overall control over the work carried out by the investigators - i.e. determined when the work started, what line it was to take and, when the cost finally became too high, when it was to finish.

The Carratu report shows that Hugh Simmonds had business dealings in the UK, Europe and North America. It suggests that money laundering and export frauds may have taken place involving North America and Africa, but this line of investigation was never taken any further: the Committee determined that the requisite standard of proof was lacking and the investigation was terminated because of its expense.

I am unaware of any links between members of the Committee or the Law Society and any Government Agencies. I am also unaware of links between Hugh Simmonds and the

The Office for the Supervision of Solicitors is an establishment of The Law Society, Law Society Hall, 113 Chancery Lane, London WC2A 1PL.

FS 3

Government or Intelligence Agencies. The only mention of such links within the report is a suggestion from yourself that this might be the case. Your theory is not substantiated at any point.

Your questions are very detailed. I do not have an answer to most of them, and can only answer in the negative to many of the others. I am sorry that I have not been of any further help, but I am afraid that you will have to find other ways of backing up your theories than talking to the Law Society. I can honestly say that your line of questionning is in no way justified by the content of a rather dull report!

In one of our conversations you suggested that you would have to point out, in your book, that the Law Society had failed to co-operate with you and had hidden what was or could be relevant information. You asked me to be creative and find a way of helping you. I was creative, have read the report and trust that you will not choose to suggest that we blocked your attempts to elicit any information. It is simply that the information you seek is not contained in the report.

You ask whether or not we would consider reopening our investigations. Naturally, we would be interested in any way of recovering costs incurred through Compensation Fund payments and Law Society activity. However, we do not have fund available to continue with an investigation which would cost the profession more money and may not be conclusive.

I am sorry that I have not been able to be of more assistance to you. Good luck with your enquiries. I hope that you manage to find the answers to your questions elsewhere.

Yours sincerely,

Zoë Etherington
Press Officer

INQUIRY INTO EXPORTS OF DEFENCE EQUIPMENT
AND DUAL USE GOODS TO IRAQ

THE RIGHT HONOURABLE SIR RICHARD SCOTT, THE VICE-CHANCELLOR

The Secretary to the Inquiry:
Christopher Muttukumaru

1 Palace Street
London SW1E 5HE
General Telephone No. 0171 238 3799
Facsimile 0171 238 3044

Geoffrey Gilson Esq
President
International Center for
       Public Policy Studies
851 Tahoe Bluff
Roswell
Georgia 30076
United States of America

30 September 1996

Dear Mr Gilson,

HUGH JOHN SIMMONDS CBE

Thank you for your letter to the Vice-Chancellor dated 24
September 1996.

For the reasons set out in the Inquiry's letter to you dated
19 August 1993, the Vice-Chancellor did not conduct an
investigation into the circumstances of Mr Simmonds' death. I
can confirm that no mention is made of Mr Simmonds in either
the Report or in the supporting documentation published in the
Appendices.

As far as I am aware, apart from in your letter, the Inquiry
has received no information about the possible involvement of
Mr Simmonds in the sale of defence equipment to Iraq.

Yours Sincerely,

Peter Edwards

pp. C P J MUTTUKUMARU

THE GENERAL ELECTRIC COMPANY, p.l.c.

1 STANHOPE GATE · LONDON W1A 1EH

0171-493 8484

FROM THE CHAIRMAN
THE RT. HON. LORD PRIOR. PC

FAX NO. 0171 409 0723

30 September 1996

P. Geoffrey Gilson, Esq.,
President,
International Centre for Public Policy
   Studies.

Fax: 706 1234567

Dear Mr Gilson

    Thank you for your letter of September 26th. I am
afraid I can shed no light on your enquiry, nor can I believe
that there is any foundation for such an allegation.

    I think I met Hugh Simmonds once or twice and it is
sad when a career ends in this way.

REGISTERED IN ENGLAND NO. 67847 · REGISTERED OFFICE: 1 STANHOPE GATE, LONDON

CONSERVATIVE

5th October 1996

P Geoffrey Gilson Esq
President
International Centre for Public Policy Studies

BY FAX

Dear Mr Gilson

Thank you for your letter.   The Chairman of the Party has asked me to inform you that he has
no comment to make regarding Hugh John Simmonds CBE.

Yours sincerely

CHARLES LEWINGTON
Director of Communications

U. S. Department of Justice

Washington, D.C. 20530

FEB 2 1 1997

CRM-970237F

Mr. P. Geoffrey Gilson
3324 Chattahoochee Circle
Roswell, GA 30075

Dear Mr. Gilson:

The Executive Office for U.S. Attorneys has referred your request of December 9, 1996, to the Criminal Division for our review and response to you. Your request has been assigned file number 970237F. Please refer to this number in any future correspondence with this Unit.

We will conduct a search to determine what records (if any) we have that are within the scope of your request. Once we have completed our search, we will notify you as to our disposition of your request. Please note that this search will encompass only Criminal Division records.

If you have any questions regarding the status of this request, you may contact Denise Kennedy on (202) 616-0307.

Sincerely,

Marshall R. Williams, Chief
Freedom of Information/Privacy Act Unit
Office of Enforcement Operations
Criminal Division

International Center for Public Policy and Social Studies

Please respond to:

3324 Chattahoochee Circle
Roswell, Georgia 30075, U.S.A.

Ms. Sue Etherington
Press Officer
Office for the Supervision of Solicitors
Victoria Court
8 Dormer Place
Leamington Spa
Warwickshire
CV32 5AE
England

March 10, 1997

Dear Sue,

Hugh Simmonds

This is a letter I feel less than comfortable writing to you. You were cordial and "creative" throughout the process of my recent enquiries. However, since it was you I dealt with then, it is you I have to write to now.

I have recently been in communication with an individual who was interviewed in the course of the investigation conducted by Carratu International on behalf of the Law Society.

That individual states categorically that, during the interview, the person doing the interviewing told the individual that the investigation had uncovered the fact that Hugh Simmonds owed a large sum of money to an acknowledged arms dealer.

The arms dealer, for whatever reason (but it is not hard to find one), had not claimed the outstanding amount, either from the Law Society or Simmonds' Estate.

In addition, the arms dealer had told the investigation that Simmonds had had expert knowledge of a handgun in use by the security services.

In the circumstances, I find it worrying that you felt able in your letter to me of October 15, 1996, to state: "The [Carratu] report does <u>not</u> cover the issues you raise or touch on the allegations you have put to me both verbally or in writing. I understand that you have several theories about Hugh

Simmonds' activities, but I have to tell you that none of these are in anyway substantiated by the Carratu **investigation** [my emphasis]".

I am sure you will understand the confusion in my mind. I am going to assume that your letter was not intended to be either deliberately misleading or a borderline exercise in semantics and dissemble.

However, the fact remains that, whether the matter was in the so-called "report" or not, the Carratu "investigation" was in possession of information which, although it might not "substantiate" my "allegations" and "theories", could certainly shed some useful light on them, bearing in mind they relate to arms sales and the security services.

Since the "Adjudication and Appeals Committee saw all information received from Carratu regarding Simmonds' activities and accounts", it follows that the Law Society must also have been in possession of the information relating to the arms dealer.

I find it difficult to believe that a firm as professional as Carratu would either have inadvertently omitted to pass on the information or have decided deliberately to withhold it from its clients.

I would be grateful if you would re-open your enquiries and furnish me as soon as possible with any and all information either the Law Society or Carratu have regarding this arms dealer and any other matter you and the Law Society, upon re-consideration, feel might be "relevant" to "my line of questioning".

I refer you to the peni-penultimate paragraph of your letter. It is solely because of the trust you inspired in me at that time that I am keeping this correspondence private, for the moment. I am hoping that that trust was, and still is, not misplaced.

Sorry to sound pompous. But it's better than resorting to four letter words.

You can write to me at the above address, or fax or leave messages on ⬛⬛⬛⬛⬛⬛⬛ Same deal as before: telephone first, then fax. Don't be put off by strangers. The occupants at the address are friends who know all about these matters and are discreet.

Yours sincerely,

P. Geoffrey Gilson

Bibliography

The Dirty War: Covert Strategies and Tactics Used in Political Conflicts
Martin Dillon (Routledge, 1999)

A Century of Spies: Intelligence in the Twentieth Century
Jeffery T. Richelson (Oxford University, 1995)

British Security Coordination: The Secret History of British Intelligence in the Americas, 1940-1945
Roald Dahl, William Stephenson, Nigel West (From, 1999)

Wild Bill and Intrepid: Donovan, Stephenson and the Origin of CIA
Thomas F. Troy (Yale University, 1996)

The CIA
Graham Yost (1989)

Allen Dulles: Master of Spies
James Strodes (Regnery, 1999)

Gentleman Spy: The Life of Allen Dulles
Peter Grose (University of Massachusetts, 1996)

Honourable Treachery: A History of US Intelligence, Espionage, and Covert Action, from the American Revolution to the CIA
George J. A. O'Toole (Atlantic, 1993)

Presidents' Secret Wars: CIA and Pentagon Covert Operations from World War II through the Persian Gulf
John Prados (Dee, 1996, Revised)

Reflections of a Cold Warrior: From Yalta to the Bay of Pigs
Richard M. Bissell (Yale University, 1996)

The Puzzle Palace: A Report on America's Most Secret Agency [NSA]
James Bamford (Viking, 1983)

Secrets: The CIA's War at Home
Angus MacKenzie (University of CA, 1999)

Defrauding America: Encyclopedia of Secret Operations by the CIA, DEA and Other Covert Agencies
Rodney Stich (Diablo Western, 1998)

The Medusa File: Secret Crimes and Cover-ups of the US Government
Craig Roberts (Consolidated, 1997)

Warren Commission Report: Report of the President's Commission on the Assassination of President John F. Kennedy
(St. Martin's, 1992)

Deadly Secrets: The CIA-Mafia War against Castro and the Assassination of JFK
Warren Hinkle, William J. Turner (Thunder's Mouth, 1992)

The Kennedy Conspiracy
Anthony Summers (Warner, 1997)

Secret Team: The Conspiracy Behind the Assassination of JFK
L. Fletcher Prouty (Citadel, 1996)

Coup D'Etat in America: The CIA and the Assassination of John F. Kennedy
Michael Canfield, Alan J. Weberman (American Archives, 1992)

Plausible Denial: Was the CIA Involved in the Assassination of JFK?
Mark Lane (Thunder's Mouth, 1992)

The Adamson Report: Zapruder/Bush & the CIA's Dallas Council on World Affairs (the George de Mohrenschildt Story)
Bruce Campbell Adamson (1999)

Live by the Sword: The Secret War Against Castro and the Death of JFK
Gus Russo (Bancroft, 1998)

Case Closed: Lee Harvey Oswald and the Assassination of JFK
Gerald L. Posner (Doubleday, 1994)

Appointment in Dallas: The Final Solution to the Assassination of JFK
Hugh C. McDonald, As Told to Geoffrey Bocca (Zebra, 1992)

The Assassination of Robert F. Kennedy: The Conspiracy and Cover-up
William W. Turner, John G. Christian (Thunder's Mouth, 1993)

Killing the Dream: James Earl Ray and the Assassination of Martin Luther King, Jr.
Gerald L. Posner (Harvest, 1999)

The Dark Side of Camelot
Seymour M. Hersh (Little Brown, 1997)

Rethinking Camelot: JFK, the Vietnam War, and US Political Culture
Noam Chomsky (South End, 1993)

The Secret War Against Hanoi: Kennedy and Johnson's Use of Spies, Saboteurs, and Covert Warriors in North Vietnam
Richard H. Schultz, Jr. (HarperCollins, 1999)

A Dereliction of Duty: Lyndon Johnson, Robert McNamara, the Joint Chiefs of Staff, and the Lies that led to Vietnam
H. R. McMaster (HarperCollins, 1997)

The Years of Lyndon Johnson
Robert A. Caro (Knopf, 1982)

Lost Crusade: America's Secret Cambodian Mercenaries
Peter Scott (U.S. Naval Institute, 1998)

Covert OPS: The CIA's Secret War in Laos
James E. Parker (St. Martin's, 1997)

RN: The Memoirs of Richard Nixon
Richard Milhous Nixon (Touchstone, 1990, Reprint)

The White House Years
Henry A. Kissinger (Little Brown, 1988)

All the President's Men
BobWoodward, Carl Bernstein (Touchstone, 1994)

Shadow: Five Presidents and the Legacy of Watergate, 1974-1999
Bob Woodward (Simon & Schuster, 1999)

Challenging the Secret Government: The Post-Watergate Investigation of the CIA and FBI
Kathryn S. Olmstead (University of North Carolina, 1996)

Born Again
Charles W. Colson (Revell, 1977)

Keeping Faith: Memoirs of a President
Jimmy Carter (Bantam, 1982)

Jimmy Carter: A Complementary Biography from Plains to Post-Presidency
Peter G. Bourne (Simon & Schuster, 1997)

October Surprise: America's Hostages in Iran and the Election of Ronald Reagan
Gary Sick (Times, 1992)

Honoured and Betrayed: Irangate, Covert Affairs, and the Secret War in Laos
Richard Secord, Jay Wurts (Wiley, 1992)

A Very Thin Line: The Iran-Contra Affairs
Theodore Draper (Hill & Wang, 1991)

Lives, Lies and the Iran-Contra Affair
Anne Wroe (St. Martin's, 1992)

Charlie Wilson's War: the CIA and the Mujahideen in Afghanistan
George Crile (Grove, 2003)

The Politics of Heroin: CIA Complicity in the Global Drug Trade
Alfred W. McCoy (Hill, 1991)

Cocaine Politics: Drugs, Armies and the CIA in Central America
Peter Dale Scott, Jonathan Marshall (University of California, 1992)

Dark Alliance: The CIA, the Contras, and the Crack Cocaine Explosion
Gary Webb, Maxime Waten (Seven Stories, 1998)

Whiteout: The CIA, Drugs and The Press
Alexander Cockburn, Jeffrey St. Clair (Verso, 1999)

Veil: The Secret Wars of the CIA during the Reagan Administration
Bob Woodward (Buccaneer, 1994, Reprint)

A Spy for All Seasons: My Life in the CIA
Duane R. Clarridge, with Digby Diehl (Scribner, 1997)

The Master of Disguise: My Secret Life in the CIA
Antonio J. Mendez (Morrow, 1999)

Inside the Oval Office: The Secret White House Tapes from FDR to Clinton
William Doyle (Kodansha, 1999)

Compromised: Clinton, Bush, and the CIA
Terry Reed, John Cummings (Penmarin, 1995)

Confessions of a Spy: The Real Story of Aldrich Ames
Pete Earley (Putnam, 1997)

Victory: The Reagan Administration's Secret Strategy That Hastened the Collapse of the Soviet Union
Peter Schweizer (Atlantic, 1996)

At the Highest Levels: The Inside Story of the End of the Cold War
Michael R. Beschloss, Strobe Talbott (Back Bay, 1994)

The First Directorate: My 32 years in Intelligence and Espionage against the West
Oleg Kalugin, Fen Montaigne (St. Martin's, 1994)

Man Without A Face: The Autobiography of Communism's Greatest Spymaster
Markus Wolf, With Anne McElvoy (Mass Market, 1999)

The Sword and the Shield: The Mitrokhin Archive and the Secret History of the KGB
Christopher M. Andrew (Basic, 1999)

Contract on America: The Mafia Murder of John F. Kennedy
David E. Scheim (Kensington, 1991, Reprint)

Crime Incorporated or Under the Clock: The Inside Story of the Mafia's First One Hundred Years
William Balsamo (Horizon, 1991)

Mafia Dynasty: The Rise and Fall of the Gambino Crime Family
John H. Davis (Mass Market, 1994)

Wise Guy: Life in a Mafia Family
Nicholas Pileggi (Mass Market, 1990)

Bound by Honour: A Mafioso's Story
Bill Bonnano (St. Martin's, 1999)

The Pizza Connection: Lawyers, Money, Drugs, Mafia
Shana Alexander (Diane, 1999)

Latin America and the International Drug Trade (Institute of Latin American Studies)
Carlos Malamud (St. Martin's, 1997)

Whitewash: Pablo Escobar and the Cocaine Wars
Simon Strong (McClelland & Stewart, 1995, Second Edition)

Drug Politics: Dirty Money and Democracies
David C. Jordan (University of Oklahoma, 1999)

The Money Launderers: Lessons from the Drug Wars - How Billions of Illegal Dollars are Washed through Banks and Businesses
Robert E. Powis

The Laundrymen: Inside Money Laundering, the World's Third Largest Business
Jeffrey Robinson (Arcade, 1996)

Evil Money: The Inside Story of Money Laundering and Corruption in Government, Banks and Business
Rachel Ehrenfeld (Mass Market, 1994)

Safe as Houses: The Schemes and Scams behind some of the World's Greatest Financial Scandals
Sam Jaffa (Parkwest, 1997)

The Failure of the Franklin National Bank: Challenge to the International Banking System
Joan Edelman Spero (Beard, 1999)

Banking Scandals: The S&L's and BCCI
Robert Emmet Long (Wilson, 1993)

A Full Service Bank: How BCCI Stole Billions Around the World
James Ring Adams, Douglas Frantz (Pocket, 1993, Reprint)

False Profits: The Inside Story of BCCI, the World's Most Corrupt Financial Empire
Peter Truell, Larry Gurwin (Beard, 1999)

Barbarians at the Gate: The Fall of RJR Nabisco
Bryan Burrough, John Helyar (HarperCollins, 1991)

Vendetta: American Express and the Smearing of Edmond Safra
Bryan Burrough

225

Holy Blood, Holy Grail
Michael Baigent, Henry Lincoln, Richard Leigh (Mass Market, 1983)

The Messianic Legacy
Michael Baigent, Henry Lincoln, Richard Leigh (Mass Market, 1989)

Key to the Sacred Pattern: The Untold Story of Rennes-Le-Chateau
Henry Lincoln (St. Martin's, 1998)

The Templars' Secret Island
Erling Haagensen, Henry Lincoln (Windrush, 2000)

The Temple and The Lodge
Michael Baigent, Richard Leigh (Arcade, 1991, Reprint)

The Dead Sea Scrolls Deception
Michael Baigent, Richard Leigh (Cape, 1991)

The Secret Teachings of All Ages: An Encyclopedic Outline of Masonic, Hermetic, Qabbalistic, and Rosicrucian Symbolical Philosophy
Manly P. Hall (Philosophical Research Society, 1994)

Secret Societies: From the Ancient and Arcane to the Modern and Clandestine
David V. Barrett (Blandford, 1999)

Dungeon, Fire and Sword: The Knights Templar in the Crusades
John J. Robinson (Evans, 1992)

The Second Messiah: Templars, the Turin Shroud and the Great Secret of Freemasonry
Christopher Knight, Robert Lomas (Element, 1998)

Secrets of Jerusalem's Temple Mount
Kathleen Ritmeyer (Biblical Archaeology Society, 1998)

Jerusalem Betrayed: Ancient Prophecy and Modern Conspiracy Collide in the Holy City
Mike Evans (Word, 1997)

The Cathars and the Albigensian Crusade
Michael Costen (Manchester University, 1997)

Born in Blood: The Lost Secrets of Freemasonry
John J. Robinson (Evans, 1990)

Secret Ritual of the Thirty-Third and Last Degree Sovereign Grand Inspector General of the Ancient and Accepted Scottish Rite of Freemasonry
(Kessinger, 1997)

Emblematic Freemasonry
Arthur Edward Waite (Kessinger, 1992)

Masonry: Conspiracy against Christianity - Evidence that the Masonic Lodge has a Secret Agenda
A. Ralph Epperson (Publius, 1998)

The Secret Teachings of the Masonic Lodge: A Christian Perspective
John Ankerberg, John Weldon (Moody, 1990)

Fraternity of the Rosy Cross
Thomas Vaughan (Holmes, 1983)

The Illuminati Conspiracy
Richard Rees (1997)

Illuminati: New World Order
Steve Jackson (Castle, 1994)

Hidden Secrets of the Eastern Star: The Masonic Connection
Cathy Burns (Sharing, 1994)

The International Encyclopedia of Secret Societies and Fraternal Orders
Alan Axelrod (Checkmark, 1998)

New World Order: The Ancient Plan of Secret Societies
William T. Still (Vital, 1990)

The Occult Conspiracy: Secret Societies - Their Influence and Power in World History
Michael Howard (Inner, 1989)

The Occult: A History
Colin Wilson

The Outsider
Colin Wilson (Putnam, 1987)

The Celestine Prophecy: An Adventure
James Redfield (Warner, 1994)

The Celestine Insights: The Celestine Prophecy and the Tenth Insight
James Redfield (Warner, 1997)

The Pagan Information Pack
The Pagan Federation International (4th Edition, 1996)

HTML Version coded by Diana Aventina, NC – Belgium

The Secret Teachings of Jesus: Four Gnostic Gospels
Marvin W. Meyer (Vintage, 1986)

The First Messiah: Investigating the Savior Before Jesus
Michael O. Wise (Harper, 1999)

Vatican Council II
Xavier Rynne (Orbis, 1999)

Their Kingdom Come: Inside the Secret World of Opus Dei
Robert Hutchinson (St. Martin's, 1999)

In God's Name: An Investigation into the Murder of John Paul I
David A. Yallop (Mass Market, 1997)

The Keys of This Blood: The Struggle for World Dominion between Pope Paul II, Mikhail Gorbachev and the Capitalist West
Malachi Martin, With Anne Kepler (Simon & Schuster, 1990)

How the Irish Saved Civilization: The Untold Story of Ireland's Role from the Fall of Rome to the Rise of Medieval Europe
Thomas Cahill (Doubleday, 1995)

The Gifts of the Jews: How a Tribe of Desert Nomads Changed the Way Everyone Thinks and Feels
Thomas Cahill (Doubleday, 1998)

The Secret War Against the Jews: How Western Espionage Betrayed the Jewish People
John Loftus, With Mark Aarons (St. Martin's, 1994)

Mein Kampf
Adolf Hitler (Mariner, 1999, Reissue)

The Occult Roots of Nazism: Secret Aryan Cults and Their Influences on Nazi Ideology - The Arisophists of Austria and Germany, 1890-1935
Nicholas Goodrick-Clarke (New York University, 1992)

The Spear of Destiny: The Occult Power Behind the Spear Which Pierced the Side of Christ, and its Significance in the Rise and Fall of Hitler
Trevor Ravenscroft (Weiser, 1987)

Blood in the Face: The Ku Klux Klan, Aryan Nations, Nazi Skinheads, and the Rise of a New White Culture
James Ridgeway (Thunder's Mouth, 1995)

Soldiers of God: White Supremacists and Their Holy War for America
Howard L. Bushart (Kensington, 1998)

Essential Law of Nature: The Creed of the White Church of God
Ben Kassem

Contract with America
Newt Gingrich, Dick Armey (Times, 1994)

To Renew America
Newt Gingrich (Mass Market, 1996)

The Silent Brotherhood: The Chilling Inside Story of America's Violent, Anti-Government Militia Movement
Kevin Flynn, Gary Gerhardt (Mass Market, 1995, Reprint)

The Ashes of Waco: An Investigation
Dick J. Reavis (Syracuse University, 1998)

Others Unknown: The Oklahoma City Bombing Case and Conspiracy
Stephen Jones (Public Affairs, 1998)

None Dare Call It Conspiracy
Gary Allen (Amereon, 1976)

Hidden Agendas
John Pilger (New Press, 1999)

Secrets of the Temple: How the Federal Reserve Runs the Country
William Greider (Touchstone, 1989)

The House of Rothschild: Money's Prophets, 1798-1848
Niall Ferguson (Viking, 1998)

The House of Rothschild: The World's Bankers, 1849-1999
Niall Ferguson (Viking, 1999)

The House of Morgan: An American Banking Dynasty and the Rise of Modern Finance
Ron Chernow (Touchstone, 1991, Reprint)

The Warburgs: The Twentieth-Century Odyssey of a Remarkable Jewish Family
Ron Chernow (Vintage, 1994, Reprint)

Titan: The Life of John D. Rockefeller, Sr.
Ron Chernow (Random House, 1998)

A People's History of the United States: 1492 to the Present
Howard Zinn (Harperperennial, 1995, Revised and Updated)

The Federalist Papers
Alexander Hamilton, James Madison, John Jay (Penguin, 1987, Reprint)

The Anti-Federalist Papers and the Constitutional Convention Debates
Ralph Ketcham (Mass Market, 1996)

The Debate on the Constitution: Federalist and Anti-Federalist Speeches, Articles, and Letters during the Struggle over Ratification
Bernard Bailyn (Library of America, 1993)

New Federalist Papers: Essays in Defence of the Constitution
Alan Brinkley, Nelson W. Polsby, Kathleen M. Sullivan (Norton, 1997)

Origins of the Bill of Rights
Leonard W. Levy (Yale University, 1999)

The Brethren: Inside the Supreme Court
Bob Woodward, Scott Armstrong

A History of the English-Speaking Peoples
Winston Churchill (Cassell, 1991)

The Oxford History of Medieval Europe
George Holmes (Oxford University, 1990)

Early Modern Europe: An Oxford History
Euan Cameron (Oxford University, 1999)

The Oxford Illustrated History of Modern Europe
T. C. W. Blanning (Oxford University, 1998, Reprint)

The Story of Civilization
Will Durant, Ariel Durant (Simon & Schuster, 1983)

From Dawn to Decadence: 1500 to the Present; 500 years of Western Cultural Life
Jacques Barcun (Perennial, 2000)

A History of the Hapsburg Empire, 1273-1918
Jean Berenger (Longman, 1994)

The Great Game: The Struggle for Empire in Central Asia
Peter Hopkirk (Kodansha, 1994)

On Secret Service East of Constantinople
Peter Hopkirk (Oxford, 1995)

Like Hidden Fire: The Plot to Bring Down the British Empire
Peter Hopkirk (Kodansha, 1997)

Philby of Arabia
Elizabeth Monroe (Ithaca, 1998)

Sa'Udi Arabia
Harry St. J. B. Philby (Ayer, 1972)

Oil, God and Gold: The Story of Aramco and the Saudi Kings
Anthony Cave Brown (Houghton Mifflin, 1999)

The Rise, Corruption and Coming Fall of the House of Saud
Said K. Aburish (St. Martin's, 1996)

Abu Nidal: A Gun for Hire: The Secret Life of the World's Most Notorious Arab Terrorist
Patrick Seale (Diane, 1998)

Hizb'allah in Lebanon: The Politics of the Western Hostage Crisis
Magnus Ranstorp (St. Martin's, 1996)

Den of Lions: Memoirs of Seven Years as a Hostage
Terry A. Anderson (Mass Market, 1994, Reprint)

Taken on Trust
Terry Waite (Coronet, 1994)

Terry Waite and Ollie North: The Untold Story of the Kidnapping - and the Release
Gavin Hewitt (Diane, 1997)

Pan Am 103: The Lockerbie Crash and Cover-Up
William C. Chasey (Bridger House, 1995)

The Price of Terror: The Aftermath of Lockerbie
Allen Gerson, Jerry Adler (HarperCollins, 2001)

Terror in the Mind of God
Mark Juergensmeyer (California, 2000)

Soldiers of God
Robert D. Kaplan (Vintage, 1990)

The Ends of the Earth
Robert D. Kaplan (Vintage, 1996)

Holy War, Inc: Inside the World of Osama bin Laden
Peter L. Bergen (Simon & Schuster, 2001)

Inside Al Qaeda: Global Network of Terror
Rohan Gunaratna (Columbia University Press, 2002)

Jihad -v- McWorld
Benjamin R. Barber (Random House, 1995)

Muslim Perceptions of Christianity
Elizabeth Gilson Aaron – Lecture (UNC-Chapel Hill, 2005)

Blowback: The Costs and Consequences of American Empire
Chalmers Johnson (Henry Holt, 2000)

Rogue State: A Guide to the World's Only Superpower
William Blum (Common Courage, 2000)

Blackwater: The Rise of the World's Most Powerful Mercenary Army
Jeremy Scahill (Nation Books, 2008)

The War Against America: Saddam Hussein and the World Trade Center Attacks
Laurie Mylroie (Regan, 2000)

The 9/11 Commission Report: Final Report of the National Commission on Terrorist Attacks upon the United States
Thomas H. Kean, and Others (Norton, 2004)

Fateful Triangle: The United States, Israel and The Palestinians
Noam Chomsky (South End, 1999, Second Updated Edition)

Israel's Secret Wars: A History of Israel's Intelligence Services
Ian Black, Benny Morris (Grove, 1992, Reprint)

Gideon's Spies: The Secret History of the Mossad
Gordon Thomas (Diane, 1999)

By Way of Deception: The Making and Unmaking of a Mossad Officer
Victor Ostrovsky, Susan Hoy

The Other Side of Deception: A Rogue Agent Exposes the Mossad's Secret Agenda
Victor Ostrovsky

The Samson Option: Israel's Clandestine Nuclear Mission
Seymour M. Hersh (Vintage, 1993)

Profits of War: Inside the Secret US-Israeli Arms Network
Ari Ben-Menashe (Sheridan Square, 1992)

Maxwell: The Rise and Fall of Robert Maxwell and His Empire
Roy Greenslade (Birch Lane, 1992)

Death of a Tycoon: An Insider's Account of the Rise and Fall of Robert Maxwell
Nicholas Davies (St. Martin's, 1993)

The Enemy Within: MI5, Maxwell and the Scargill Affair
Seamus Milne (Verso, 1996)

Robert Maxwell – Israel's Superspy: The Life and Murder of a Media Mogul
Martin Dillon, Gordon Thomas (Carroll, 2002)

Foreign Body
Russell Davies (Bloomsbury, 1996)

The Arms Bazaar: The Companies, the Dealers, the Bribes
Anthony Sampson

The Shadow World: Inside the Global Arms Trade
Andrew Feinstein (Farrar, Straus and Giroux, 2011)

Death Lobby: How the West Armed Iraq
Kenneth R. Timmerman

Arming Iraq: How the United States and Britain Secretly Built Saddam's War Machine
Mark Phythian, Nikos Passas (Northeastern University, 1996)

Spider's Web: Bush, Saddam, Thatcher and the Decade of Deceit
Alan Friedman (Diane, 1999)

The Shell Game: A True Story of Banking, Spies, Lies, Politics - and the Arming of Saddam Hussein
Peter Mantius (St. Martin's, 1995)

Arms and the Man: Dr. Gerald Bull, Iraq and the Supergun
William Lowther (Macmillan, 1991)

Guns, Lies and Spies: The Inside Story of the Supergun
Christopher Cowley (Hamish Hamilton, 1992)

The Unlikely Spy: Inside Matrix Churchill
Paul Henderson (Bloomsbury, 1993)

Betrayed: The Inside Story of the Matrix Churchill Trial
David Leigh (Bloomsbury, 1993)

The exchange of letters between the UN and Iraq – governing the rights of UNSCOM
May 1991

The Monitoring Plan [UNSCOM]
S/22871/Rev.1 of October 2nd, 1991

Notes on a meeting between Hussein Kamal and UNSCOM and IAEA
Ammam, Jordan – August 22nd 1995

The export/import monitoring mechanism
S/1995/1017 of December 7th, 1995

Twenty-six Reports of UNSCOM to UN Security Council
October 25th, 1991 through October 8th, 1999

Note on the establishment of the three panels
S/1999/100 of January 30th, 1999

The "Amorim Report" (panel concerning disarmament and future ongoing monitoring and verification issues)
S/1999/356 of March 27th, 1999

Draft Work Programme of UNMOVIC [successor to UNSCOM]
March 17th, 2003

Unresolved Disarmament Issues: Iraq's Proscribed Weapons Programmes
UNMOVIC Working Document – March 6th, 2003

Twenty-five Reports of UNMOVIC to UN Security Council
June 1st, 2000 through May 30th, 2006
Compendium Summary
UN document S/2006/420 of May 30th, 2006

Report of the Inquiry into the Export of Defence Equipment and Duel-Use Goods to Iraq and Related Prosecutions (including Appendices)
Richard Scott (HMSO, 1996)

Unclassified Report to Congress on the Acquisition of Technology Relating to Weapons of Mass Destruction and Advanced Conventional Munitions, January 1st Through June 30th, 2002
Central Intelligence Agency

Iraq's Weapons of Mass Destruction
British Government, September 2002

"A Decade of Deception and Defiance": White House Background Paper for President George W. Bush's September 12th, 2002 Speech to UN General Assembly on Saddam Hussein's Continuing WMD Program
US White House White Paper

Iraq's Weapons of Mass Destruction
Central Intelligence Agency, October 2002

The Decision to go to War in Iraq: Ninth Report of Session 2002-2003
UK Parliamentary Select Committee on Foreign Affairs, July 2003

Iraqi Weapons of Mass Destruction: Intelligence and Assessments
UK Parliamentary Intelligence and Security Committee, September 2003

Report of the Inquiry into the Circumstances Surrounding the Death of Dr. D. Kelly, CMG
The Right Honourable The Lord Hutton, January 2004

Review of Intelligence on Weapons of Mass Destruction
The Right Honourable The Lord Butler, July 2004

Comprehensive Report of the Special Advisor to the DCI on Iraq's Weapons of Mass Destruction
Iraq Survey Group, September 2004

The Report of the Special Advisor to the DCI for Strategy Regarding Iraqi Weapons of Mass Destruction
US Senate Committee on Armed Services, 2005

Report to the President of the United States by the Commission on the Intelligence Capabilities of the United States Regarding Weapons of Mass Destruction
President's Commission on Intelligence Capabilities, March 2005

Knee Deep in Dishonour
Richard Norton-Taylor, Stephen Cook, Mark Lloyd (Orion, 1996)

In the Public Interest: An Account of the Thatcher Government's Involvement in the Covert Arms Trade
Gerald James (Warner, 1996)

Thatcher's Gold: The Shady Financial Dealings of Mark Thatcher
Paul Halloran, Mark Hollingsworth (Simon & Schuster, 1995)

Once a Jolly Bagman: The Memoirs of Margaret Thatcher's Fundraiser
Alistair McAlpine (Weidenfeld & Nicolson, 1997)

Dirty politics, Dirty times: My Fight with Wapping and New Labour
Michael A. Ashcroft (MAA Publishing, 2005)

In Defence of the Party: The Secret State, The Conservative Party and Dirty Tricks
Colin Challen, Mike Hughes (Medium, 1996)

The Price of Power: The Secret Funding of the Tory Party
Colin Challen (Vision/Satin, 1998)

The Path to Power
Margaret Thatcher (HarperCollins, 1996)

The Downing Street Years
Margaret Thatcher (HarperCollins, 1993)

One of Us: A Biography of Margaret Thatcher
Hugo Young (Pan, 1993)

The Conservative Party from Peel to Major
Robert Blake (Heinemann, 1997)

Disraeli
Robert Blake (Prion, 1998)

This Blessed Plot: Britain and Europe from Churchill to Blair
Hugo Young (Macmillan, 1998)

Conflict of Loyalty: The Memoirs of Margaret Thatcher's Foreign Secretary
Geoffrey Howe (Pan, 1995)

Mrs. Thatcher's Minister: The Private Diaries of Alan Clark, former Conservative Trade Minister
Alan Clark (Phoenix, 1994)

John Major: The Autobiography
John Roy Major (HarperCollins, 1997)

In Office
Norman Lamont (Little, Brown and Company, 1999)

The Liar: The Downfall of Jonathan Aitken, former Conservative Minister for Defence Procurement
Luke Harding, David Leigh, David Pallister (Fourth Estate, 1999)

Pride and Perjury
Jonathan Aitken (HarperCollins, 2000)

Open Verdict: Strange Deaths in Britain's Defence Electronics' Industry
Tony Collins

Smear!: Wilson and the Secret State
Stephen Dorril

The Silent Conspiracy
Stephen Dorril (Heinemann, 1993)

The Conspirators' Hierarchy: The Committee of Three Hundred
John Coleman (American West, 1992)

Enemies of the State
Gary Murray (Simon & Schuster, 1994)

The Committee: Political Assassination in Northern Ireland
Sean McPhilemy (Rinehart, 1998)

Thatcher's Private War: The True Story of a Secret Agent and Hitman Working or Thatcher's Government
Nicholas Davies (Blake, 1998)

SAS, the Illustrated History
Barry Davies (London Bridge, 1997)

The Feathermen: Protectors of the SAS
Ranulph Fiennes (Bloomsbury, 1991)

A Web of Deception
Chapman Pincher (Sidgwick & Jackson, 1987)

Traitors
Chapman Pincher (Sidgwick & Jackson, 1987)

Faber Book of Espionage
Nigel West (Faber, 1994)

Faber Book of Treachery
Nigel West (Faber, 1997)

The Illegals
Nigel West (Hodder & Stoughton, 1993)

Counterfeit Spies
Nigel West (Warner, 1999)

The Cambridge Spies: The Untold Story of Maclean, Philby, Burgess in America
Verne W. Newton (Madison, 1991)

Spycatcher
Peter Wright

GCHQ: The Secret Wireless War, 1900-1986
Nigel West

MI5: British Security Service
Nigel West

Defending the Realm: MI5 and the Shayler Affair
Mark Hollingsworth, Nick Fielding (Deutsch, 1999)

Inside Intelligence: Memoirs of an MI6 Officer
Anthony Cavendish (HarperCollins, 1997)

MI6: Fifty Years of Special Operations
Stephen Dorril (Fourth Estate, 2000)

Diana: Her True Story
Andrew Morton (O'Mara, 1997)

Diana in Focus
Mark Saunders, Trevor Anthony Holt, Glenn Harvey (Blake, 1996)

Death of a Princess: The Investigation
Thomas Sancton, Scott Macleod (Weidenfeld & Nicolson, 1998)

Who Killed Diana?: An Investigation into the Various Conspiracy Theories concerning the Death of Princess Diana and Dodi Fayed
Simon Regan (Scallywag, 1998)

Diana, Queen of Hearts - CIA/MI6, the Princedom of Darkness
Dennis McDonough, Bruce Campbell Adamson (1998)

The Bodyguard's Story
Trevor Rees-Jones (Little, Brown and Company, 2000)

Dead Wrong 2: Diana, Princess of Wales
Richard Belzer, David Wayne (Vigliano, 2013)

***

The Thirty-Nine Steps
John Buchan

Tinker Tailor Soldier Spy, Smiley's People, The Honourable Schoolboy, The Secret Pilgrim, The Russia House, A Perfect Spy, Our Game, The Night Manager
John Le Carre

Berlin Game, Mexico Set, London Match, Spy Hook, Spy Line, Spy Sinker
Len Deighton

The Day of the Jackal, The Odessa File, The Dogs of War, The Fourth Protocol, The Fist of God, The Devil's Alternative, The Negotiator, Icon
Frederick Forsyth

The Spy in Question, Spy Shadow, War Dance
Tim Sebastian

GBHP1
http://www.btinternet.com/~chief.gnome/gordon1.html

The Shoes of the Fisherman
Morris S. West

Black Lamb and Grey Falcon: A Journey through Yugoslavia
Rebecca West

Foucault's Pendulum
Umberto Eco

The Brotherhood of the Rose, The Fraternity of the Stone, The Covenant of the Flame, The Fifth Profession, The Totem, Double Image, Assumed Identity, Extreme Denial
David Morrell

The Once and Future King: The Legend of King Arthur and the Holy Grail
T. H. White

Index

V

W

Y